CHISELED

A MEMOIR OF
IDENTITY, DUPLICITY,
AND DIVINE WINE

PRAISE FOR DANUTA PFEIFFER'S
Chiseled

AWARDS & HONORS

GOLD MEDAL NON-FICTION DRAMA
Readers' Favorite International Award

ERIC HOFFER AWARD FINALIST

GOLD MEDAL NON-FICTION AUDIO BOOK
Readers' Favorite International Award

WRITER'S DIGEST AWARD SELF-PUBLISHED E-BOOK

RECIPIENT OF FIVE STAR REVIEWS
from Readers' Favorite International

"*Chiseled* makes *Wild* look tame!"

—Amazon Reviewer

"I come away from reading *Chiseled* with tremendous respect and admiration for her. This is a powerful and courageous memoir filled with one stunning twist after another. She reveals truths about herself that are as excruciating as they are liberating. The takeaway for me: the truth will set you free, even if it hurts to tell it."

—JOHN DEDAKIS
Former CNN Senior Copy Editor
(The Situation Room with Wolf Blitzer)

"...a wonderful book, splendidly written."

—ANDREW MORAVCSIK, Professor of Politics and International Affairs, Princeton University

"A compelling memoir, an excellent storyteller, a powerful voice, a talented writer, and her story well-told."

—*Writer's Digest* Self-Published Award

"I highly recommend *Chiseled*, as Danuta Pfeiffer eloquently shows that truth can be more dramatic and fascinating than fiction. Readers be prepared to be angry—and possibly shed a few tears—but in the end, feel inspired."

—KRISTINE HALL
Readers' Favorite reviewer

"This is an amazing story, and I had to keep reminding myself that it was a biography and not a work of fiction because the trials and struggles that the young Danuta went through defies belief....It is a tribute to the author that her writing was so descriptive and emotive that I was unable to put it down until the end. This story will stay with me for a long time.…I give enormous credit to the standard of writing that made this a truly memorable read."

—JANE FINCH
Readers' Favorite reviewer

"The writing style is fast-paced and engaging, and her voice comes across as genuine and authentic…a gripping memoir and one that I enjoyed reading tremendously."

—GISELA DIXON
Readers' Favorite reviewer

"The story reads like fast-moving fiction!"

—KATHERINE COLE
The Oregonian, OregonLive

"I could not put the book down. I found myself poring over the pages in my car, in a park, during work hours two days in a row. I was entranced…"

—HILARY BERG
Oregon Wine Press Magazine

"I found it gripping, one of those books that is not easy to let go of. As well as being the true story of her journey to find herself, to find the real truth about her life and her family, it's also a story that encourages others to start their own journeys."

—ANNE-MARIE REYNOLDS
Readers' Favorite reviewer

"The journey to Alaska, told with snippets of a life she leaves behind, adds an element of thrill and expectation that makes the reader read on and on. In the final part of the book, her father's story and her crumbling marriage make an interesting juxtaposition. And just as we think we know how her story ends, it takes another turn that is completely unexpected. Hers is an extraordinary life told in a remarkable way!"

—MARIA BELTRAN
Readers' Favorite reviewer

"She allows the reader to see behind the cameras of her life and in telling her story, she explores love, trust, deception, forgiveness, faith, courage, and endurance. Buckle up for this one folks. I loved the book and could not put it down."

—J. WARD, Amazon Review

"This is an amazing book! It is difficult to find adequate adjectives to describe it. Danuta is a great storyteller, and she takes the reader on an incredible roller coaster ride.

—JOHN D. SYNDER, Amazon Review

Experiences cited from *Chiseled* have been quoted by Pulitzer Prize-winning author Chris Hedges in his book *American Fascists: The Christian Right and the War on America.*

CHISELED

A Memoir of
IDENTITY, DUPLICITY,
AND DIVINE WINE

DANUTA PFEIFFER

LUMINARE PRESS

EUGENE, OREGON

Printed in the United States of America

Cover Design: Claire Flint

Luminare Press
442 Charnelton St.
Eugene, OR 97401
www.luminarepress.com

LCCN: 2015931338
ISBN: 978-1-937303-43-3

For Paul and Troy, my sons: thank you for being in my life;
For Robin, the love of my life;
And for Patricia, my mother, who made it all possible.

*We must be willing to get rid of the life we planned,
so as to have the life that is waiting for us.*

—Joseph Campbell

Contents

PART TWO
THE BLACK, THE BLONDE, AND THE BAPTIST

PART THREE
THE WHITE POLE

PREFACE

I AM OFTEN ASKED HOW I CAME TO BE THE cohost on *The 700 Club with Pat Robertson*. How was it that a journalist, who was a liberal Democrat and a feminist, could be associated with that conservative, right wing, charismatic Christian television program and become, as the *Washington Times* proclaimed, "The most visible woman in Christianity today." Even more, I am asked why I left and what has become of my faith and my life.

This is a memoir, my best recollection of what happened. I have taken care to reconstruct the scenes and conversations to the best of my ability with the understanding that memory is wickedly elusive and necessarily subjective. Ultimately, this is the memory of a lie. That lie stalked me to the coldest regions of the globe, and drove me to gods real and imagined.

This is a story of how that lie carved a greater space for my soul.

PROLOGUE

THE FIRST TIME I MARRIED MY FATHER, I WAS five years old.

In the summer of 1954, when the Canadian sun still freckled my nose and warmed my father's heart, we made our vows in the backyard of our rented house. I wobbled in my mother's shoes and gripped a bouquet of dandelions as I plowed across the grass toward the shadow he cast over me. I strained to see him, but he had eclipsed the sun. To me he had become a god: fiery, unreachable, invisible. How could I not love him?

Mummy stood between Daddy and me and sang "Here Comes the Bride." She wore a white dress with black polka dots, a good match for her hair—black locks bubbling onto her shoulders with a single white streak of hair, her "skunk stripe," as she called it, sweeping over her brow as if God forgot to finish painting her.

Mummy concluded the song, then removed her wedding ring and slipped it on my finger. "By the power vested in Mummy, I now pronounce you Daddy and wife." She clapped her hands. "You may now kiss the bride."

Daddy reached down and kissed me. The warm, familiar smell of roasted tobacco floated up from his cigarette. I hugged his neck. "I love you, Daddy," I whispered, content that my world was in order.

Eleven years later, I would once again slip my mother's wedding ring on when my family stopped playing games.

PART ONE

THE ESCAPE

Danuta and Bruce the cat, taking a break somewhere in the Yukon

The Escape

UNFORGIVING. UNTAMED. UNCONDITIONAL. The Last Frontier. The westernmost, easternmost, northernmost state. Alaska, more than twice the size of Texas, a birthmark sprawled on the top of the globe, a place where everybody had a story. Some go there for adventure, others seek haven from a past. For my mother and me, Alaska was a gamble, 4,000 miles from Michigan and my lost home. Alaska loomed over us, a vast expanse of shameless proportions. For anyone in 1965, Alaska was a godawful challenge, a camouflage of beauty hiding an icy interior where the weak perished and the strong merely survived.

The odyssey was upon us: my mother, a month-old baby, my four-year-old brother, my grey tabby cat, and me, barely seventeen, traveling perilous roads to Alaska during an arctic winter, and crossing the Rocky Mountains at unforgiving altitudes. We tucked into a borrowed Ford sedan with no snow tires and aimed for redemption.

The first day of our exodus took us through the coldest reaches of the United States: the Upper Peninsula of Michigan, through Minnesota to Duluth, south to Minneapolis, Saint Paul, to Fargo, North Dakota, and on to Winnipeg, Canada. Snow battered the windshield. Winds buffeted the car and rocked us like a cradle, and baby Paul slept through it all. We left behind a different kind of storm: the shouting, the threats, the chaos.

"We're close to the Canadian border. And it's already freezing cold." Mom sounded worried about the weather, but as mile after mile of frigid landscape rolled by, my mind traveled back to our troubled departure from what had been our home. I thought of my brother's face as he stood in the living room that day, an hour before leaving. Rick announced, "I'm not going." He had poked his nervous fingers through a button hole in his plaid jacket.

"What?" Mom and I blurted together, startling baby Paul who whimpered on a blanket beside us. My youngest brother, Michael, sat on a suitcase playing with a toy soldier.

"I want to stay with Dad until you get back." Rick was fourteen, a quiet boy who seldom took a stand on anything and ducked like a prizefighter whenever trouble brewed. And in our family trouble brewed more often than coffee.

Mom and I had been sitting on the floor wrapping our few possessions in tissue paper: her porcelain figurines from England, my set of Beatles albums, some books and teacups. We would secure our little valuables in a storage chest in the garage until we returned. "You're coming with us," Mom insisted, wrapping more and more paper around a porcelain figurine.

"And we're all packed," I said, pointing to the Beatles' *A Hard Day's Night* album that topped the records piled on the floor, music of the girlhood I would be leaving behind. Bundles clustered along the far wall would be the baggage we'd take: a laundry basket stuffed with a pillow for the baby's bed, four small suitcases—one for each of us, Michael, Rick, Mom, and me, plus boots, scarves, and down-filled jackets, a bag of oranges, a loaf of brown bread, a jar of peanut butter, and a baby's bag filled with bottles, formula, and diapers.

I glanced up at Rick, my tree-house companion, my bunk-bed partner, and my silent confederate in pain. "Why would you want to stay?"

He scanned the floor between his feet. "Dad needs company."

"You've always been afraid of him. You're coming," Mom huffed. She finished tying her Pied Piper ceramic with a gold string.

"He needs me."

"He doesn't."

Rick fiddled with the loose threads on his jacket.

"I want to stay."

"I don't believe this." She tore at the tissue in her lap, looked at her half-wrapped treasures, and sighed. "A boy needs his father, I suppose. Maybe you'll get to know one another. Maybe. A man and his son . . . if you're sure." She scanned his face looking for any sign of doubt.

"I'm sure. I want to stay." He picked up his suitcase and stood still as a mouse.

"If you're sure." Mom resumed her wrapping. "We'll be back in a few weeks, anyway." Her tone was overly reassuring.

Rick, age 15

Rick quickly ducked out of the room. Later that morning, we placed our travel itinerary against a cracked, white cup on the kitchen table with the hope that my father would write to us along the way. Rick appeared at the door.

I pecked a kiss on his cheek, "See ya."

Our eyes locked momentarily, blue blinking at blue, sharing an unspoken sorrow in an uncertain season.

"See ya."

Mom hugged him. "We'll be back, Ricky," she said. "Take care of your father." She twirled a tangle of dark brown hair off his forehead and laid her hand softly on his cheek.

"Don't worry, Mom," Rick said, "I'll be all right." The pimples on his chin made him look too young to be left behind, but for a moment he seemed taller and older than his fourteen years.

My father stood in the hallway as our little procession passed by him to the door. My mother, who was holding Mike's hand, paused briefly in front of Dad. "Michael, my son . . ." Daddy said, blessing my brother with a touch to his young face. He said nothing to Mom.

Cradling the baby in my arms, I stepped past my father. "So, you're going then." His gentleness unnerved me.

I nodded and kept my eyes riveted on the ground all the way to the car. I placed baby Paul in the laundry basket in the back seat, where Michael sat next to the basket waving bye-bye. I got into the front passenger side, softly clicking the door shut. Mom slid into the driver's seat, closed the door and stared straight ahead, unflinching at the wheel. As we drove away, I turned and saw my father's stoic figure at the window, rooted, immoveable, watching us. I gave a little wave. We turned the corner before I could see if he waved back.

How could he let us go? I hoped, in some small space

where hope still dwelled, that he would catch us before we slipped away. There would be time to write along the way, and time to mend what was broken, but still, how could he let us go?

MY THOUGHTS WERE INTERRUPTED AT the Canadian border by Michael's plaintive voice from the back seat, "I'm cold." I was cold, too. Mom and I both reached for the dashboard dials. Cold air blasted from the vents.

"This is not the time or the place to run out of heat!" she said, slapping the dashboard, as if that would help. If she had hoped for a mechanic at the border, she was disappointed. The checkpoint consisted of a dismal hut with two Canadian agents huddled inside.

"Excuse me," my mother rolled down the window when an agent came out, "but would you know why I'm not getting any heat in the car?"

"No heat, ma'am?" He poked his head in the window and saw our shivering troop. "It could be your radiator. I'll take a look." He opened the hood for a few moments and then returned to Mom's window. "Radiator's leaking," he said as he wiped his hands on a piece of paper. "You're losing antifreeze. Temperature's twenty below. Hoses could freeze."

"Is there a gas station where I can get it fixed?" My mother gazed into the darkness ahead.

"Nothing for eighty miles, 'tween here and Winnipeg." The earflaps on the agent's hat flopped when he talked.

"Look at his funny hat," Michael whispered.

"He looks like a big old dog." The girl in me giggled with him.

"What's your destination?" he asked.

"Anchorage. Alaska." She sounded apologetic and gripped

the steering wheel as the preposterous idea hit her.

Doggy Ears poked his head in the window again. "Did you say Alaska? Just you and the kids? This time of year?"

"Just us." She gave a sickly smile.

He stepped back in the hut and a minute later dashed out with a teakettle.

Was he going to give us a cup of tea? I was amazed at the kindness of these Canadians.

But the kettle wasn't for us. He poured its steamy contents into the radiator and fixed a piece of cardboard in front of it. The agent slammed the hood down and walked around to my mother's window. "Ma'am, you'll have to drive slowly or the engine will overheat and stop. There are no towns or services until Winnipeg, so you'll need to keep driving. There's a bad storm coming. Good luck to you." He stood under a puddle of light from the lamppost, tipped his hand to his hat, and watched us go.

The contradictions of our situation did not escape my mother, who was accustomed to contradictions. "Money short, speed a must, but now we need to go slow." She rubbed the windshield with her sleeve as snow streaked into the headlights, striking the windshield, banking into ice at the edge of the thrashing wipers. We drove through the night as terrifying gusts of wind slammed into the car, slicing through the doors and floorboards in icy streams, threatening to bring us to a standstill while snow piled up deeper and deeper on the road ahead. At the time, we were unaware that we were driving through Winnipeg's fiercest winter and the "Snowstorm of the Century," with winds gusting at 70 miles per hour and temperatures that week plummeting to minus 49 degrees.

"If we stall in this temperature we could freeze to death

before anybody found us. Talk to me, Danny, for God's sake, keep me awake."

I shined our flashlight on the map. "After we hit Winnipeg we turn west onto the Trans-Canada Highway to cross the world's second largest country." Swinging the light across the brightly colored paper, I said, "Then, we drive, oh, 350 miles to a place called Regina. And then, just a sec, I ran out of directions." I unfolded more sections across my lap. "Okay, 475 miles later we end up in Calgary, Alberta, and then a couple hundred miles north to Edmonton." I glanced up at my mother. She stared at the road.

"And then a hop, skip, and a jump, and we arrive in Dawson Creek."

"How far is that?"

"Four hundred miles. And then it's the Alcan, the Alaska Canadian Highway. It says here under "Notes," that the Alcan is 1,500 miles of sub-Arctic terrain." I shot a look at my mother again. She didn't take her eyes from the road.

I brought the map up to the light and continued reading, "Soldiers built the road in one year to defend Alaska after the attack on Pearl Harbor. The Alcan gets to forty below zero. That's when metal turns brittle. It says it was so cold that the soldiers' feet and hands froze in their rubber boots and woolen mittens and food froze in their bowls before they could eat it. They had to keep their bulldozers and trucks running twenty-four hours a day to keep the engines from freezing. And listen to this, the Alcan is a road of logs in many parts—built like a giant raft—whole trees were rolled over what it calls 'vast stretches of sinking mud bogs that in the summer act like quicksand.' There's this little ditty written by a soldier who helped build the Alcan:

The Alaska Highway winding in and winding out
Fills my mind with serious doubt
As to whether the lout who planned this route
Was going to hell or coming out!

I laughed, but Mom just kept driving.

"Jeez, Mom, the Alcan goes over glaciers, the Rocky Mountain Range, really high passes, then Fort Nelson in British Columbia in the northern Rocky Mountains, and by the time we hit the Yukon Territory, we will have driven more than 3,000 miles. And then it's about a thousand miles more to Anchorage."

"Turn the flashlight off." She sighed, "You're wearing out the batteries."

And so we talked about our favorite food and what we'd have for dinner in Winnipeg. We spoke hopefully of receiving Dad's letters, maybe by the time we made Fort Nelson.

"We might turn around and go home, if we get a nice letter, right, Mom?"

"Maybe."

For a while, we talked about everything except what was most on our minds, the event that drove us away. There was nothing to say about it anyway. We were both there; we knew what had happened. But, after a long, silent lapse in our forced chatter about the deteriorating weather, igloos, and whether they had ice skating rinks in Anchorage, I had to ask one question. "Do you think we did the right thing? Do you think Dad misses us?" I pulled a blanket over Michael who had fallen asleep and checked the baby in the laundry basket.

"Reliving the past is unhealthy. Besides, what's done is done." Mom tested the fan for heat. "What's important is the future. We're doing everything we know to do."

She was right. Why bring up the nightmares of our past? Nevertheless, we were painfully aware of what our conversations avoided.

At the time, I never questioned that silent pact between my mother and me. Today, I can only speculate why she was so willing to embark on that desperate journey to Alaska away from my father, and why she couldn't talk about it. To protect me I am certain, because without her shield, I may never have survived the trauma of those past few weeks. But she may have had other underlying issues. After suffering abuse at the hands of her parents, she was raised by nuns in a cloistered environment where silence was a virtue and hugs unknown. Perhaps she succumbed to my father's early signs of tenderness, only to be seduced into another life of isolation and pain by the only man she ever loved. With no little words of warmth or encouragement, my father withheld from her the very thing she needed most—simple affection. Perhaps the rage and rejection we both endured at the hands of my father in the weeks leading up to our flight was beyond even her capacity for hope, much less explanation.

As for my silent resignation, I thought that if I shut my eyes at night, the images of that boy in that car would disappear. Maybe I thought that if I didn't talk about the rape and the consequences, I could go on as if nothing had happened.

MOUNTAINS

THE TEAKETTLE AND CARDBOARD GOT US TO Winnipeg. Mom had been driving for thirty-three hours. Exhausted and cold, we were ready for a warm bath and cozy bed, but due to the storm, Winnipeg had shut down for the night. Although vacancy lights flashed up and down the empty streets of the silent city, we could not rouse a soul to open a door. Desperate for a place to rest, she turned into a police station and they escorted us to a motel for the indigent and the destitute.

It wasn't the best place in town. The stale room smelled of cigarettes and urine. The sheets were unchanged from the last tenant and the jukebox from the bar downstairs blared through the floorboards. A slimy, black wood pallet covered the drain in the shower stall. We would forego the fantasy of a warm bath. Touching the sink and faucets was an uneven transaction inviting more bacteria than we were parting with, so we skipped washing altogether. "A stable would be better than this," Mom said and flopped down on the sagging bed.

The four of us slept, fully clothed, on top of the covers for a few hours before hurrying back to the relative comfort of the car where we ate the last of our peanut butter sandwiches and gobbled down a couple of oranges. It cost fifty dollars to repair the radiator. Mom didn't bother to ask how much a new one would cost.

The Trans-Canada Highway funneled us west, across

Manitoba, and into Saskatchewan's capital city of Regina. We passed through Moose Jaw, Swift Current, and Medicine Hat. North from Calgary, through Red Deer, Ponoka, and Leduc. High clouds formed before us, but as the hours went by, we realized those towering clouds were actually the Rocky Mountains.

"Look! Mountains," Michael hollered, pointing his stubby finger on the window. We had never seen anything so imposing, nor so serenely beautiful. At times, clouds cut the mountains in half, releasing the peaks from their bases—mountains floating in a misty sky. By the time we reached Dawson Creek, we had seen hundreds of snow-capped peaks.

"Look, Michael," I said. "More mountains!"

"Yeah, yeah." Michael said, "There's nothing but mountains."

The drama of car wheels crunching through snow somehow assured us that with every tick of the odometer we were forging ahead and in control. But sadness overwhelmed me. Part of me died the day I was attacked. I believed that when a boy said he loved me, he wouldn't hurt me. I believed that if I had a father who loved me, he wouldn't abandon me. I believed that if I had faith in God, He wouldn't forsake me. I was wrong on all counts.

Paul slept like baby Moses in his reed laundry basket, rocking through the wilderness with the gentle motion of the car. We fed him bottles of formula warmed in small cafes along the way. In heeding my mother's warning that I didn't want my breasts to sag at sixteen, I had moved another step away from being a mother, but I didn't want to think about that.

In Edmonton that afternoon, using the cardboard we saved from the radiator, I made a sign, "ALASKA OR BUST," and placed it in the back window of the car. The sign made a big impression. People shook their heads in disbelief. Most were amazed that we were going the distance alone, but we weren't alone. We had each other, Michael and Paul, Mom and me. The sign did not convey why Dad wasn't with us; we couldn't even bring ourselves to talk about that.

At a grocery store, a tall, Lincoln-esque man offered to help my mother carry groceries to the car. When he saw the "ALASKA OR BUST" sign in the window, he sighed, "I've always wanted to go to Alaska, but it's too late for me now."

My mother searched the craggy landscape of his face and said, "It's never too late."

He glanced at the car filled with babies and Bruce the cat and looked back at my mother. "God go with you," he said, taking her hand in his and shaking it gently.

Under the stranger's benediction, we continued north toward the Peace River Bridge, a spectacular span of steel girders. As we swept over the river, once known for transporting millions of dollars of furs in giant canoes, my mother, who loved bridges, said it was rivaled by only the Golden Gate in beauty. Peace River would be the last solid, steel threshold for almost two thousand miles. From here on, there would be more than 125 bridges on the Alcan, most of them rickety and unreliable.

I read the map as my mother drove. "The Alcan determined its own route when they bulldozed it through old Indian trails, rivers, and a few winter roads for fifteen hundred miles!"

She tried to laugh, "I bet we're the first Ford sedan with a bad heater, no snow tires, and two babies escaping down trails made by Indians in the middle of the godforsaken winter."

We checked the post office in Fort Nelson—no mail

waited for us. *Maybe in Whitehorse*, I thought, walking back to the car. I drew up the collar of my jacket against the cold wind. The cold made me think of sunshine, and the song Daddy used to sing, bouncing me on his knee:

You are my sunshine, my only sunshine,
You make me happy when skies are gray,
You'll never know dear, how much I love you,
Please don't take my sunshine away.

My heart broke a little bit more and I felt tears burning my eyes.

Mom never took her eyes off the road. She was focused, a soldier, unemotional and practical. At a small service station outside of Fort Nelson, the young man pumping our gas said the road ahead of us wasn't too bad, "Once you get over Steamboat Mountain."

Mom shook her head. "He said that too casually for comfort."

We were on one of the world's most challenging highways and now heading towards its highest pass.

Witches in the Woods

DARING AN UNFAMILIAR JOURNEY IN A FIERCE, cold season in an unpredictable car could seem like a terrible predicament for normal people. But we were far from normal and we were used to roughing it, sometimes with only a tent and a bonfire. That was when life was simple and I was happy.

It was 1956, the best summer of our lives together as a family and the warm season of my father's love. My brother Rick was six and I was eight the year we all camped in the woods while building our first home, a one-room cinderblock cabin in northern Michigan. My parents had scrimped and saved to put a down payment on a wooded parcel of land dotted with white birch trees and giant ferns. A country road wound by the property and led a short distance to the Au Sable Ski Resort where my father was the head ski instructor during the winter.

The convenience of living close to work and the fact that the land reminded Dad of Poland made the place ideal, with or without a roof over our heads. The best part of living without a house was sleeping under the stars. The blazing hollow of an old tree served as our heat, our stove, and our light. The bad part was going to the bathroom at night. The routine was to carry a shovel and a roll of toilet paper, and, while holding a flashlight, trundle into the forest. One night, the glint of eyes in the light had me clutching my pants with both hands, screaming, and dashing back to the safety of the campfire.

DANUTA PFEIFFER

Daddy laughed softly. He wasn't afraid of the wilderness. Ruggedly handsome, his erect carriage and broad shoulders stood against the dark things in the night like a Roman sentry. "It was maybe raccoon or deer, maybe scared of you too." He stirred a pot of soup, a bubbling mixture of powdered milk, beets, potatoes, and mysterious things he picked in the woods. The soup was especially good when flavored with fairy tales he told, stories that always began with the witch who lived in the woods.

"A woman lived in a small hut in the corner of the forest, away from the world. She charmed everyone into thinking she was a dazzling beauty with golden hair. But in reality, she was a wrinkly witch, with one eye burned shut."

"No one knew she was an ugly witch?" Rick squirmed on the log next to me.

I elbowed him. "Shhh!"

"Her power made her ugliness invisible. She cast a spell on everyone and even the owls didn't see her true identity."

I sat closer to Rick.

"Daddy, you made that up, didn't you? Witches aren't real."

My father added salt to his soup and threw another log into the fire. Sparks erupted into the night and buzzed around the shadowy outline of his head. He sat, reached for a cigarette, lit it, and stared for a long time into the fire. Rick and I stared with him.

"Tomorrow we have two witches coming here with their wands."

"Real witches?" Rick sounded nervous.

Dad flicked the cigarette ashes into the fire. "You will see. But now it's time for sleep."

With witches coming, he got no argument from us. We tucked into our sleeping bags around the fire and tried to sleep. Witches! Coming here?

The next morning, an old 1949 Ford pickup turned onto the dirt drive that led to our campsite. One headlight was missing. A rusty scratch ran alongside the driver's side from the headlight to the back bumper, and the roof of the cab had partly caved in. The witches who stepped out of the car didn't look much better. Surprisingly, they were men. One was short, the other was tall, and they smelled bad. Dark smears on their khaki pants looked like blood and their plaid shirts had holes in the elbows. Their suspenders were probably red once, and their boots were stiff with mud, the toe of one ripped open completely. The witches' teeth were nubs of brown and yellow, and they had thick Polish accents, like Dad.

"This is the best thing that happened to us, ever," Rick gushed, as the short witch leaned into the truck and pulled out a mason jar filled with what looked like water but smelled more like paint. He sloshed down a mouthful of the water, and wiped the drippings with the back of his grubby hand. The witch tripped over my brother, hovering behind him, and he hollered out something in Polish. Rick ran for a nearby tree, but five minutes later he was right back with the witches, underfoot and in the way. We dogged those witches. Everywhere they went, we went.

Their magic wands, lying in the back of the truck, looked more like y-shaped sticks. After a lot of talking and walking around with the jar of water, the tall witch spit on the ground. Then, he rubbed his hands together, grabbed both handles of the stick and slowly started stepping gently forward, the tip of the stick pointing ahead of him. We scuttled a safe distance behind him, fascinated and fearful of what sparks might fly out of the wand. He made a big circle, squinting at the wand as if he were casting a spell. Suddenly, the tip of the stick cranked down so fast that the green bark of the shaft wadded up in his hand. The magic wand pointed straight down at the ground, hovering, as if a giant magnet held it in place. The witch spat again. "Water. There." He grinned at us with those yellow nubs.

I didn't see anything that looked like water except that smelly old Mason jar, but that summer we built our cabin around a shiny red pump that would mark the kitchen sink and the well where the water witch spat.

Dad was right, witches were real. I never doubted him again. I was in awe of his knowledge of the world. Sometimes, he took us for late night walks deep into the woods to an old fallen tree that had rotted out. He reached his hands into the thick humus of warm, decaying wood, and pulled his hands out glowing green in the dark. His explanation of a phosphorescent worm spoke to me each time of nature's magic, which he imparted to me even when he took me deer hunting.

Hunting was the only source of meat in our diet, but Dad had strict rules. He said he hated guns, something about the war, so he hunted with a bow and arrow. "Besides," he said, "guns aren't fair to the deer. And you never hunt a doe, no matter how hungry you are, because one day she will be a mother. Only hunt daddy deer, the ones with antlers."

One cold, damp morning that dripped heavily with dew, we had tracked a deer since dawn. Dad pointed out a grassy berth in the meadow looking more like the nest of a huge bird than a deer's bed. Plunging his fingers into the deer tracks in the ground, as if reading the temperature of the earth, he said quietly, "He walked here a few minutes ago. Let's move downwind."

The ferns grew thick and hip high. My breath puffed out

like clouds of smoke. My nose was runny and my fingers and toes curled in the cold. Hungry sounds gurgled in my stomach. I wanted to go home. Just then, Daddy tapped me on the shoulder. In a clearing stood a large deer with a twitching, white tail and antlers that looked like twin trees. He nibbled on a small bush. Grinding a mouthful of leaves, he turned his head and stared at us.

Daddy drew an arrow to his bow, raised the bow, fixed his sight along the barbed shaft, and pulled back the string. The buck stopped chewing. My muscles hunched tight. A bead of sweat trickled down Dad's temple. His arm began to shiver, the bowstring still drawn back to his eye. Suspended between beauty and duty, my father paused, groaned. Just then, a resonant *twang*, and the string broke. The arrow fish-tailed through the air like a kite losing wind and impaled the ground inches from the buck's hoof. With a flash of his tail, the deer bounced into the woods and disappeared.

We stood there for a moment staring at the arrow.

"He was beautiful, wasn't he?" Dad said.

He never could shoot a deer. That's why we usually came home with a rabbit or nothing at all. The only venison on the table was if a neighbor accidentally hit a deer with his truck and we ate the road kill.

While hunting and sleeping in the woods conveyed to us a sense of wonder and adventure, nothing would prepare us for the magic of the tent we lived in. Four weeks into our summer in the woods we had an unexpected visit from the local Catholic priest, Monsignor Kaminski. He had a gift for us. "It's a circus tent, donated by Ringling Brothers when they came through town. I heard you were living out here without shelter. Thought you could use it." He signaled a flatbed truck that backed up our dirt path. It carried bulging masses of gray canvas looking like misplaced elephants, draped over stacks of long, thick poles. Ropes as thick as garter snakes coiled under the poles. Accompanying the priest were several hefty parishioners who followed behind in cars to help Daddy unload all the paraphernalia.

I imagined two hundred people a day watching lion tamers and dancing girls in the same tent that would become our bedroom, a tent so big that Dad allowed trees four times his size to grow under the canopy.

"Tent is temporary, trees are forever," my father said.

Over the course of several days, using the station wagon and ladders, ropes, pulleys, pile drivers, and the help of the monsignor's men, my father raised the 75-foot round, silvery Big Top above the forest floor. Canvas flaps rolled down for the walls and dozens of stakes, ropes, and poles held the top aloft. Live birch trees became bedposts, plywood planks our bed; the round canvas corners converted to closets, sawhorses and wood planks made up our dining table. The fibers of the canvas carried the smell of buttered popcorn and the musty scent of manure. In the autumn, leaves fell on our bed from the trees left standing in the tent.

While we lived in the tent and built the house, it was my mother who paid the bills. During the week she worked as a nurse in Detroit and lived at the YWCA. Riding seven hours on the Greyhound bus every weekend, she brought us cherries and cheese and fresh vegetables. By the time she reached us, my gentle English mother made the remarkable transition from operating room nurse to ditch digger and brick mason with the uncompromising strength and versatility of an early pioneer. Mud and sweat streaked her face as she shoveled gravel along the driveway and helped dig the foundations for the house. She hammered two-by-fours and hauled water to mix cement all weekend long. Sunday night, she rode the midnight bus back to Detroit where her calloused hands nurtured the sick and dying for another week.

That summer of water witches, the circus tent, and Daddy's glowing hands made me believe that anything was possible and everything was true.

I continued believing in my father even when he began to change.

His change took place the way a shoelace comes undone, gradually unraveling what was once secure. When our real house replaced the tent, Dad seemed lost, as if he preferred canvas to cement, as if concrete were too permanent, the block walls too real. During the ensuing years, he pined for his homeland and considered Michigan a substitute for his true home far away. He viewed the rolling hills and breezy birch trees near the Au Sable River as the scenery and stage settings for his "inauthentic life," as if my brother and mother and I were fakes, a fill-in family substituting for the real thing. Once, when I asked to go to a school dance, he scolded, "Why don't you stay home and learn to sew like your Aunt Danuta?" And he often complained that Mom's cooking, "Doesn't touch what mothers do every day in Polish kitchens." We paled in comparison to the genuine articles back in Poland: his brothers' loyalty, his father's garden, his family's joys. In his wallet he even carried a photo of his fiancée who had died in Auschwitz, her dark eyes accusing us of living her life.

And so we lived, bound to a longing that was not ours and to a past we couldn't share, imposters attending my father's counterfeit life.

Man of Seasons

JOHN RYLKO WAS MANY THINGS TO MANY people. He was the embodiment of charm, athleticism, and talent. So great my father's achievements, versatile his talents, and enduring his courage, that his light filled the room. People heard about his Olympic medals and the citations for bravery in World War II. They knew the stories of the Polish soldier who escaped the Nazis and saved those who suffered with him. And they idolized his work as a master sculptor. In churches throughout Europe, Canada, and America, his name adorns massive angels and saints chiseled from chunks of wood and stone. To the outside world, he was irresistible.

My father was a Gemini, born under the sign of the twins, good and kind and mean and moody, religious and self-righteous. He had two careers, a skier in the winter and a sculptor in the summer. He cheated on my mother. He was hard as hammers on us, but he also exhibited fragile, almost delicate qualities, a duality that always kept us guessing. People loved him. At five-foot-seven, he seemed so rooted to the ground that the very earth seemed to hold him up higher than the rest of us. When he spoke, his audience leaned into him, bathing in the golden haze of his stories, as if hobnobbing with a hero could redeem their gray and unchallenged lives, as if some part of his charm might rub off on them like lint on a black wool suit.

Clearly, he gathered adoration from friends and acquaintances, but as his family, we never really knew him, not then anyway, not when we lived under the same roof, recycling his war stories.

My father was a hero. We experienced his nostalgia and memories daily even though we were insulated by thousands of miles and more than a dozen years from World War II. By the time John F. Kennedy ran for president, we owned our first television set and Chubby Checkers had invented a new dance called the Twist. For Rick and me, the accounts of Dachau and starvation and torture were from another world. In our world, we threw snowballs, built tree houses, and traipsed through the woods in our Daniel Boone hats. Still, the war became a solid part of our lives, a habit-forming companion at dinner or bedtime, slipping into casual conversation.

"How'd you get that scar on your chin, Daddy?" referring to the three-inch scar underscoring his lower lip.

Dad rested his arms on the table. His shirtsleeves always rolled to the elbows, exposed lean forearms massing into his Popeye the Sailor muscles. "Gestapo. With a rifle, they knocked out my teeth. Bashed me in the face." He touched the scar. "I lost three teeth in front. Spit them out of my mouth. Drink your milk." Folding his hands in front of his face, blocking the scar, he stared at his food. His hands were wide and solid, suited to the squarely rooted body of a five-foot-seven inch athlete, but he had the long perfect fingers of a priest, except they were strong and not delicate.

I reached for my milk. "How come you have teeth now, Daddy?"

"The Polish army made me new false teeth. The Germans, they were butchers."

Rick and I hardly noticed our food, transfixed by the superhero at the head of the table, until my mother intervened. Without looking up from her plate she said, "John, not now, not at the table."

"Eat." My father brandished his fork at us. "And be glad that you have food and drink."

We processed one more unfinished story without a beginning or an end, filling in the blanks with our own imaginations. Sometimes his stories were brutal:

"The Butcher plunged the pointed end underneath my thumbnail and locked the pliers down from the top. The burning point of metal under my thumb held me up. I didn't feel anything at first; my body tried to understand what was happening. Then adrenaline blasted through me. I lost my breath. And pain! Intense, fiery pain! 'Would you like to talk now?' The Butcher laughed."

There were hundreds of other vivid tales alluding to suffering and pain, Gestapo disguises, and daring escapes echoing his past. We listened, wide-eyed and never sleepy, when my father sat by our bunk beds and told us a story.

"We were slaves in the high hills in the Hirschrot Camp. Building highways and starving was the name of the game. One small loaf of bread had to serve twenty men."

"Tell us how you had to march six miles every day." I hung off the side of the bed from my perch on the top bunk. I liked the top bed where I could view the whole of our brick house in a single glance, one big room where Daddy's life-sized carvings lived in the center like a silent family. I could see Mom and Dad's dark bed in the opposite corner, and the kitchen sink next to the door. I loved the big fireplace adjacent to our bunks, where Daddy lit logs every winter morning, melting the ice from the uninsulated concrete walls before we got up. My bed was as high as the TV balanced on the refrigerator. Many nights I snuggled in my bed and watched the TV's light dance on the wall above my head as I fell asleep to the comforting sounds of the *Huntley Brinkley Report* and the chipping of Daddy's chisels.

"Tell us about the empty truck," Rick chimed in from his bottom bunk.

Daddy reached for cigarettes from his shirt pocket, sometimes Chesterfields, sometimes Viceroys, but mostly they were Camels. "After this bit of food, we marched six miles to work every morning. An empty truck followed us. We carried tools, picks, and shovels. The truck carried the dead." He knocked the packet against his fingers three times and tugged on a cigarette that popped out of the box.

"The stone quarry was at the bottom of a hill. Our job was to crush the stone by hand and load a little wagon mounted on a small track." His cigarette lighter clicked open and he thumbed the flint into a flame. The tip of the Camel burned bright red. He snapped the lighter shut, tilted his chin up, and exhaled, his eyes following the long wisp of smoke into the air.

"It took eight men to push the wagon up the hill," Rick reminded him.

"That's right, four men in front pulling ropes and four men pushing behind as rifle stocks of the German soldiers pushed the prisoners, bashing them in their backs and ribs. We were hungry, wet, cold, and weak, and sometimes men slipped and tons of stone rolled back over them, crushing their miserable, meager bodies." With his cigarette hand, Daddy plucked a shred of tobacco off the tip of his tongue with his pinky finger and thumb.

I wiggled back into my warm covers.

Daddy shrugged. "But there was no mercy. If a man died, the Germans threw him onto the truck and buried him somewhere." He tapped the cigarette ashes into a saucer he held in his lap.

"And for lunch all you had was half a cup of soup made of leaves, with no fat or salt in it. Just leaves and boiling water." I added my two-cents worth, as my mother used to say, thinking of the soups Daddy made when we were building our house.

"Tell us about the monkey-face." Rick crinkled his freckled nose.

My father chuckled, and wafted more smoke in the air. Crossing his legs and leaning back in his chair, he continued. "One of the engineers was a German who looked like a monkey. The quarry contained a layer of slate, a soft, black stone when wet, hard and gray when dry. As a small diversion, I flattened some nails and sketched the face of this gorilla onto the stone. The boys got a kick out of it and some were laughing as a guard passed by. The guard grabbed the carving and smiled, 'Could you make portraits of all of us?'"

"They paid you two loaves of bread for each portrait," I said.

"Yes, two loaves for each portrait." Daddy stared past our beds, past the flickering television set and the sounds of laughter from the *I Love Lucy Show,* past Mom rattling dishes in the sink on the other side of the room, and back to a memory of a desperate time. Against his fair complexion, Daddy's eyes shone like blue stars in an alabaster sky and his hair, blond and combed straight back, made him appear as if he were hewn by a blast of wind.

No matter how many times he repeated the story, we listened in awe.

"What a treasure! Every evening, when those exhausted men came back to the barracks, they had an extra bit of bread waiting for them. I kept us all alive with my stupid little portraits." He stubbed out the cigarette.

"And nobody died." I reassured myself of a good ending.

"When I think back on it, children, I didn't do those carvings for bread. I did it for lives."

As he always did at the end of a story, my father wagged his finger at me gently. "Danuta, you have the good English. One day, I will tell my whole story, and one day you will write it."

"I promise, Daddy," I said, accepting the precious covenant between us and reminding myself of the promise with each passing tale. I would write his heroic story, like the stories of Zorro, except the man in the mask would be Daddy.

John Rylko in the quarry

My father was a sculptor. I grew up for years watching him pound at wood with mallet and chisel in that cabin in the woods. The cabin was our home, but far more important, it was his studio. Strewn across the floor were dust and tools and planks of wood glued together with iron clamps.

We shared our dining room table with his furled sketches of *Abraham Sacrificing His Son* and a statue of *The Virgin Mary* molded in plasticine. A banquette of wood balanced on saw horses bore the outlines of *The Last Supper* and the roughed out contours of the face of Judas. Our beds, the refrigerator with the television on top, and the kitchen sink all lined the walls while my father's extraordinary talent monopolized the center of the room.

By the age of eight, I would crouch for hours in a corner hugging my knees, eavesdropping on his secret life. He caressed wood like a lover, fingering the grains, reading the cambial Braille, fondling the sinews and muscles hidden in the fibers. My father was an alchemy of flesh and steel swinging his mallet, chiseling rhythmically into the wood. Long into the night my mother, brother, and I slept to the lullaby of the sculptor's song: tapping tools and the gentle rasp of wood chips spiraling to the floor. By dawn, curled shavings rustled underfoot like crisp autumn leaves, remnants of his long night of lovemaking.

His tools were both delicate and destructive. Sometimes he coiled bits of wood with an instrument as dainty as a dentist's probe and other times he lunged at a carving with a chisel shaped like a soup can. His mallet was a rounded stump of wood concaved from years of pounding, held by a rolling pin handle. I often marveled at how his biceps looked as round and hard as his mallet.

I watched in wonder as shape emerged from the unshaped. Grotesque at first with the effort of becoming, body parts wrenched themselves from the fibers: fingers arthritic with unfinished knuckles; a coarsely hewn arm; a chin stubbing out from the grain; a rib as new as Adam gave to Eve. Before my eyes, Jesus was born next to the refrigerator.

Jesus is chiseled to life in the living room of the Rylko family home.

Christ Crucified was bigger than life—at eight feet tall, massively graceful, more than human, less than God. Christ's arms stretched upon a timber cross, shoulders strained, tendons drawn and aching beyond endurance, hands and feet ruptured by nails, his diaphragm heaving for air. The eyes of Christ, bathed in extraordinary sadness, peered down on his creator, my father, with peace and forgiveness. Our Savior, who was born and baptized in our living room, was installed in Saint Paul's Church in Onaway, Michigan, where thousands of people now worship Him.

Of all his carvings, *The Holy Trinity* was his masterpiece. Ponderous black walnut the size of a barn door became God the Father, a vision of cumulus robes flying in divine wind. In God the Father's outstretched hands, a life-sized crucifix with Jesus limp in death, his soul gleaming through the polished wood with resurrected life. Between the heads of the Father and Son rose the dove of the Holy Ghost. The chest of the dove was barreled with power, the feathers chiseled like armor. Oiled and rubbed to a high gloss, the black walnut was an explosive creation, boiling with my father's energy, bursting beyond the wood, dwarfing us all.

As much as my father loved wood, I think he loved marble more. The air would fill with white powder as he polished massive boulders to a finish as smooth as his cheeks after a shave. Stone dust clung to the hairs on his arms and settled on his head and eyelashes until he appeared to be part stone himself, leaking his human warmth to statues while he slowly turned cold. This was, in part, his genius.

It was also his flaw. His creations seemed to claim bits and pieces of his life; their muscles flexed with his strength; their tendons tensed with his will; their faces filled with his sorrow . . . until slowly, agonizingly, bit by bit, Daddy became the man on the cross.

It seemed as though every Catholic in the northern hemisphere made a pilgrimage to see my father's sculptures. Bishops from Chicago and Detroit, student sculptors from Germany, tourists from Toronto, all made the journey of faith to see the saints in Daddy's studio, our living room. A bus full of nuns fell to their knees before *Jesus on the Cross* and said the whole rosary in the driveway. Some shed tears. They marveled at the life emerging from rock and wondered over the blood coursing through veins of wood.

When the cardinal came to visit, Dad kissed his ring. Then Rick and Mom and I kissed the ring, too. The high priest's nails were shiny and clean. I didn't think he ever built a house. My father showed him *Jesus on the Cross* and *Mary with Child*. He showed pictures of *The Last Supper, The Twelve Apostles*, and the *Stations of the Cross*. The cardinal nodded and sighed.

Our cottage in the middle of the woods was not a place one expected to find holy men with fine clothes and ruby rings, but nearly every day, the Church came to us. My mother rummaged through her meager cupboards to prepare tea and cakes, slapping away the wood chips from the dining room table with her dishtowel. Mom always made something special for priests, and if we were lucky, we got to eat some too.

"How long would it take for you to carve a crucifix for me, John?" The cardinal glanced around the room but didn't sit down.

"About four months, Your Excellency." My father put his pictures aside and squared his shoulders toward the priest. "But I would need to be paid in advance for the wood. I haven't been paid for my last two statues yet. It's been over a year now and as you can see, we could use the money."

"God will provide, my son," the cardinal said, walking out of the room and stepping to his big black car, where a chauffeur-priest opened the door for him. "When can you begin the new work for me?"

The cardinal didn't want to see our single room dotted with beds in the corners. The cardinal did not care to know how the frost gathered on the unadorned walls and bare cement blocks inside the house on below-zero mornings. He certainly didn't care that the Church frequently forgot to pay my father for his remarkable statues. He had little need for the lowly thoughts of compensation. My father had a gift for creation; whether the Church honored that gift was unimportant to it. Holy men only wanted to see divinity in the wood. Dad must have felt used. At least the Germans had paid him with bread for his carvings. The Church didn't seem to care about him at all. As a child, I thought that was why he didn't go to Mass.

Had it not been for my mother's efforts we would really have been in trouble. She showed Dad's pictures to design companies and churches and negotiated his commissions. Weary from working double shifts at a local hospital, she'd slap pictures of his work on the desks of agents or wood company executives in Traverse City or Detroit, and say, "Here's his work. He's talented. Interested?" Her brevity must have surprised them, and sometimes her efforts got him paying work. Sadly, my father wasn't affected by my mother's devotion. I rarely saw them hold hands or kiss or even smile at each other.

While Mom worked nights to pay the mortgage and buy the groceries, and took care of us during the day, my father drank long cups of coffee in the morning and watched the afternoon slip into night. Between artistic inspirations, he spent days with an aimless friend, played chess, filled ashtrays with cigarette butts, and in the evening piled up empty wine bottles around his chair.

Within this fortress he drifted through the present like a dream, preserving the past as his only true life. As children, we sensed his depression in the long hours of brooding silence, in the stories he told of Poland, and the family he missed there. His true life had already been spent, poured out like an overturned bucket of milk, lost and irretrievable. Eventually, his emptiness filled us all.

MY FATHER WAS A SKIER. He taught me that snow builds legends. And John Rylko was the greatest legend of them all. He was a man of seasons, a sculptor in the summer and a skier in the winter. If I had to choose which element most suited him, I'd choose ice over fire. Dad was at his emotional best when his feet lengthened into skis. Laced into boots and locked into skis, he belonged to the snow. He was intense and self-assured, puffing steam clouds in the air, fired up, ready to move.

On skis, he made a simple turn spectacular. Ordinary skiers turned on the snow. My father turned directions in the *air*. He'd cross the face of the slope, plunge his poles in front of him and vault above them, body and skis angulated against the sky like a blue heron. Whipping around the tops of his poles, he'd slap to the ground, facing the opposite direction, skiing with his arms open wide, embracing the sheer joy of it all, as if switching directions in the sky were second nature to him. How could it be otherwise to an Olympic medalist?

Dad told us the story a hundred times. Germany and the 1936 Winter Olympics. He skied for Poland in the cross-country marathon. Acting out the drama in the middle of the room, picking through the trail of snow, his energy drummed against us with every stab of his ski pole, every lunge of his boot against bindings.

"Near the end of the race, I was exhausted with only three kilometers to go. Over the ridge I saw crowds of people. The loudspeaker announced, 'It looks like the White Pole is taking first place!'

"The White Pole? Then I realized they were talking about me! I was dressed completely in white: white stockings, white gloves, a white parka, even my skis were white. I knew I was doing good time, I had passed a lot of skiers, but I didn't know I was winning!

"I came to a slight hill with a sharp bend to the right and then another incline of about thirty feet. From there, it was straight down to the finish line. But when I heard my name called, I pushed even harder. I climbed the incline, exhausted after almost fifty kilometers."

"That's twenty-six miles," I explained to Rick in a big sister, know-it-all sort of way.

"I know that." He dug me with his elbow.

"I jabbed at the snow. My bamboo ski pole stuck in a tree stump. Snapped in half. Jerked me back. I shook it off my hand. Left it behind. Climbed with one pole. My lungs ached, my heart pounded in my head. I got to the top. I ran, downhill, through the checkpoints and over the finish line. I lost first place by three-tenths of a second."

"You lost just by a ski tip." I pinched my fingers together.

My father pinched his fingers together. "Just a ski tip!"

"Remember, Danuta, one day I will tell my whole story."

"And one day I will write it."

Daddy winked. "That's right, one day, you will write it in your good English."

John Rylko with admirers at the ski lodge

Rick and I were destined to be in our own Olympic trials one day. I learned to ski between my father's legs, my arms wrapped tightly around his knees as he coaxed my wobbly skis into compliance inside the corral of his sharp edges. He built a ski jump and taught Rick to land with his arms "spread like an eagle." At eight and ten, Rick and I were among the youngest unofficial ski patrol members in the country, working at the resorts where my father taught, flagging injured skiers, helping the ski bunnies to their feet, shoveling icy patches, leveling moguls—first on the slopes in the morning, last on the runs at closing. We raced nearly every weekend during the winter and each time I made my winded encounter with the finish line I felt indelibly linked to the White Pole.

Olympic medals opened doors at ski resorts where Dad became the ski pro. Reporters and photographers trooped to our cabin and took his picture and wrote down his stories. Winter and summer, skiing and sculpting, it was the one-two rhythm reinforcing the power of his life.

Unfortunately, there were other characteristics of my father that were not so well documented. He had a quick, fierce temper that he often turned against my mother. I hated to hear my parents fight—their angry voices ring in my ears even now, decades later. Shouting and tears, voices charging at one another, my mother pleading, "John, how could you?"

"Shut up, you think the whole world should hear your voice?"

"I hoped you'd be grateful."

"Grateful? To such a wife?"

"I'm shy, you know that."

"Shy. You are not shy. You think you are better than other people."

I didn't understand their quarrels. They were just words, but loud, harsh words that made my stomach ache. But there were plenty of clues that pointed to the source. My father attracted women. A newspaper clipping from the *Gaylord Herald-Times* in 1959 shows my father's charismatic smile, his arms around two ladies. The caption reads:

"Two pretty skiers who drove all the way to Au Sable Ranch and Ski Club from Toledo, Ohio, for its opening week 'round-up' pose briefly in front of the warming house with John Rylko, the ski instructor, before taking a lesson."

He looks charming. Downright handsome. He's sleek in his dark blue form-fitting ski pants. Pale blue wind jacket tucked in at the waist, goggles riding high on his forehead. The "pretty skiers" are giggling.

At night, my father became an expert of another sport in the ski lodge. "He could put his ski boots under my bed any day!" At the time, I didn't know what the lady in the red ski pants meant, but apparently Dad's ski boots saw lots of bedsprings and we felt the effects of his dalliances. My parent's muted relationship became defined not by words that were spoken, but what was left unsaid and by my mother's sadly, soulful brown eyes. "It was the war," she said, excusing the infidelities of her husband.

To us, "the war" meant patches of recollections, bits and pieces told in moments of deep reflection, or gleaned from newspaper articles. One read: "John's tank ran over a land mine and he was sent to Dachau, possibly the worst of the German concentration camps. He and his brother dug mass graves in the forest where many prisoners were hung and buried."

We carved wide margins of forgiveness for my father due to those experiences. He piled his despair upon us until we became the storehouse of his grief, stockpiling his wounds like dusty trophies. We clung to his pain like a legacy, because for the hundreds of times he disappointed us, there were the hundreds of stories that forgave him.

It was the war, we told ourselves.

"We are from a long line of the House of Jasterowski," my father taught us, and Rick and I repeated it like a mantra: "Jasterowski, the Polish count who fought the Czar and escaped to the Carpathian Mountains. He changed his name to an anagram from his coat of arms. The wild boar, the lion, and the sword became our name, Rylko. Our name was conceived by a count and passed on through our grandfathers to us."

"Never forget," my father said.

How could we do otherwise when confronted time and again with newspaper reports detailing my dad's brutal background and his stunning survival skills? How could we not be proud as we read newspaper articles from Detroit proclaiming his glory?

SCULPTOR NEAR GAYLORD POSED AS GESTAPO AGENT

This man escaped from concentration camps twice during World War II. John A. Rylko's biggest thrill was winning second place for the Polish cross-country ski team in the 1936 Olympic games at Garmisch, Germany. John studied at the University of Fine Arts in Krakow for seven years and was working for his Master's when Hitler invaded Poland. The only thing that mattered then was to free the homeland from the shouts of 'Heil Hitler.'

We paid homage to the blood, believing in the qualities that surged through our Polish veins: bravery, honor, endurance, and achievement. These were the themes of our heritage, told time and time again in my father's stories. His courageous life stamped us like a birthmark. My father expected Rick and me to navigate our way through life fearlessly and confidently, possessed of star quality and noble birth. Because my father had suffered and survived, we forgave the stings of injustice we suffered at the end of his belt.

PATRICIA MICHELLE

MY MOTHER FORGAVE HIM BECAUSE SHE LOVED him. She said it like an apology into a dark confessional: Bless-me-father-for-I-have-sinned-but-I-loved-him. Through the lonely winters of my father's "socializing" and the moody summers of his "artistic temperament," through his bitter rebukes and his countless infidelities, my mother loved him.

She loved him the moment she first set eyes on him in a London hospital after the war. She was eighteen, a student nurse. He was sick with jaundice.

When we had been living in our newly built cabin in Michigan for less than a year, she told us the story of how they met. Due to our nomadic life up until then, Mom confided in her children, having few friends of her own. Rick and I, seven and nine years old, listened, equal victims of unrequited love.

"What's jaundice?" I looked up from my geography book. Rick stopped drawing.

"It's a liver problem when your eyes turn yellow. God, he was handsome!" She paused, and stared at the pictures in my book, silently adoring my absent father, who was in the ski lounge gathering adoration from others.

"I loved his high cheek bones. Square jaw. Blue eyes. He only knew 'yes,' 'no,' and 'cigarettes, please.' He always used the dictionary and got so frustrated sometimes; I had to duck when he threw it against the wall. That was okay, though. He was homesick."

When they met, my father was already a thirty-one-year-old veteran of many miseries, but my eighteen-year-old mother was a veteran of another kind of war, accustomed to bruises on her arms, welts on her back, and the occasional broken bone from her parents. She was used to ducking out of the way. I didn't learn these things as a child, however, and my curiosity went only as far as a fairy tale could take me.

Patricia Michelle and John Rylko 1948

"When did you get married and live happily-ever-after?" I asked.

"A year later. We made a fine pair. I couldn't speak Polish and he didn't speak English. But I saw him through the lens of love. And if Daddy is grumpy sometimes just remember that unimaginable misery must have some effect on a human being. The war and what your Dad went through, you know what I mean? All he needs is patience and love. Lots and lots of love."

My mother believed love was supposed to fix everything, even the cold stares of the British who hated foreigners. Back in 1948, strangers felt compelled to chide her, "Isn't an Englishman good enough for you?" Jobs were tight. Foreigners threatened English workers.

Mom probably thought if her love were strong enough, it would comfort her not only from a disapproving society, but also from the abandonment of her parents. As it turns out, love did not rescue her and she remained as isolated as her childhood.

Her eyes spoke the language of her loneliness. A hooded expression and a slight tilt of her head lent her a shy appearance, yet she was not as fragile as she seemed. While misery has countless victims mired in helplessness, in my mother unhappiness built a reservoir of strength that some might call stubbornness. She never cowered from my father. Instead, under his rebuke she stood firm, regarding him in a steady gaze of brown eyes softened by pain. Her beauty bypassed pretty. The features of her heart-shaped face—a long nose, deep brown eyes, full lips, a porcelain complexion—assembled themselves toward a quiet elegance. Dad used to say Mom's nose lacked proportion (whatever that meant) but I thought she looked regal. Her black curls bounced on her shoulders as she marched rather than strolled down the street. I can still see the navy blue cape she wore over her nurse's uniform billowing with each step of her long, sure stride. Her simple dresses flattered a perfect figure. She wore a watch, her only adornment, on the back of her slender wrist for taking a patient's pulse.

It seemed like Dad never saw her beauty, inside or out, and Mom must have been disheartened by the way he treated her. She told me years later that after I was born Dad used sex like a favor, and religion like a club. On birthdays and holidays, sex was a present he didn't have to buy. He told her sex was against the Catholic faith except to make children. We still lived in England when Rick was conceived. She seduced him with wine, apparently during a night he forgot. That's why a few months later he roared at her, "Go to the father of it!" I was only a year old when Dad stomped off and disappeared, leaving my pregnant mother to fend for herself.

By 1950, England was still early in the process of recovering from the war; jobs were scarce. All Mom and Dad could afford was the rent on a small gypsy wagon. The three of us lived in a ten-foot-long, uninsulated wooden box. When it rained, it leaked, and, after Dad left, Mom tried filling the holes with straw. Seven months later, Rick was born and the hospital refused to release a young mother with two babies and no father to care for them. The government tracked Dad down, threatening to withhold his wages unless he came to the hospital. Mom said he showed up grudgingly to collect us.

On the train ride back to the wagon, my mother remembered that my father didn't talk about his whereabouts and offered no apologies. It took him an hour to ask about his new son, Richard.

"His head is too long." He was still mad.

"It's from the forceps."

"Humph," was all he said.

Two years after Rick was born, Dad's mother died in Poland on New Year's Eve. Dad fell into a black hole, drinking and weeping for weeks. Mom said he blamed her for putting "a ball and chain" around his neck, for "trapping" him with children, and keeping him from his beloved home. He raged at her, "You and Churchill. If it wasn't for you, I'd be back in Poland."

My mother refused to move to Poland with two small children when Poland lacked bare essentials like aspirin, shoelaces, and penicillin. Besides, she reasoned, there would be no turning back; in the communist world a visit was permanent. My father seemed stuck, pining for what he said was unattainable and blaming my mother for it, even though he could have gone back to Poland without us. Sometimes, I wondered why he didn't.

Eight years would go by before the birth of my youngest brother, Michael. Dad would melt into smiles holding him, as if the annoyance of another child had never occurred to him. By that time, we would also be nearing the full brunt of his bitterness. That time was yet to come. And Mom still had to get us ready for bed.

After telling us the story of how she met Daddy, Mom said, "Okay, brush your teeth and thank your lucky stars you don't have to brush with salt."

"Salt?" Rick screwed up his face at the thought of it.

"That's what we used in the Carmelite convent. I've told you how the government sent me to the Convent of Jesus and Mary in Willsden after my mother beat me."

As a little girl, my mother prayed to Saint Jude to rescue her, but the beatings continued. She sought sanctuary in the church, a safe place where she could stop the bleeding, away from her mother's broom handle. Hiding and shivering in the anteroom of a church on Park Lane in Wembly, she covered herself with a rug from the floor. Hours later, her enabling and timid father, who never raised a finger to protect her, found her washing the blood from her socks in the cold water of the presbytery sink. Without saying a word, he took her hand, and brought her home again. Saint Jude finally answered her prayers at the age of six when somebody notified the Royal

Society of Prevention of Cruelty to Children and placed her in a convent to be raised by nuns.

"They treated us like little nuns," my mother said. "We slept in a long dormitory on iron cots with a white canvas surrounding each bed for privacy. At four a.m. each morning, we washed our faces and hands in cold water and brushed our teeth with salt that burned our lips."

I sat on the edge of my bunk thinking Crest toothpaste wasn't so bad.

"We went to Mass for an hour-and-a-half. Ate breakfast by seven. Took a bath in a bucket of warm water once a week. And we weren't allowed to speak."

"You couldn't talk?" I thought she was joking.

"No, the nuns seldom spoke, they took the vow of silence, and so did we. We did everything—chores, schoolwork, and meals—all in silence. But when you can't talk, you listen." She put her finger to her lips. "I recognized the nuns by the sound of their footsteps."

Mom stood up with a glint in her eye. "Sister Joseph was tall, with a long, pale face and a measured tread, and her beads slapped her skirt in time with her steps." Mother strode around the room and we jumped off our beds and marched in behind her.

"Now, Sister Anne was like lightning." Mom spun around, her voice sounding more and more like a young girl. "She hurried everywhere and played field hockey with us by hiking her habit between her legs." I figured Mom was more like Sister Anne than anyone, quiet as a nun around most people, but the few times she laughed, it sounded like music.

"Nuns run?" I tried imagining a nun with legs.

"Except the Reverend Mother." Mom's voice lowered. "She saw to the spiritual balance of the convent and prayed. She kept her distance so as not to be disturbed. Her little feet took bird-like steps, and we stood to one side to let her pass."

Mom tiptoed around the floor. Her black locks fell into her face and she seemed more like my big sister than my mother. "And then there was Mother Francis de Salles, the Mother Superior, a tank of a woman with a stony face, who always looked for the worst in us. She walked like thunder, all six feet and 220 pounds of her, her enormous black habit swaying heavily in the breeze." We all marched around the room swinging our arms and collapsed on the bed laughing.

Mom spent her entire girlhood, from six to sixteen, in the convent. "After ten years, I was a nun by osmosis." Rick and I didn't know the word *osmosis*, but we figured Mom was almost a saint. When her parents refused, in writing, to give their permission for her education as a nun, she bargained for medical school, hoping to become a doctor. Her parents wrote back that it was not an occupation for ladies, at which point she settled for nursing. They didn't like that either, but they reluctantly gave in.

Mom motioned me towards her, and she brushed my dark blonde hair, twining it into a long pigtail down my back. "You can be anything you want to be. Don't ever let anyone tell you differently."

"I'm going to be a ski racer, like Dad," Rick clapped his hands.

"I'm going to the Olympics." I climbed up to my bunk.

Osmosis at work, from Daddy to us. I wonder if my mother noticed that, even then, the goodness she gave us could not deter our devotion to Daddy's life, that he pulled us into him and we could not see the Moon for the Sun. Looking back, I now understand that my mother was the source of my resiliency and focus, gifts I would need to escape from him. And later, I would need her capacity to forgive. But back then, not one of us could break the obsession with my father.

Though my mother was as soft as an English mist, she was stubborn as a London fog, and she would wait up for my father all night long as the black and white television flashed shadows of the Marlboro Man on the wall.

On my bureau today rests a framed photo of my mother and father the year they were married. She was not yet twenty, sitting on a high-backed bench with my father, his legs crossed, a cigarette casually held in his hand. She is smiling with unparted lips, a modern Mona Lisa. With her first love at her side, a handsome Polish soldier, she gazes at the camera as if she were finally happy.

On the opposite side of the bureau is a faded newspaper photo of my father posing with his chisels beside his stone *Madonna*. The caption beneath reads:

"John Rylko is an outstanding sculptor, who has finally found the life he desires away from the turmoil and tragedy of the old country."

Neither got what they bargained for. Not my father who could never return to Poland, nor my mother, escaping to Alaska from the man she loved.

Bridges

WE LOST THE ROAD AT THE HIGHEST POINT ON the Alaska Highway. Fluffy, white snow camouflaged a varnish of ice up Steamboat Mountain as the Ford snorted against the incline. The temperature gauge inched into the red zone. Steam belched from the hood. My mother pounded the steering wheel. "Come on. Come on!" Coughing and choking, the car had finally reached the summit at Milepost 392, an elevation of 4,250 feet.

The landscape before us would have made a beautiful postcard if it weren't so diabolically real. Snowcapped peaks circled us like tepees. The snow had become a silent menace lying deep about us, concealing the road. The anemic sun cast half-hearted shadows across the landscape of ridges, boulders, and embankments. The bony branches of buried trees sprouted from gnarly mounds of snow like tangles of wire. Summit Lake spread before us enshrouded by a dusty cerulean fog that made the lake look like it was floating in midair.

The instant Mom and I stepped out of the car the atmosphere seemed to crackle with cold, the icy air biting into my flesh like fire. We dashed ahead to survey the road, if you could call it that. The passage forward was more like a suggestion—a narrow depression—and in some spots, the icy blanket flattened out to no suggestion whatsoever.

"Could use some tire chains about now," Mom said under her breath as we hightailed it back to the car. "We'll have to pussyfoot through here." We crept around curves, zigzagged up switchbacks, and twisted into shallow valleys, occasionally stopping to make sure the road was beneath us. It was hard to tell; the road was gravel and dirt and ice below the snow, just like everything else in the Yukon. The route was pretty obvious in another way: either plow into a glacier bulging over the road or fall off a cliff, chances were pretty good that the road was somewhere in between. There were no guard rails, no motels, no signs of humanity at all. We pussyfooted for 202 miles without seeing another soul on the road. This wasn't anything new, really. We were used to being lost.

I nodded off and on in a fitful space between wakefulness and nightmares, never sure which was the dream. At times I'd be cowering in my room as my father blasted through the door in all his fury and thunder, and other times I'd be insulated back in our 1965 Ford sedan traveling four thousand miles through burning ice. I found my bearings in my mother's riveting focus on the road ahead and in the holy cargo tucked in the back seat: my four-year-old brother, Michael, my tabby cat, Bruce, curled up in his lap, and my baby, Paul, sleeping in the wicker basket.

Mom hadn't slept for two days. And she never turned the car engine off. Never. It was the unwritten code of harsh winters even back home in Michigan. Cold kills. Engines freeze. If she had shut the engine down, we probably would have frozen to death in that icy tin can. As it was, we could have ended up at the bottom of a gorge had my mother not answered a call to courage.

I woke up when I heard Mom say, "Oh, oh." It was early and ice fog filtered the light through a gauzy, frozen lens. The linen sky cast no shadows on the Yukon landscape. Thick, scruffy trees and still pines sprouted from the snow and hedged the road. A snowcapped mountain mocked us in the distance as if to bar our way. Ahead of us appeared a narrow passage in the brush.

Mom stopped the car and hollered, "You've got to be kidding."

We saw what could only jokingly be called a bridge. The structure was about a hundred feet long and thirty feet wide. It was made of logs rolled together perpendicular to the road and spanned a steep gully of boulders leading to a frozen chasm of ice fifty feet below. A rickety railing of tree limbs leaned out of reach from the sides, warning of imminent collapse if touched. Crossing the logs were two tracks of four-by-six planks nailed to the logs, wide enough for a single tire. Nothing seemed to hold the bridge up in the middle, no crisscross boards, no slats, no pilings. Only a stack of more logs under each end held the span to the opposing bank.

"It's a simple bridge," my mother said. She loved bridges and was always fascinated by their supports and suspensions, bridges that spanned the gaps from one impossible bank to another. She often said were she not a nurse, she'd be a designer of bridges. The snow crunched under her knee as she knelt to examine the structure. "There may be a girding, or something underneath, but I can't see it. If it can't hold the car. . . ."

Her sentence drifted off as she glanced back down the road, perhaps wondering if the bridges we left behind were better than the bridges ahead. Maybe she hoped a repair truck might come barreling up with extra pilings or a serviceable railing or maybe another way around the chasm, but the Alcan was a desolation of wilderness filled with bears and godawful cold. No one would save us but ourselves.

"Okay, we've got to get across this thing. There's no going

around it." She pulled off her gloves and stuffed them in her pocket. "But just in case, we're going to walk across it first. You and Michael go ahead of me. I'll carry the baby. Then I'll go back and drive the car across."

"What do you mean, just in case?" I asked.

"If the car doesn't make it, at least you children won't be at the bottom of the gorge." She said it with flint in her eyes.

"But, what happens if . . . "

"No ifs. Just do as I say." That no-nonsense tone of a British nurse made her sound perfectly reasonable. She took Michael and Paul out of the car and zipped Mike's jacket tight, putting him in front of me. "Hold his collar and don't bloody let go," she commanded. She clutched the baby and we faced the bridge.

"Wow," Michael said, pointing to the abyss below, "Look at that."

"Never mind. Don't look down." Mom nudged me towards the bridge. "I want you to walk slowly. Keep your eyes on the other side. Michael, you go first. Danny, you next, hold onto the collar of his coat and for God's sake don't let go of him."

We walked in a tight single file, without side rails, or posts, or anything to hold on to. Air above and air below, we walked the plank, one foot in front of the other. The distant bank wobbled in my sights. I felt seasick on the sweeping space about me. I looked down at the narrow board suspending me at a breathless height. The logs beneath the four-by-six planks were not tightly set and in some spots the snow fell between them, revealing spaces wide enough for someone my size to slip through.

"Keep your eyes on the other end." My mother's cool voice came from behind. "And don't look down."

The bank grew closer and leveled out to a firm promise.

When we planted our feet on the opposite side, Michael stomped his boots into the snow, confirming solid ground. We stood quietly staring back across the bridge at the car we left behind. The Ford looked small and abandoned. Our breath hung suspended in icy clouds above our heads. The sweat on my face burned as it froze on my nose and cheeks.

I took Paul from my mother's arms and held Michael's hand, and she walked back across the plank to the car. The three of us clung to one another, watching her. She sat in the car, staring at the bridge, bargaining with the gods, and finally gave a little wave. We waved back. Mom started the car forward and sighted it with the bridge. She got out and came around the front to make sure the tires aligned with the planks. Her stomach must have been doing flips.

What if she fell through the bridge? What were we kids supposed to do, standing in the middle of the Alcan? I guess my mother believed we'd have a chance on the road; maybe a car might come along before it was too late. There would be no chance at the bottom of a crevasse. I figured we'd be goners, either way.

Michael called out to her, "Mommy, are you coming?"

"It'll be okay." She sounded far away.

"Shush, Michael. Let Mommy drive the car." I squeezed his little hand.

The front tires inched up onto the planks. The bridge groaned. The car stopped. Mom leaned her head out. She let up on the brake. The front wheels rolled on and the back tires ran up each plank. The car crept onto the bridge. The crevasse below and the bridge above held our lives suspended as we bargained on my mother's dead reckoning. The bridge creaked and the planks moved slightly under the weight. Eternal seconds later, the front wheels crunched into snow and the back tires followed onto terra firma. Our lives were back.

"Yay!" Michael clapped his hands. Mom jumped out of the car and hugged all of us.

"You did it!" I bounced Paul in my arms.

"Had to." She gave her British no-nonsense nod.

As we sped away, I wondered if we would ever have to cross a bridge like that again.

WHITEHORSE

IN WHITEHORSE THE TEMPERATURE PLUM-
meted to minus thirty degrees. I never saw daylight so dim.
Dull fog absorbed all the colors of the world. Trees and poles,
rocks and roads appeared and vanished in a matted haze.

There was no mail waiting for us at the post office.

"Maybe in Anchorage," I said, trying to sound hopeful.

"Maybe." Mom tried, too. She yanked her dark hair off
her shoulders and wrapped a scarf around her neck. I thought
how sad she looked, how faint her voice. I thought she would
cry.

We mailed our postcards for Rick and Dad with pictures
of the Rocky Mountains and a pencil line indicating the
Alcan skirting impossible ridges. I figured if we showed Dad
our perilous journey on postcards, he might show a sign of
concern. A letter back from him would mean love. A letter
would mean forgiveness. A letter would repair our shredded
family. I carried that torch of longing across the tundra.

Of course, looking back on all this now, I can see how
impossible that would have been. Dad had no intention of
writing to us. And Mom had no intention of going back.
Words must have been said and deeds done that could not
be undone. I was not privy to what transpired between my
parents during the two weeks leading up to our departure.
In those bleak days, I was sick and weary, faint and fearful,
locked in my room, emotionally drained. Mom took the

brunt of it. I felt only the margins of my dad's anger, but the power of his rage was fierce. I think Mom must have finally drawn the line in those two weeks. Enough was enough.

But at the time, during the journey, I still wondered if my father ached with the empty spaces around him. Did he miss us? I honestly believed my daddy wouldn't just let us go, no matter how bitter he was. Yet, I questioned whether it was better to have no father than a father who is mad with rage, and if my mother decided it was better to have no husband than a husband who doesn't love back.

But why did Rick stay with a man like that? My brother always tried so hard to win my father's approval, struggling at school, falling into a vortex of underachievement. Teachers claimed that he didn't try, and that infuriated my father. Out came the belt and another day of Rick's wailing and fear and going to bed without dinner, as if Daddy thought he could beat the grades out of him. So Rick cowered before Dad and kept his distance. He got picked on the most.

Not me. I always had good grades. Always. If my brother was bullied into underachieving, I responded just the opposite way. I overdid everything, as though my first attempts might not be good enough. If my teacher wanted a volunteer, I volunteered twice. Two pages for a report? I did five. One book report? I wrote two. Next to Rick's grades, mine dazzled. The more I accomplished, the less Rick achieved. I was the first born, and my father's approval passed on to me and overlooked Rick completely, although my dad did not spare the belt and the lashings on me, either.

Rick went underground; his sensitivity thrived in the dark, below the surface, where his meticulous mind and creative instincts existed in relative safety from the storm that blew above. He read Superman comic books and drew pictures and whittled at small carvings that he kept hidden in a box. He disappeared like the furniture, noticed only when needed.

Rick and I were scales, counterbalanced against my father's emotional excesses and my mother's resignation. My brother's gentle and submissive nature weighed in direct proportion to my anxieties to please. And for years we played our parts in trying to stabilize our rickety family structure. Maybe Rick stayed because he wanted to show Dad his loyalty, and he wouldn't need to compete for space and time with his father. Maybe, in spite of his fear, Rick needed Dad's love more.

Back on the Alcan, the faint-hearted sun courted the southern hemisphere for most of the day and wouldn't climb to our horizon until late afternoon, and then only briefly, barely lighting the dim fog before plunging us back into the dark. The swift-running rivers of summer were now solid and silent, jammed into mounds of ice that would not give way for months. Like the still and frozen land, we were inert, awaiting the animation of a warmer season. But this was only February and the frost lay thick upon the rivers, and ice fog draped us like a shroud.

THE CONTRADICTIONS

"ONE-TWO-THREE, ONE-TWO-THREE, ONE-two-three. Don't look at your feet, listen to the music." I was five years old and the "Blue Danube" played on the hi-fi as my father swung me around the floor, laughing at my awkward feet, nodding with approval when I got it right. "One-two-three, one-two-three." Daddy swept me around and around the floor until I learned to dance without counting. The strains of the "Vienna Waltz" rings in my ears like the whistle of my father's belt when he beat me. He rarely spared his temper, even when we were little, and the memories burn me like a brand.

Before Michigan, we lived in Canada in the rented attic of a house next to a bean field—one that got us into a lot of trouble. Rick and I had just come home from school, and our parents were still at work. Mom worked the midday shift in a hospital and Dad carved for an agency in town. That small interlude between supervision and the lack of it caused the welts that rose on my back later that day.

"New things are few and far between," my mother used to say, so when she bought us new trench coats, we treasured them and wore them everywhere with pride, even into the bean patch. It had rained earlier and the mud was thick as chocolate pudding. Rick got stuck first. Up to his hips. His new coat ballooned around him like a poodle skirt. He couldn't wrench himself out and started to cry. I slogged out to help him, only to find my own boots sucked down in the goo. We were both stuck. From a bird's point of view we must have looked like two lonely flowers, trapped by the petals of our new coats, swaying in a black field. No one heard us cry for help. Eventually, we crawled to the safety of a ditch, our boots left behind in the mud, and our new white coats soiled the color of coal.

I don't know what scared us more, the quicksand of the bean field or Daddy's quick temper. We were desperate to clean ourselves up before our parents came home. Six inches of cold water in an old aluminum tub only made our coats look worse. The next best thing to do was hide. We bundled our clothes into muddy black balls and shoved them under the bed, then we put on our pajamas and pretended to be asleep when our parents came home a few minutes later.

They saw the clothes, the tub of dirty water, the mud splattered on the floor, and one sock stuck to the wall. This might have seemed pitifully funny to some, but not to Daddy. He was furious.

"We get you new coats and this is what you do with them?" He yanked me out of bed. "You hide your coats? You think we will not find them?" I trembled before him on knees made of jelly.

I wanted to say that I tried to save Rick, that he was crying and stuck in the mud. I wanted to say I was stuck too, but nothing came out. What was important was the mud on my coat. And the hidden clothes. He did not like to be deceived—although I'm certain that if the clothes were out in the open, his anger would have been the same. The lesson was fixed in my mind. Telling the truth hurts as much as hiding it.

"Daddy," I pleaded. I danced on my tiptoes and tried to explain.

He wasn't in the mood for explanations. I remember my terror in minute detail, the way people report absolute awareness during an accident. The rattle of the buckle under his fingers. The hissing of the belt whipping through the loops of his trousers. My mother screaming, "No, John, don't!" The pajamas becoming warm and wet as I peed in terror. My eyes blinking uncontrollably. The buckle jingles. The leather snaps. A quick inhale and flinch before the pain. The belt cracks across my bottom. Whips on my back. I exhale in a fearful cry. Red welts rise up under my pj's. He presses my head against the side of his leg with one hand and flogs me with the other. In a hellish waltz around the floor, we swing in furious, howling circles, one-two-three, one-two-three. Jingle, snap, crack, jingle, snap, crack.

I hear my mother's voice, begging him to stop. She covers Rick's face, trying to shield the terror from his eyes, but he still shrieks and clings to her with both hands, as my father whips me again and again. My mother grabs the scissors. "John, so help me, if you don't stop!" She brandishes the steel talons above her head like an eagle protecting her young.

My father drops me to the floor like a sack of flour. "You would do this?" he gasps, breathing hard out of his furious trance.

"My god, they're just little, John," she cries, throwing the scissors on the floor, and propelling Rick and me outside, down the stairs and into the car. We spend the night in the pews of Saint Mary's Church while the parish priest goes to the house to calm my father down.

Unlike my mother when her parents terrorized her, I did not pray to Saint Jude for help. My mother protected me. She intercepted the terror between her own childhood and ours. Her empathy came from what was withheld from her—protection, love, joy—and she imparted those prizes to us. We enjoyed much happiness on the bruised and battered back of my mother's youth, shielding us from the scorching heat of my father's blazing temper.

But it was Dad's temper that also saved us from the nuns. When we lived next to the bean field, Rick and I attended the Canadian Catholic schools taught by Dominicans. We studied arithmetic, geography, and reading, all in French.

"Many times knowing languages saved my life." My father always told us we could be interpreters for the United Nations. He spoke eight languages and taught us to read and write Polish by night while we learned French by day. It seemed a given that we, too, would be great linguists like our father, but our first French school was a nightmare.

My third-grade teacher, Sister Mary Teresa, was a humorless woman with a massive, bulldog face who had no tolerance for children and who seemed exquisitely suited to terrorizing us into loving the Holy Mother Church. My run-in with Sister Mary Teresa came as we prepared for our First Communion and our first confession. Sister had a way about her. She used a small storage closet as a "pretend confessional" and put herself in the role of confessor to help us "practice."

Unlike a confessional booth, the closet was totally dark and unlike a confessor, she was an inquisitor, grilling us for our sins, real and imagined. When six-year-old Rick went in the closet, Sister Mary Teresa gleaned from him that we slept together on the same straw mattress in our attic room. When it was my turn for the closet, the nun was ready for me.

"What do you and your brother do when you are in bed together?"

I was a little scared. It was dark. "We sleep, Sister."

"But you don't always sleep, do you?" Her rosary beads

clattered against her skirt that smelled like mothballs. "Your brother told me what you do in bed. You tell me, young lady, right now!"

I hunted for the right words. "We jump around and. . ."

Sister grabbed me by the shoulders and shook me. "You do more than that. You touch places on each other. You lay on top of each other and you sin. Tell me!"

My legs wobbled. What did she mean? I was scared. "I don't know, Sister."

"You sin."

I felt woozy and sick. I stumbled around in the closet, frightened and in tears, scanning the walls, searching for the door. "Let me out! I have to get out!"

"You disgust me." She shoved me out the door.

When I got home, I told Daddy what Sister Mary Teresa had said.

Dad said a lot of words in Polish and banged around the house. My mother tried soothing him, but he waved her off. The next day Daddy took us to school, holding our hands as he marched into our classroom. Sister Mary Teresa was in trouble.

"Sister, did you hear my children's confession?" His voice bounced off the walls and boomed into the ears of every kid in class. This was new, someone shouting at Sister. The third-grade pillars of salt came to life, fidgeting with the prospect of a real scrap between Sister and my daddy. Boys rested their chins on their folded hands and watched without blinking. Others shifted from side to side for a better view. All eyes were focused wide and waiting.

"Now, Mr. Rylko. . ." The nun put her hands up like she was being arrested.

"Did you take my children into a closet? Did you pretend

to be a priest and scare my children?" Daddy's hand was shaking in mine.

"Mr. Rylko, I come from a large family, and I know what goes on—"

Daddy exploded. "Sister, shame on you! And shame on your family. Your sick family is not my family."

Whatever they were talking about sure made Sister look like it was her turn to wet her pants. Daddy stomped us right out of that horrible school and we never saw Sister Mary Teresa again. Unfortunately, it wasn't the end of the nuns. Within the week we were new students at the other Catholic school across town. It wasn't any better.

On my second day in the new school, I said hello to a girl standing in line for the water fountain. Talking in line was apparently against the rules. A nun kept me after school. When everyone was gone, she reached into her desk and uncoiled a long, thick leather strap with ridges cut into it. She led me to the water fountain and shoved my hands under the spigot. Grabbing my wrist, the nun raised the strap and whacked into my wet hand. The strap hissed across my knuckles and burned into my palms. My mouth opened wide but no sound came out. All I could do was blink and suck in little bits of air with each scourge of the lash. Ten times on each side, twenty times in all. Then she did the same to my right hand.

As my skin fried under the whip, the curious sound of that collision echoed down the hall and ricocheted off children's pictures of snowflakes and the star of Bethlehem. It careened off pictures of the baby Jesus lying in a manger and reached the ears of my little brother, who watched from an outside window. He cried for me. His little face streaked with tears as the strap bit into my hands.

We walked home, both crying. My boiled and blistered hands had ballooned to the size of boxing gloves and my horrified mother wrapped them in bandages. The next day, my father escorted us to school again.

"Sister, look what you have done to my child." He looked like he was going to hit her. "You're witches in nuns' habits. Frustrated witches!"

We bolted away with our daddy, our hero. I couldn't use my hands for weeks but that was the last of Canadian Catholic schools.

There were many reasons to love my father, although his contradictions made him difficult to love. He taught us to ski and to read and write Polish. He told us bedtime stories, but at other times we couldn't talk to him. He protected us, but sometimes we needed protection from him. He entertained archbishops and cardinals but never went to church. He was a hot-blooded man with a cold heart. He was a flame in the snowy corner of northern Michigan.

The contradictions emerged in Dad's choice of friends, as well. "John," I often heard my mother ask, "Why is it that you have so many German friends and you don't have any Polish friends? I thought the Germans treated you so badly during the war?" Dad only shrugged in response, signaling the capacity to bend an idea and make both ends true at the same time.

I was not immune to his contradictions and developed some of my own. I loved my father although he frightened me, and this duality also influenced my faith in God: we sought sanctuary in the Church to escape my father, but we also sought refuge in my father to escape the Church. Both my father and God were associated with considerable pain and fear. As I grew up, it seemed natural to love what I feared.

I feared two Gods. My Savior was Christ who suffered under Pontius Pilate, was crucified, died, and was buried and rose again from the dead, amen. My savior was also my father who suffered under Hitler, was tortured, left for dead, and rose from the grave. My father's skillful hands conceived *The Christ* who hung upon the cross, and people worshiped these statues. In the eyes of my childhood, my father was Father, Son, and Holy Ghost. And I tried to be worthy of them all.

Born to Be Special

I WAS RAISED A CATHOLIC. OUR EUROPEAN roots instilled an easy acceptance of Old World ritual and traditionalism. Linked directly to the Rock of Saint Peter, I was baptized, catechized, and authorized with an exclusive pass to heaven, side-stepping my doomed Protestant friends who would spend their eternities in hell. In my youth, it seemed a very practical and simple solution to getting everyone to believe in the One True Church (and woe to those who didn't).

I never questioned why God the Father murdered His own innocent Son in order to forgive guilty wretches deserving of eternal flames. Or why any father would do that. I never questioned how God could be like a stalk of celery: the Father, the Son, and the Holy Ghost, three branches on the same stem. Why He would kill Himself to satisfy His own rules and then rig the plan, to be killed but not really die—the *deus ex machina* in His own play. And why make that bargain anyway?

As a child, it never occurred to me that I prayed every day to a man suffocating under the weight of his own body as his palms tore apart from the nails in his hands, or what the Crown of Thorns really meant. Immersed so totally in the Blood of Christ, I was blind to the graphic details and deaf to the story. I never really imagined a crucifixion until I saw the movie *King of Kings,* and then swooned over Jeffrey Hunter, falling even more in love with Jesus. The scene where he died on the cross made me want to devote my whole life to the Christ with the tortured blue eyes. That's when I decided to become a nun. I was in the fourth grade at Saint Mary's School in Gaylord, Michigan.

"How many children here are special?" Sister Paul had our attention. Everyone shot up their hands. Everyone was special.

"Ah, but do you know what it means to be special?" Sister walked between our desks. "To be special means to be called by God, to become nuns and priests." She stared into us, looking for that special ingredient. "Now, who in this class is being called by God to be special?" Her gaze locked into mine. It was a sign. This time fewer than half of us held up our hands, but mine was still among them. By the eighth grade, I was the last special kid in class. I was called by God to remain unsoiled and untouched. As a nun, my virginity would be my virtue, my symbol of worthiness, and when God took inventory and counted hymens, blessing those that were still intact, He could count on mine, that veil of skin, that noble filament woven like a spider's web guarding my goodness. To my Catechism mind, my hymen was my holiness. It was 1964.

My commitment to be a nun evolved from my mother's sympathies growing up in a convent and my father's work as an itinerant sculptor. I don't know how I managed to romanticize her experience—brushing her teeth with salt and bathing in cold water—into my own rosy expectations, but becoming a Bride of Christ to the movie version of Jesus seemed a better life than the one I was living.

My father's work carving statues for churches had us moving every few months without establishing roots, making friends, or learning to love one place over another. With my parents fighting constantly and loudly, mostly about money and his roving eye for the ladies, my decision at fourteen to become a nun arose partly from the romantic notion of marrying God and partly as an escape into monastic solitude free from the chaos at home. Neither choice had anything much to do with the complex issues of God or religion. The austere vows appealed to me in a raw and uncomplicated way. The monastic order offered a simplification of life: no more new schools and new towns, no more isolation being the new kid in class, but rather, a communal life among kind and like-minded nuns, embraced in unconditional love. Where some may have seen such a life as limiting and Spartan, I saw it as freeing and uncluttered. Tranquility.

The sequestered environment was a stark contrast to my parents' ongoing turmoil, such as the argument they had when Dad gave away the only home we ever loved.

"Shut up!" My father spun around at my mother, "I am sick of your voice."

"John, why didn't you tell me? We could have saved it."

"Never mind. It's done."

"Never mind? I paid for this house. I bought every one of those concrete blocks. I helped dig the foundation. You sold it because you forgot to pay $300 in taxes? You sold us out?"

"It's finished!"

I stopped breathing. We lost our house? Dad never told Mom about the taxes we owed, and in one terrible moment he sold the tax problem and our whole house for one dollar to a man he met at the ski lodge.

I feared the pounding of my heart might make a noise. I wanted to evaporate into the cinder block walls, the walls we loved, and the bricks I kissed and counted when we built the cabin. The house was no longer our home. Out of the corner of my eye I saw Rick grab his Daniel Boone hat and his BB gun and slip out the door with Ranger, our collie dog. I was stuck on the bunk bed. They'd see me if I got up. I squeezed my eyes closed, praying for our house, wishing my parents would stop shouting, but their voices fired into me.

"To hell with it," my father roared again.

"John, are you insane? You sold our home for a dollar to get out of paying the taxes?"

"It was nothing. A noose around my neck, like you."

I pounded my head with my hands. *Think. Think. Think. Remember a better time when Daddy loved us, when it wasn't like this.* I thought back two years ago when we lived in the tent and worked so hard to build our lovely cabin.

Rick and I helped Daddy pound the nails on the roof. We helped mix the cement for the blocks. I fought the monsters in the woods to go potty. We ate soup all summer saving money for bricks. Now our cabin, and everything in it—Dad's workshop, our living room and bedroom and the big fireplace—didn't belong to us anymore. It was all gone.

I never understood it. None of us did, especially my mother, who was taken completely by surprise. A crash, and Dad's sawhorses and tools smashed to the floor. My father had kicked the makeshift table.

"To hell with you and Churchill and the whole bloody world," Dad roared.

Mom cried.

And I wondered, where were we going to live now? And could we build another magical house in the woods ever again?

Not surprisingly, the Bride of Christ never made it to the altar. My parents couldn't afford the room and board, my vows were never consummated, and after only three months, the convent sent me home. This time, home was a rented house in the farming community of Bellaire, Michigan.

NAMES AND IDENTITIES

WHILE IT WAS COLD ALONG THE ALCAN, WE didn't experience frigid until Tok, ninety-three miles inside the Alaskan border.

"According to the map," I read aloud to Mom, "Tok, which rhymes with poke, sprang to life as a highway construction camp twenty-four years ago. Considered the gateway to Alaska, it consists of 133 square miles of beautiful Alaskan wilderness."

"I'm not impressed," Mom said, scanning an oasis of service stations, a motel, several bars, shops, and few diners in the middle of a mountainous nowhere. "At least we can warm the baby's formula," she said. Only six weeks old, baby Paul had to be fed every three or four hours; and we usually warmed his milk by the car heater.

"I'll just be a minute." Mom grabbed the bottle, left the car running, and ran into the diner. A few minutes later, as she made her way back to the car, the warm, moist air from the diner trailed behind her, freezing into frosty clouds suspended above her head. Before she made it to the car, the warm bottle of formula had frozen and burst in her hand.

Mom dove into the car. "It's what they call a wind chill factor." Her face looked sunburned. "Wind combined with the temperature. It's minus sixty degrees. Can you believe it?"

The cold was a two-faced demon, fire and ice, burning and numbing. At sixty below zero fog freezes, paralyzing the air to something close to solid. Breathing hurts as the air scalds its way to the lungs. Frost forms in your nose. Wind chafes your eyes and tears freeze on your eyeballs and cheeks. Even the streetlights changed in the cold, funneling through the fog vertically to the ground like a flashlight, giving an odd, sickly yellow hue to the gray gloom, puddling at the bottom like pee holes in the snow. Nothing was as it seemed. Desolate and white, the sky and the ground converged into a single, looming nightmare without dimension. Matter transformed in this frigid place: air froze, ice fogged, cold burned, light dimmed. It made me wonder if I had converted into something else as well. Were any of us who we thought we were? A year ago, I was a girl who still loved dolls—a girl who was proud to carry the name of a saint.

My father said he named me after Saint Danuta, a fifteenth-century Polish martyr whose legend was sealed when Nordic invaders mutilated her breasts as she burned alive at the stake. I grew up embracing the spirit of that fabled saint until her fortitude became a part of me. Naturally, I skipped the grisly details of her martyrdom, just as I had circumvented the savage concept of the Body and Blood of Christ, so familiar to my childhood faith that it became a sanitized, unbloodied, and painless sacrament. In much the same way, I consumed the Eucharist of my father's chivalry, gnawing on the lessons of his heroism, while overlooking the details. I believed I had embodied his very backbone. Much later I would realize my resolve springs not from my father's grit but from my mother's guts.

But as a young and traumatized teenager, I still idolized the man I feared, and navigated a cold sweat of emotions, stumbling over fear, deception, and pity. And yet forgiveness was what I wanted—for him, for me, and for my family.

But that virtue didn't come to us as easily as our pride. We had little in those hardscrabble days as European immigrants. College educations constituted the sum total of my parents' wealth. The true family treasure was our heritage. It played a huge part in my family's life, compensating any hardships we faced with the promise of destiny, as if the glory days of our ancestors would one day burst upon us in a karmic rain.

My father fueled that expectation in the mantra that once again rang through me in that Yukon cold. "We are from the long line of the House of Jasterowski and the Polish count who fought the Czar and escaped to the Carpathian Mountains. He was inspired by the images on his coat of arms: the wild boar, the lion, and the sword, and he created our new name, Rylko. Ours was a name conceived by a count, passed on through our grandfathers to us. Never forget," he said. And I never did.

While our surname rooted us in the resilient blue blood of our ancestors, our first names had no such grounding. At school, no one could pronounce Danuta, so they abbreviated me to Danny. As I grew older my name grew shorter, to just Dee, until I almost disappeared. Later, during my career in broadcasting, I resurrected my full persona as Danuta and, tired of rhyming Rylko with Bilko, dropped my last name altogether.

My mother never used her real name. Christened Agnes at birth, she tried distancing herself from her abusive parents by adopting the name Patricia. Later, she changed her name to Michelle. For a time, she went by Alexandra. In the latter part of her life, decades after this saga, she adopted PM, an elegant formula designating her as Patricia and Michelle at the same time, an alloy of the past and the present.

Reinventing our names seemed as natural to us as relocating our homes, replacing our friends, and remodeling our citizenship. We were immigrants in a new country, seeking a new life, and our names became as fluid as our lives. But, while my mother and I managed to fuse our identities through time, my father added a twist to his, exploiting the power of his personality. He was a Mobius man bound to the single threshold of his character, captured in a timeless orbit of his own weaving. He wielded his name like a sword and wore it like a crown. Sometimes he hid behind it.

MY LIE

WHEN I TRY TO FORGET, I REMEMBER MORE: Steve yelling, "You goddamned tease! You think a guy's got no feelings?" The car swerving across the road. He screamed and then began to cry.

The '56 Chevy cut an erratic line down the country road. "Steve, slow down!" I cried.

Steering recklessly with one hand, he pawed at me with the other. I squirmed away, hugging the door. "Steve, you're scaring me!"

At sixteen, I still had hopes for the convent, but I also bloomed into a teenager who enjoyed occasional dates and high school dances. Steve was my friend, a football player. Everything about him was thick and wide and square. His neck was the same width as his head, a bowling ball resting on a ledge of shoulders. His thighs chafed against each other as he walked. He was eighteen, a senior, bigger and beefier than other boys because he was held back a year in elementary school. I liked him. He let me wear his leather jacket. He made me feel small and secure like a big brother would, like a father should. He made me feel safe, until now.

The car skids across the road, lurches into a ditch, heaves to one side. I slam into the passenger door with my arm twisting under me. My head hits the window. My neck hurts. He's on top of me. I can't breathe. He's heavy on me.

"You'll see, it's not so bad."

"Steve! Get off!"

"I'm not taking any more of your shit."

It hurts. Can't breathe. No. Please God.

My fingernails bite into my palms. Eyes squeeze shut. Must be brave! My tears, his sweat, the steam of his breath—all smear together on my face. And finally, it ends.

He is out of breath. I am crying—a wretched mess, lying in a wrinkled, sodden heap, my neck cranked in an odd position against the window.

He heaves himself up and off of me and sits back behind the steering wheel, adjusting his jeans, zipping his fly. "You're all right," he pants, swiping his hand over his face, wiping the sweat from his eyes. Then he looks at me and extends his hand. "Stop crying. Here, get up."

"Don't touch me!" I sob, trying to kick at him with my feet still tangled in my pants. Suddenly aware of my nakedness, I grab at my clothes and pull them around me while still lying awkwardly against the passenger door.

Steve starts the car and puts it in reverse, spinning the wheels in the mud until they catch traction and mercifully we are back up on the road. But there is no reversing this moment. He drives me home without speaking another word as I cling to the door handle as if it were my only friend in the world.

Arriving at my house, and overwhelmed with guilt, I slowly open the car door. Steve says nothing, but he is clenching the steering wheel as if he wants to throttle it. I slip out, gently shutting the door behind me—closing an irreversible part of my life. Steve spins out of the driveway spewing gravel and dust in his wake. What did I do to make him so angry? Wasn't he supposed to be my friend? My neck hurts and I have a bump on my head and I find it difficult to walk. I glance up at the house where my parents are, where my bedroom waits. I must hide. I can't tell Mom and Dad what happened. I have no words. I can't stop trembling.

From the porch I can see the blue glow of the television set and the dark outlines of my parents in the living room. My hand rests on the front-door latch. I am afraid. What if they confront me? I quietly turn the doorknob and step inside the unlit hallway, softly clicking the door closed behind me. I stand in the dark. I desperately want to cry—to run to Mommy and throw my arms around her and tell her—everything. I want Daddy to stroke my hair, tell me I am still his sunshine—to protect me. Instead, I tiptoe past those desires and the living room where Mom and Dad are watching the news. Walter Cronkite is saying something about Vietnam and on the TV screen wounded soldiers are rushed to waiting helicopters in the jungle. I want to be rescued, too, but I'm not sure from what.

I move slowly to the safety of my room upstairs. Cuts and dried bits of blood on my palms. My hands still tremble. I'm bleeding "down there." Should I take a shower? I still have homework to do. I find my algebra book. Take out paper from a folder, a pencil from the bedside table. I sit on the bed and stare at the blank sheet. Maybe I should feed my cat. I get up and open the door and close it again. Not a good idea to go downstairs. I stare out the window to the driveway below. What if Steve comes back? I check to make sure the window is locked. I need to change my clothes—ripping them off me as if they were on fire, kicking them under the bed. All of a sudden, I am exhausted and curl up in a tight ball on the bed, pulling up the covers around me, sobbing in the blanket so no one can hear.

I long for our cabin in the woods. The cabin we lost when Daddy didn't pay the taxes. The cabin he sold for a dollar. I want my bunk bed, to sleep on the top, next to the cool cement blocks. I want the black and white television to lull me to sleep with its flashing shadows on the wall and the sound of Daddy's tools tapping into the night. But the sturdy concrete blocks of our cabin are gone, replaced with the groaning old wood of a Victorian house that creaks in the wind.

Who would help me? In the spring of 1965 I couldn't tell anyone. I was in the ninth grade, a good girl who made no sounds when she was afraid, perhaps because I was innocent. But innocence would not let me off the hook. Innocence led to my guilt. And I bore the guilt alone. My silence would extend into months of unarticulated despair.

Until the nightmare in the car, I preserved my chastity as a symbol of God's ownership, but now the way to Him was ripped and torn. I would never be a Bride of Christ. In my Catholic upbringing, there were no shades of gray. No matter the circumstances, I was as guilty as Eve, as guilty as all women for causing the Original Sin.

As for Steve, he tried to make up the next day in the lunch hall saying I shouldn't make such a big deal out of it; all the kids are doing it. But I couldn't face him, I felt humiliated and dirty. A few weeks later he was dating another girl.

The rest of the story is as old as humanity: an unwed girl whose shame swells pink and round like a peach in her belly, a story of guilt that grows with each passing month into the full flower of humiliation. It has always been a brutal place for the Hester Prynnes of the world.

I didn't think about it when I missed my period, and when I threw up in the morning, I thought I had the flu. I refused to consider the alternative. I wasn't like other girls who were "sent away" suddenly during the school year; the kind of girls people whispered about, the "easy girls," the girls who "did it." The girls boys liked. Those girls, who always had dates, who never got A's, were never called by God, and didn't go to Mass. That wasn't me.

The country living of northern Michigan didn't produce street-smart kids. Sex wasn't on television or talked about in casual conversations. It was a nonsubject, just like girls who got "in trouble" were nonpersons. It was way beyond me. Those kind of girls always seemed older and more mature in ways that had them living on another planet as far as I was concerned.

But my mother knew.

I had fainted again at school. Mom had picked me up at the nurse's station and took me home. I was in my room in the old house we rented by the lake. I lay on the top blue cover on my bed and she sat facing me. Then she asked the awful, awful question, dreading the answer, "Danny, are you pregnant?"

"No!" I acted shocked. But then I saw there was no way out. And then, "Yes, I think so."

My mother cupped her mouth, forbidding words to tumble unguarded from her lips.

"Please, Mommy, don't tell Daddy. Promise you won't tell him." In that same moment when I feared my father the most, I wanted to run to him. I wanted to rush into his arms, protected, embraced, and forgiven. "Suffer the little children to come unto me," Jesus said, but I knew there would be no mercy for me, not from God the Father. Certainly not from my father, the god. I could not bring myself before either of them.

There would be hell to pay for letting God down. My father didn't fight a war for this. Jesus didn't die for this. They expected an Olympic contender, a linguist at the United Nations, a nun, but not this, not pregnant at sixteen. Hadn't they sacrificed enough? The capacity of their love was spent and I had fallen beyond the reach of the gods.

When I told my mother about Steve and the night in the car, distress lined her face. "My God, Danny. You should have told us. Damn that boy!"

"But what about Daddy? He wouldn't care how it happened. I'd rather die!"

Mom gripped the fringes of the blanket. "It would be better not to tell Dad, anything would be better."

She understood. How could we run to the man who beat the living tar out of a little girl for getting stuck in the mud? If he didn't spare me then and a dozen times before, he would not excuse me now. We took the only way out: spare the truth and spare the rod. We lied to my father. The weight of that lie finally collapsed the fragile foundations of our family.

THE WRONG ROAD

IT WAS EASY TO GET LOST. OUTSIDE OF TOK, AT the end of the Alcan, we came upon a forked road with no signs. From the map, the Richardson Highway would take us north to Fairbanks, the other, south to Anchorage. With a 50 percent chance of getting it right, we got it wrong. Through a hundred miles of ice, we drove deeper into the tundra, the sky dimming with ice fog, the day fading into night. Before us loomed a spectacular mountain that seemed to split the heavens. Mt. McKinley, the highest mountain in North America, failed to tip us off to our error until we saw a sign that read, "University of Alaska, Fairbanks 60 Miles."

"Oh my God. This isn't right." Mom lurched the car to a stop. A look at the map showed that we were just 260 miles south of the Arctic Circle. The single-lane road seemed abandoned; not a single vehicle had passed us in hours. The temperature was dropping again, and I could feel cold air creeping through the baseboards of the car, wrapping my ankles in a permanent chill. Paul began to cry. I reached over the seat and picked him up from his basket. Rocking him in my arms soothed us both as Mom turned the car around. A storm had swept in with the darkness. Snow swarmed about us and ice formed along the edges of the windows. Just then, along the side of the road, we saw a gate with signs on a wire fence proclaiming, "No Entrance Allowed." Pulling up to the gate, Mom honked at a soldier sitting in a small guardhouse.

She cranked the window down a couple of inches and an icy blast of wind whipped about our heads. "Where are we?" she asked.

"This is an early warning military installation," the soldier said. When Mom asked for a place to spend the night, the soldier said, "There's a lodge that's always open down near Paxson."

"Can you tell me anything about the road?" Mom had to shout through the window and against the wind and her voice sounded muted and worried.

"Oh sure, the road's good." He waved us off and hurried back to his guardhouse.

Bad advice. The highway had been closed ahead of us and behind us due to the storm. That night we drove with the angels, along the tops of mountains, and the winds howled like angry dogs. We drove along the edge of possibility through Isabel Pass and through tight bends and steep pitches. A roller coaster ride in the dark.

The "lodge that was always open" was closed, the windows boarded up. We had no choice but to continue on to Glennallen. In daylight and with good weather, the town was an hour's drive away, but not in a horrific snowstorm. A white, trackless expanse bobbed in the headlights as we inched our way to Glennallen, then suddenly, the road was gone.

Mom calculated her thoughts aloud. "We're descending. All we have to do is assume the road follows the lowest spot ahead and point the car in that direction." It made sense, I guess.

Eventually a dark, long patch came up alongside us. "I assume that's a river." Mom pointed to the right, "Let's use that frozen line as a guide for the road's outer edge."

We assumed a lot, but they were good guesses.

The engineers of this road must have known of its treachery and planned a series of mini-rescue stations along the way. Food caches showed up every fifteen miles or so along the way, small huts on high platforms out of the reach of bears. They contained biscuits, an oil stove, and other survival items for travelers who got stuck. We wrote down the mileage as we passed each one, just in case we stalled, were forced to turn back, or worse.

Paul

IN CHOOSING NOT TO TELL MY FATHER ABOUT my pregnancy, my mother and I also denied the reality to ourselves. We went on as though nothing were wrong until another kind of response would be necessary. As my stomach grew bigger, my presence grew smaller. I hid in bed.

Since my mother was a registered nurse, no questions were asked when she told my father that I had a chronic kidney infection and needed rest. He never saw me grow. Nobody did. Teachers sent school lessons home with Rick. My father questioned me only once about my health and then said nothing more. My mother and I never spoke of it either. Perhaps we started believing our own lie that with a little rest things would get better.

One February morning, an ice storm slipped down from Canada. Wind summoned speed across Lake Superior, gathered ferocity over Lake Michigan, and blasted past Torch Lake. By midmorning it slammed into our house, thundering against the boards, lashing at the doors.

I didn't feel well. Maybe I needed something to eat. A cold draft coiled around my ankles as I stood in the kitchen frying an egg. My bones ached. Maybe I had the flu. During breakfast, a twinge of pain reared and faded quickly. Food didn't help. A charley horse wrenched my back. Better go to my room and lie down. Before I got up from the table, another cramp. My legs buckled. I grabbed the table for support.

Heartburn. I found a couple of antacids and chewed them on my way back to bed.

Lying down didn't help. The flu just got worse. Thrashing around on the bed. No good. A terrific pain! I cried out. Breathing hard. A jolt of fear. My parents were in Traverse City. Rick was in school. No phone. No neighbors. Sick, and alone.

Pain grew more and more intense. Sweat trickled down my neck. Fever. Need an aspirin. Another sharp arrow lanced my back. "Help!" Only wind and snow answered.

Bolts of pain traveling along currents of terror shuddered through me. Tremors wormed through my legs, shaking them uncontrollably. Another strike. "Help!" Searing heat. Spasms wouldn't let go. "Somebody. Please." Suddenly, a horrendous jolt. I screamed. From the depths of me came a blistering red-in-the-face scream. I screamed for all the times I held back. And the wind screamed with me. Tears. Sweat. Fear. Terrorizing pain assaulted me time and again. "Mommy!" But Mommy didn't come. No one came.

Between bouts of agony, I tried to reason it out. Food poisoning. The egg. Maybe I'm dying. Each time I struggled to understand what was happening to me, it happened again. But each time I thought I'd die, I didn't. Finally, between the heated rounds of torment, I wondered if this was labor. I had heard the word before, when my cat had kittens. I remembered being shocked by little, bloody heads emerging from the swollen place between her legs. Was that happening to me?

I reached for my dictionary among the schoolbooks strewn on the bed. The book trembled in my hands as I tried to read the many definitions listed for labor. "1. productive activity; 2. persons engaged in work; 3. fatiguing work; 4. pangs and efforts of childbirth." Childbirth?

Another jolt of pain. I gritted my teeth and held my breath and tried not to scream until I had to. Godawful aching drew my body tight and tense. My spine felt like it would snap. I screamed long and hard and loud until the pain subsided.

Now I pushed, involuntarily, like a bowel movement. I couldn't stop pushing. I writhed on my back, tearing and gripping at the blankets, heaving myself forward and upward, and then, in a mighty burst of power and pain and fright, another voice. A muffled whimpering. The misery stopped as quickly as it began. I sat up, panting, like waking from a bad dream, except this was no dream. Between my thighs, squirming in gooey puddles of blood and awfulness, lay a wet and shining creature. So big. So little. A baby.

At sixteen I never really, really imagined that I would have a baby. Pregnant was a word, an interminable condition, a long, dark, tunnel with no purpose, a seemingly endless heaviness of body and soul. But now this. He made puppy sounds, and pulled with arms and legs going nowhere. I reached down and picked him up. He was slippery. Wiggly. What do I do now?

Cradling him in my arms, I slipped out of bed and ran to the bathroom to wash him off in the sink. An ugly-looking cord tied to his stomach tugged on something inside of me. A purple, bruised-looking, twisty kind of rope as thick as my thumb linked us together. What was I supposed to do with that? Then I remembered. The mamma kitty chewed it off.

Back in bed, I laid the baby next to me and picked up the rubbery cord and squeezed it. I felt nothing. The baby didn't seem to feel anything, either. I felt too tired to look for scissors. Reluctantly, squeamishly, over the course of twenty minutes, I severed the purple cord with my thumbnail. It didn't bleed, probably because it took so long to cut and the blood had time to clot.

All this mess on the bed, Mom's gonna kill me. I stumbled into the garage and gathered old newspapers from the dirty floor and heaped them on the bed over the offending red stains. Baby and I fell asleep on the grimy newsprint, both of us exhausted, unwitting partners in the great dance of life, both of us on unfamiliar ground.

The school bus dropped Rick off early, due to the storm. At fourteen, he was stupefied and speechless at the sight of the baby.

"Don't ask any questions, just help," I managed to say, feeling drowsy and hot.

Rick took the sheets off the bed, rolled them up, and dumped them in the garbage. I dressed in a fresh nightgown and went to my parents' wide, clean bed.

The storm had subsided but still threatened with a second and more ominous front. My parents, delayed by the weather, arrived later that afternoon. Mom came in to see me first.

"Look what happened while you were gone, Mommy." I pulled back the covers to reveal the baby boy nestled under my arm.

"Oh my God," she whispered. "What happened to the afterbirth? Are his eyes all right? What about the umbilical cord? Did you tear?"

I couldn't answer any of those questions.

She left the room, perhaps to collect herself for what would happen next.

My father walked in. "I see you're in our bed."

For the first time in my life, I had no fear, none at all. "Daddy, look what I have." I pulled back the sheet.

A curious distance separated me from my father's reaction,

as though I were a nonparticipant in the play that unfolded before me. My father went white. Then red. And then he blew his top.

"What in God's name? Who? Steve?"

I winced under the blare of his voice. The baby stirred under my arm.

My silence must have answered his question.

"I'll kill him! I'll kill the son of a bitch!" He whirled around as though the guilty boy were hiding somewhere in the room.

"No Daddy, please . . ." I begged as my father raced out of the room.

He returned with a gun. It was strange to see him with a gun. He hated guns.

"He's not getting away with this." Dad rushed out of the house and into the storm.

Good thing he couldn't find Steve, because Dad would have blown his head off. Had he known I was raped, he would have killed him for sure. It was better not to tell him about that. By the time he returned home, Dad's rage had subsided. Now he wasn't trying to kill anybody but he still acted like a silverback gorilla, shouting and banging things around.

I lapsed in and out of consciousness, grasping a few scenes and some sounds. Voices. Shouting. Blessed sleep.

I woke up once to find Rick standing in the room. "Rick, what's going on?"

"Boy, Dad is really mad." He sat on the floor by the bed, facing the door.

I felt hot and dizzy. Rick told me I had a really bad infection from lying on those newspapers and that Mom wanted to get some medicine for me. Dad had the keys to the car and wouldn't give them to her. There was an argument. That's when Mom started to walk across the lake. Rick said the ice started to crack. He could hear it pinging like the radar in submarine movies. Apparently, Dad heard the pinging too, and he threw the car keys at Mom. She had to dig around the snow looking for them. Hours had gone by and she wasn't back yet.

"Rick, can you get me a drink of water? I'm really thirsty."

Rick's eyes darted toward the door.

"Where's Daddy now?" I whispered.

"He's in the living room, walking around and around." Rick looked scared.

"Forget about the water. I'm too tired to drink it anyway." I slipped away again.

I'M COLD.

A white cloud floats above me, waving, like a flag. It drops down and tickles my skin and then it snaps up again, curling like white smoke, blowing its snowy white breath against my hot, sticky skin. Goose bumps run up and down my arms and legs.

I know why I'm cold. I'm swimming in a river. Trying to get away, but I can't. Three nuns hunt me, their faces hidden by hoods. I'm swimming underwater with scuba gear, but the nuns breathe naturally underwater. Their black and white habits make them look like killer whales or witches in hoods. I can't escape. The nuns become white fish, then white clouds, billowing above me. I can't run. I'm helpless in a frozen place. I cry.

"Danny! Wake up! Can you hear me?" My mother's voice.

"Mommy?" Cold and shivering, I opened my eyes.

"Shhh, you've had a fever." She tucked me in a warm blanket all the way to my feet. "The snow helped bring it down."

"Snow?"

"Bags of it. Then I washed you in witch hazel." Mom felt my forehead with the back of her hand.

"Washed with witches?"

"It's like alcohol. I fanned you with a sheet. Evaporation worked like magic. The penicillin should knock out the infection."

"Rick said you tried to walk across the lake."

Mom sat on the bed. "I had to get antibiotics. Dad heard the ice breaking, I guess, and he threw the keys at me. 'Take them and may you choke on them!' he said. Anyway, by the time I found them in a snow bank, it was dark."

"What time is it, anyway?"

"Almost three in the morning." Mom's hair had fallen into her face and she wore a deep frown. "I drove too fast on the ice. Big storm. It's still coming down. Rolled into a ditch." She ran a cold washcloth over my face.

"An accident?"

My mother put her fingers up to her lips, "Shhh, don't wake your father. I'm okay. But the strangest thing, out of nowhere came this man in a truck, with a chain on the back end. Didn't say a word to me, just hitched up the chain and pulled me out of the ditch. Then drove off. Makes you believe in angels. And I got the penicillin."

I felt so sorry for her. I had put her through such an ordeal. "Thanks, Mom." What else do you say to your mother after she saved your life?

"You get some sleep." She took a peek at the baby. "He looks healthy. You're lucky." She sighed and left the room. I fell asleep comforted by the blue lampshade on my bedside table, the fringes on the shade tattered from years of loving it, the base, a little girl holding a lamb.

For the next four days I never strayed from the bedroom.

I rocked my baby to sleep and fed him bottles that my mother prepared. It never occurred to me to breastfeed the baby, besides, I didn't know how. Lactating was just another weird thing happening to my body, and I soaked up the liquid in towels stuffed into my bra.

I watched the snow heap high above the windowpane, heard the wind howling, and shivered when the draft crept under the sill. The terror came when the baby cried. The sound ignited my father's smoldering temper. Half a dozen times he crashed through the door like a rhino.

"Keep that bastard quiet," he bellowed, a threatening finger thrust in my face. "Do you hear me? Shut it the hell up."

A fist swung. I ducked the punch. The baby screamed. Another fist. And another. Each time I dodged the swings.

"You whore. You filthy whore." My father punctuated each curse with a fist, slogging at the air, off balance like a drunk who couldn't hit his target. "You are garbage. Nothing. You'll never be anything and you'll never amount to anything. Slut. Worthless. No man will have you. Liar. With a bastard." He swung wildly and hit the blue lampshade. The girl and the lamb crashed to the floor in a thousand pieces.

"No, Daddy." I clutched the wailing baby. My father screamed. My room was a cauldron of pain for all three of us. His swings missed me. Maybe he didn't really want to hit me. Maybe he just thrashed about in frustration never meaning to connect, because if he had he would have smashed every bone in my face. I almost wished he had.

I couldn't blame him for being angry with me. I lied. I may have been from the long line of the house of Jasterowski, but unlike my ancestors, I grew up a coward and had now become just another source of pain added to his bitter heap.

Whore. Slut. Judas. I accepted my father's analysis; I was

all those things. I felt dazed, but strangely unaffected. A chill swept over me. The Bride of Christ was lost.

Meanwhile, my mother walked a high-voltage tightrope. She avoided my father, clashed with him when she had no choice, took care of four-year-old Michael, and helped me with the baby. When she ran out of her own money buying diapers and baby food, bottles and clothes, she pleaded with Steve's parents to help support the infant.

They made her an offer. My mother dutifully reported the offer to me.

"They gave you one hundred dollars and said Steve would marry you." My mother sighed.

It came out of the blue. What a strange situation. As if my father's rage were not bad enough, now a marriage proposal by the parents of the boy who raped me. A nightmare.

"Marry? I'm not old enough to get married." How could my life come crashing to a halt in a miserable compromise with the brute who hurt me?

"They said you can always get a divorce later when all this blows over." My mother sounded flat, and sad.

I laughed at the thought of it. Mom gave a thin smile. We spoke no more of marriage.

Just then, the baby whimpered and the tension grew thicker than blood. My attempts to hush the baby failed. The more I tried to keep him quiet, the more anxious I became. The baby grew agitated and nervous and finally wailed and wouldn't stop. The infant's cries awakened another angry surge in my father. He kicked the door in; this time it flew off its hinges and slapped onto the floor.

"I told you to keep that bastard quiet. You think I will help you graduate? Never. You're through being my daughter!" His loud baritone shook the walls.

My mother stepped between us. "That's enough. Get out of the room, John."

He stared at my mother and me—traitors, liars, and deceivers.

"Daddy," I managed to quiver, "Daddy."

He locked his gaze on me, calm as the eye of a hurricane, but still breathing hard. He whispered, "You lie to me and you call me Daddy? Never call me Daddy again." He came closer, his finger in my face, his blue eyes pale and cold as the winter sky. "Give that bastard up, give him to somebody else to raise, and I'll let you stay here until you're eighteen. Then you're out." His face now so close to mine I smelled the tobacco on his breath. Close enough to kiss me. Close enough to hit me.

Each time he called this precious little child a bastard, I winced. It wasn't the baby's fault. Why take it out on him? Why call him names? Why should I have to give him away?

"Daddy, please, I can't do that." But he had already left the room.

Could it be that only three short years earlier, when I was thirteen, I still believed in Santa Claus, making his list, checking it twice? Was I a whore? What an awful word! I was only in the tenth grade. I wasn't ready for any of this.

Time passed slowly in the weeks that followed; my father continued to rage and threaten. Little Michael clung to Mom constantly. My baby cried. Trauma crippled me. Rick moved about as silent as a gravedigger and my mother looked drained. It was impossible to stay. But first, a doctor. Four days had elapsed, the baby needed a birth certificate, and I needed stitches. My mother made an appointment with a doctor in another town.

Just before entering the doctor's office, something happened that would cause another permanent shift in the order of my world. My mother slipped her wedding ring on my finger. "You are Mrs. Patricia Rylko. You are married to John Rylko. He is your husband and the father of your baby. Do you understand?"

I understood only too well. We were still hiding. This was the early Sixties and times were not yet a changin'. The Women's Liberation Movement was in its infancy and Billie Jean King wouldn't beat Bobby Riggs for another eight years. A woman's place was in the home, it was still a man's world, and a woman's reputation had to be preserved. Wearing my mother's wedding band would save my reputation and give legitimacy to the child. Legitimacy was a big deal.

More than willing to follow my mother's instructions, I behaved like a robot, moving in the direction given until told to stop. I let Mom do the thinking. My responses were sluggish and bewildered. I saw without seeing, moved without feeling. I was lucky to be alive.

Ten years earlier, I wore my mother's wedding ring when I married my father for fun. This time it was no game. How bizarre, that our innocent little make-believe ceremony would serve as a twisted rehearsal for my future. The events seemed prescribed, driving me down a road of inevitable consequences.

"WELL DONE," THE DOCTOR SAID in the examination room. "You're lucky there were no complications. And the name of your son, Mrs. Rylko? The name. For your son? For the birth certificate." The doctor held a clipboard and a pen. He looked at me as if I should know the answer.

I glanced at my mother, who shrugged, "It's your decision."

"I hadn't thought," I said, unaware of the understatement. "Well, I like the Beatles, and Paul McCartney. How about Paul?"

"Paul it is." The doctor clicked his pen into action. "And the middle name?"

I scrambled for another answer. "After my brother, Richard . . ."

"Good, good, then Paul Richard Rylko it is." He scribbled the name on his form and I heard my son's name for the first time. Then, almost to himself the doctor spoke as he wrote, "Son of Mr. and Mrs. John Rylko."

My son had just become my brother.

Unaware of the implications in that moment, I followed my mother's lead. There were no other choices. The child had a name. I kept my baby. We avoided a scandal.

The Plan

MY MOTHER MOVED INTO HIGH GEAR. DETER-mined now to keep us all safe, she came up with a plan. "I'm going to Detroit," she said on our way home. "We need a car and they advertise in the paper for drive-aways."

Mom said it's when drivers deliver new cars to their owners all over the country. A car dealer in Detroit said they had a car destined for Florida. It was warm there. She could get a job as a nurse. Let things cool off at home. For the first time in ages, a smile came from deep within her, springing up like a daffodil. She was thirty-eight years old, but just then, she almost looked like a teenager herself. But Detroit was four hundred miles away.

"I'll hitchhike. I can do it," Mom said. "I'll get a car and I'll be back as soon as I can." She added an unnecessary precaution, "Stay away from your father." She caught a ride with a couple leaving the ski area the next day. They drove her to the outskirts of Detroit, to a small car dealership advertising a drive-away to Miami.

Back at the house, my brother Rick seemed to disappear. When the arguments erupted between my parents, we usually ran to our tree house or sat beneath the ferns in the woods, nervously petting the dog, absently soothing ourselves, waiting for the clash of angry voices to subside. The hellish week Paul was born, Rick had the advantage of school taking him away, and Dad still had work to do in Traverse City. So, peace came for me during the day when the house fell quiet and the baby slept in my arms. I felt more like a sister than a mother. Still, his hands, tiny and wrinkly, and the way his lips formed a perfect cherry-red vise around the nipple of a bottle fascinated me. He was one of my dolls to dress and bathe and pin diapers on, except, I had to remind myself, this doll was real.

The warm, golden promise of a beach in Florida washed away with the tide when my mother arrived in Detroit. The car dealer had lied. The only car available was not bound for balmy Miami, but for Anchorage. An airman stationed at Richardson Air Force Base in Alaska had ordered the car and would reimburse the driver for gas and mileage upon its delivery. Mom was stuck at a car lot with an impatient salesman who wanted to close the shop for the night. She had no transportation back home, and no time to find another dealer. She took the car and acquiesced to a journey north. A fifty-dollar deposit would be reimbursed when we arrived in Anchorage. That left her with exactly seven dollars in her purse.

"Is that all you have left?" the dealer asked when he saw the money in her bag.

She nodded.

He filled up the gas tank, no charge. That would get her two-thirds of the way home and the seven dollars would be enough money to make it back to the house.

It was clear to my father that we were leaving when my mother returned home with the new car.

"John, this is not how a family is supposed to live. We need a time-out, for all of us."

My father barked at her, "What do you mean, supposed to live?"

"A family is supposed to be like a wagon train when it's under attack. It should protect people who live inside. But here, the attack is within. This family is threatened." She paused. "We're going to Alaska."

For the first time in six terrible weeks, my father listened, the roaring replaced with a stupefied silence. We had no money, but my mother had purchased a new oil heater for the house with her savings. She returned the heating unit, still in the box, and got the full $250 refunded. Fifty dollars went towards a thirty-day travel insurance policy, which paid my father in case we died on the road. She was still being practical. The remaining $200 would have to take us to Anchorage.

We picked up a map on the way out of town.

BORN OF ICE

THE TERRAIN CHANGED AGAIN FROM THE tundra and the black edge of a frozen river to the sudden iridescence of turquoise walls. The tires lost traction and the car began to slide sideways.

"What the . . . " Mom released her foot from the gas and the car drifted to a stop against the sheer face. A cave of ice enveloped us. Smooth and glassy as an eyeball, it seemed to come out of nowhere. Wide bands of blue and green air bubbles arched overhead like frozen 7-Up. To the right, a wall bulged with gleaming veins of white and blue. To the left, the turquoise cascaded into a white and frothy fusion, sudsy as vanilla malt. Strange prisms of violet and red and blue twinkled around us.

"What *is* this?" The ice enchanted me.

"A tunnel, maybe." Mom leaned over the dashboard to get a better look and said, "Listen. Do you hear something?" She rolled down the window. Above the hum of the car engine we heard the sound of water, trickling and plopping, echoing through the cavern as if we were in a huge tin can.

"Sounds like rain," I said.

"Too cold for rain." Mom rolled up the window.

"It's a waterfall, Mommy," Michael said, jumping excitedly up and down on the backseat.

Mom put the car into gear. "Let's get out of here."

She nudged the car forward and after a few reluctant spins

of the tires, we made our passage slowly through the ice. It seemed as if Moses had parted this frozen blue sea just for us. And then, as quickly as it came, the ice cave vanished. The lost road that Mom assumed followed the river miraculously reappeared before us in the dark.

Half an hour later, at 11:30 at night, we approached Glennallen. According to the map, the village formed the junction of the Wrangell, Chugach, and St. Elias ranges, a monstrous kingdom of glaciers representing a *Who's Who* of peaks in North America topping above 16,000 feet. And we'd trekked right through the middle of it.

After losing the road in a whiteout earlier in the day, climbing down a mountainside blind, and then creeping through all that weird ice, we were exhausted. The lights of the town promised comfort and hospitality. But this wondrous illuminated oasis turned out to be a small, smoke-filled tavern. Inside, unshaven, burly trappers, who looked like they'd spent too long in the bush, slumped around tables and slouched over the bar. The smoke and the stench of stale beer mixed with the onion-like odor of unwashed bodies made my eyes water. The clamor of the tavern fell to a hush and disbelief swept across the faces of the men, as if they'd never seen a mother with children before.

"Excuse me," my mother addressed the bartender, whose drab apron held back a bellyful of beer. "Is there a place for us to stay the night?"

"Did you come down Highway 4?" the bartender said, loud enough to be within earshot of the curious patrons.

"Yes, and we've been driving for hours. We're very tired." Mom made a motion toward us. I held Paul, and Mike clung to Mom.

"But the road's been closed for days. How'd you make it around the lake?"

"Didn't see any lake. We drove through a tunnel, under some ice."

"Tunnel? That was no tunnel. It's the fuckin' river! 'Scuse my language, lady, but nobody could get through that. River crested just before the big freeze, poured straight off the mountain. Washed over the road, into the lake. Jesus, Mary, and Joseph, you say you came *under* it? Shit, that ice fall is gonna blow anytime." He turned to the other men in the bar, who whistled and shook their heads.

"My children and I need a place to stay."

The bartender wiped his hands on his filthy rag. "We have a bed upstairs," he said, "but I don't think you want it."

"Actually, we want it very much." My mother sounded extraordinarily British in this unrefined setting.

"You can check it out. Up there." He tilted his head to a loft above the bar. Below the loft, nailed to the wall, was a makeshift ladder of two-by-fours. It looked like a ladder built by kids, nailed to the trunk of an oak, leading up to a tree house. The whole tavern watched Mom climb the improvised stairs. I cradled Paul and held Michael's hand.

At least she was wearing ski pants and not a dress, I thought, as the men watched her. She clung to slats above her and wedged each foot sideways on the steps. After she scrambled into the loft, the men turned their eyes on me. From every corner of the quiet bar, hungry eyes drilled into me, leering at me, clawing at my clothes, stripping me naked. I remembered groping hands, and sticky breath, and being trapped behind steamy windows. I wanted to scream. Wanted to run. But their eyes paralyzed me and I could barely breathe.

"Ow," Michael winced as I squeezed his hand too tightly.

After what seemed like an eternity, Mom climbed back down.

Dusting off her hands she said, "I don't mind the single bed shoved next to the wall. I don't even mind the lack of clean bedding. But the smell's unbearable. Toilet's plugged and overflowing. It needs to be fixed."

"Ha!" The man wiped the bar with his rag, "It ain't broke. Just needs water. You gotta melt snow to flush it. Pipes froze. Got no water."

"What about drinking water? What about the baby?"

"Sure sorry 'bout that. I feel for you, I do. But the pipes are froze. Need water, you gotta melt snow. We got whiskey, beer, you know."

My mother scanned the tavern, searching the faces of the other men. I guess she didn't want to know where they were sleeping, because she didn't ask.

They weren't melting snow, I thought. They went outside. How could we be sure we would be using clean snow? I guess Mom didn't want to know the answer to that, either.

"I'll pass," Mom said. "Thanks anyway."

"But you can't go back on that road." The bartender surveyed the room for agreement. "It's closed."

Mom clenched her jaw and squinted her eyes in a way that said she meant business. "I've come this far, I can make Anchorage." She gathered us like chicks as a stunned silence followed us out the door and back to the car. With no room at the inn, we drove through the night. I slept against the door. The boys quietly slept in the back seat. Mom was the only one who didn't close her eyes.

Early the next morning, the seventh day of our journey, Mom jolted me awake. "We made it, kids!" Anchorage rose in the dark light of the Alaskan dawn. Buildings and streets and flashing neon lights reflected in the snow like Christmas. I scooped Paul from his laundry-basket bed and Michael climbed over and sat between Mom and me.

"We made it, baby. We made it." I kissed Paul and bounced him on my lap.

Mom looked at me. "You can do anything you set your mind to," she said. "Never forget that." At that moment Mom radiated beauty. Not in the pretty sense of the word. It was more like she glowed with a powerful fierceness about her and the kind of pride that comes from beating a dare.

Civilization sprang upon us without warning when we turned onto a wide street called Northern Lights Boulevard and stopped at a red light. It seemed strange to stop at an intersection, as if there were rules again, and driving codes, and other people in the world. As if nothing had happened to us. As if people didn't understand what we'd just done and where we'd just come from. I thought how trumpets should blare. Parades of people should clap and shout, "Well done! Welcome! Bravo!"

I loved the gritty drifts of dirty snow mounded in gutters and the antlers and snowshoes decorating storefronts. The cold wind lifted wisps of snow off the rooflines like streamers lining our parade route.

"Look." Michael pointed to a figure bundled in a parka. "There's someone wearing a fur helmet. Is that an Eskimo?"

"Could be," Mom said.

A few cars passed by. "Jeez!" Michael said. "Cars. Tons of 'em. But where are the igloos?"

Turning onto The Milky Way Drive, a sign on a tow truck read, "Moose Snort for Hire, Push, Pull or Tug." Farther down, a sign over a Mexican restaurant displayed a cartoon of a moose eating a taco. A stuffed brown bear standing in a window snarled in frozen menace at passersby. There would be no more mileage charts and mountain passes, no more taverns and timber bridges. We were safe at the top of the world, halfway between New York and Tokyo, as far away as we could get from our past. Now it was time to rest our heads on clean pillows and sleep the sleep of the saved.

Our exodus was complete, or so I believed.

Danuta, West Anchorage High School
Graduation, 1967

False Spring

SPRINGTIME IN ALASKA, AND LIFE SPARKED A fierce revival. The noisy plunder of "breakup" provoked calamity and wild awakenings to scores of frozen rivers. Solids turned back to liquids. Columns of ice heaved upon boiling waters, piling along the shore in monumental collisions. Trickling springs burst into avalanches of water and mud, plowing up trees. Rivers raced under the waking sun.

My mother and I knew little about the grand dimensions of Alaska. We had no meaningful understanding of this vast state. Our imaginations froze on images of seal hunting and Eskimos. I pictured Anchorage a village of igloos, cauliflowers dotting a desert of ice. Instead, I found a city of fifty-thousand people, two high schools, a television station, two military bases, and a municipal airport. The tallest building in town, the McKinley Building, stood five stories high. It was pink, as out of place here as a flamingo, and it was scarred. The 1964 Good Friday Earthquake cut a black, uneven fissure up its side, deep enough to devour my fingers. Just two years earlier, the largest quake ever recorded in North America, registering 9.2 on the Richter scale, devastated the city. It shifted whole villages, obliterated others, and redesigned geography. Anchorage remained shell-shocked, the fractured, pink building a graphic reminder of the trauma.

The savage and the civilized coexisted here under an awkward truce. The Iditarod Sled Dog Race started in the middle of downtown. Airplanes from the military bases buzzed overhead. People joked about the ravenous mosquitoes, calling them the state bird. Earthquakes and rain rattled and soaked the landscape and glaciers gleamed like new teeth between the crowns of the Chugach Mountains. Bear and moose wandered downtown so often they hardly drew a shrug from an unflustered population accustomed to living on the wild side.

Alaska boasted of having more bars than banks, and more Quonset huts per square mile than any other spot on earth. This was a place where men outnumbered women five to one, and where strippers took to wearing red long johns and forced the reversal of a law against nudity in bars. You could still pan for gold, stake a claim, and disappear. In Alaska you could start your life all over again.

No letter came from my father, not the day we arrived in Anchorage nor the days and months that followed. Hope of going home faded and dimmed. My father, who was all too visible in his fury, now plundered my confidence by his invisibility. I felt as empty as the mailbox.

Mom found a job at the local hospital, and accommodations in converted army housing. The following week we delivered the car to its rightful owner, but felt nostalgic about giving up our faithful friend that ushered us safely across the wilderness. I attended Anchorage West High School to finish out my sophomore year, and Mom worked nights at the hospital, our schedules arranged so that one of us was always there to watch Michael and Paul.

The high school harbored a noisy and bewildering student body with six hundred names and faces in my class alone, more than all the students in my entire school back home. I couldn't find my locker; I got lost in the halls and showed up late for classes. Everything went too fast, and I felt relieved when school let out for summer.

For six months, we lived our lives on hold. I made no friends. We leased our apartment month-to-month, and my mother worked as a relief nurse, prepared to leave at any time. Letters to Dad and Rick went unanswered. "We'll come together over this," Mom would say. "We'll be stronger in the long run." All the while, we hungered for a letter from home.

It finally came. The envelope, postmarked Bellaire, Michigan, lay on the table. We stared at it as if by wishing we could make it hold the words we so desperately needed. Mom picked it up and held my gaze for a long moment. I wanted to shout, "Go on! Open it! What are you waiting for?" But I swayed on the edge of an emotional abyss. The envelope possessed a universe, amassed within the seal of its paper fold—a great unknown. Unsure and unsettled, vertigo swirled in me, and neither breath nor words would come. All I could do was nod my head.

Standing beside the table, Mom tore the envelope open. Her fingers scrambled for a letter. Finding none, she looked inside and frowned, and then tapped the contents of the envelope onto the table. A slip of newsprint, as light as a feather, floated to the tabletop, its edges torn, ripped from the classified ads section of a newspaper. She read the scrap aloud, "A divorce decree was granted to John Rylko, on the grounds of desertion by his wife, Patricia Rylko."

Mom let out a cry and dropped to the chair. The news clip shook in her hand, its ugliness made worse by the contempt of the sender who informed us of our status through heartless anonymity. I felt like I'd been slugged in the stomach.

Dad may have been an insensitive, womanizing bastard,

but Mom loved him. How could he not love her in return? Those terrible, long years of abrasive, cold offenses did not lead to reconciliation and commitment but to a newspaper announcement proclaiming his righteousness.

"Damn him!" Mom crumpled the paper to her face and wept. "How could he do this?" she sobbed. "We didn't abandon him, we *escaped* from him. It was only supposed to be a cooling-off period. Isn't that what we said, a time-out?" She looked so vulnerable and distressed, I began to cry. As we both sobbed, the two little ones saw us crying, so they cried too. That day, we all grieved the death of our family.

Now, we were truly on our own. With no attempt to reconcile, my father divorced both his brides. In my father's world, this was our punishment, the price we paid for our betrayal of his trust and love. But we didn't feel like deserters. We were his wife, his daughter, his young son, and his grandchild, severed from the body of his family, carved away and disowned.

We hoped for reconciliation behind the silent lapses in our conversations, though perhaps my mother understood all along that it would never come. Maybe she even wished for an end to the relationship with a volatile husband, but it distressed me terribly. The rejection symbolized not what was, but what could have been. Going back to Michigan would have signaled restoration—to my father and to myself, and to all things familiar. Now all I felt was fear, fear of an undefined future, fear of my own guilt, fear for my mother. What would happen to us? How would we live? Where would we go? And what about Rick? Would I ever see my brother again? How could things have gone so wrong?

It was all because of me. If I hadn't lied, we'd still be a family. I'd split us apart. Remorse was not enough to make up for what I had done. "Father, forgive me," I cried. But my father was gone.

SLEEP REFUSED ME BOTH REST and peace. My dreams skimmed the shallow surface of slumber: feathers, ripped from the wings of birds, fell from the sky, bloody and torn, turning to slips of paper and into my mother's tears. Exhausted and troubled, one night I ambled out to the steps of the apartment. I expected the blue wash of moonlight, but found instead, a yellow glow, not from the moon, but from the pale midnight sun. It floated through the night, beaming at me from the brink of the horizon, unblinking, not giving way to the dark. Maybe it was a sign that I was not to give in. If only I could be that strong.

Through the night, I stayed on the steps in the dusky light of the false dawn and watched the sleepless sun rise up in an arc, like a smile, to a reclaimed day. Could I do that? Maybe I could rise above a dark day. Maybe. At least, I thought, if this were to be our home, it had strange and wonderful treasures.

The first treasure came a few months later, as an opportunity. Mom put her teacup down and pointed to the newspaper, "It's the Miss Anchorage Contest. They're looking for contestants. You could do that."

"Do what?" I asked.

"Compete in the Miss Anchorage Contest." She put the paper down and looked at me with the same intensity as when we crossed that bridge in the Yukon.

"Are you crazy? You've got to be a virgin to be in those contests. That's why they call it *Miss* Anchorage!"

"Danny, they won't know."

"Boy, Mom, one look at me and they'll know! Everybody will know. I'm a ruined woman." My father's words still pounded in my head.

"Danny, all they'll see is a beautiful girl."

"How could I, Mom? I need a dress and shoes and how could I just get up there in front of God and everybody?"

"You just walk on that stage like you own the bloody joint, that's how."

"Well, I think you're crazy," I said, secretly hoping she was right.

MEMORY IS A YELLOWING THING, faded as old newspapers, brittle as old bones. Years later, leaping out at me from a scrapbook, I scan the saffron pages of the *Anchorage Daily Times* from 1966. There is a picture of a young woman in a white chiffon gown with a wide cowl neck, her hair piled and pinned upon her head. She is seventeen, and smiling; walking across a stage as though she owns the bloody joint. The caption reads,

> *Danuta Rylko, winner of the talent contest and second runner up in last night's Miss Anchorage Contest. She read an original poem called, 'The Epitaph of Bernie Loftus.'*

Funny, that a poem about a pirate lost at sea would win a talent contest in a beauty pageant; funnier still, that the girl who penned it wrote it while she was pregnant and hiding in bed. She made quite an impression to win the talent contest, reciting the poem dressed in pirate garb, a patch over one eye, a sword at her side, and a Rachmaninoff concerto playing in the background as she began the poem:

> *At the junction of thirty and forty beware,*
> *For an eerie tryst awaits you there,*
> *Where stifled air meets deadly calm,*

A desolate brig drifts, wearily on,
Old sea memories haunt tattered sails
And the rotting boards
Held by rusting nails,
Putrid souls immersed with time,
Slick the deck with their fleshy slime,
And enshrouding the brig are fingers of mist
And a spectral psalm that you must resist,
For it cries, it wails,
But take no heed,
Or you die with those
Who can't be freed,
And the blood it bleeds
Will be the blood of thee.

The girl in the dated picture is not Miss America–pretty with a little nose and valentine lips. This girl has a strong Roman nose and cheekbones that make ledges for her eyes. You might call her handsome. She seems radiant, defying the yellow relic of newsprint, oblivious to the future, even happy. But her happiness is short lived. She is walking a tightrope, without knowing it. Her smile seems fearless, as if she is unaware of the clouds forming overhead. She looks, but she does not see.

I want to warn her; I want to reach back in time and have her eyes look into mine and tell her where she must go. I want to be her counselor, her big sister, and her friend. I want to teach her how to avoid the sinkholes and chasms of her life. I want to give her a sip of my wisdom and a piece of my mind, but I can't.

Instead, I hold a picture of a girl living a false spring and I cannot save her.

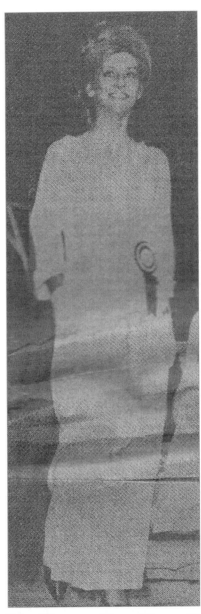

Talent Winner and Second Runner Up
in Miss Anchorage Contest, 1966

WILL

THIS IS THE NATURE OF THINGS: YOU SQUEEZE through the eye of a needle, tempered by pain, counseled by caution, thinking you've been saved. You find little use for prudence, that graceful shepherd of your past, and in favor of the present, abandon yourself to joy. The dazzle of this good fortune renders you blind, has you thinking that happiness is an open account with unlimited funds.

I began my senior year in high school fresh on the heels of talent winner and second runner up to Miss Anchorage. I scored enough self-confidence to audition for *The Varsity Show*, an *American Bandstand*–type television program, hosted and produced by high school seniors. Applicants had to dance, and tryouts were held at the sponsoring TV station in the basement of the scarred, pink McKinley Building.

The studio was cold and dark as a cave, a blank space waiting to be filled with the imagination of lights and props and colors. Outlined in the dark, a Jurassic black camera peered down from a pedestal and pointed to a spot of light. A husky red-haired man directed me to the spot and told me to dance when I heard the music. He disappeared, and moments later, Mick Jagger's voice blared out of a speaker, singing about satisfaction. Uncomfortable at first, I eased into the rhythm of the Rolling Stones, swaying and rocking my arms, swinging my head to the music. It was just me and the music in the spotlight, the surrounding darkness luring me into a sense of solitude. But I wasn't alone.

When the music stopped, the silence embarrassed me as if I were caught dancing in the reflection of a shop window. I fiddled with my skirt and blouse, waiting for someone to tell me what to do. The burly man reappeared, grinning. "My name's Chuck." He put his hands on his hips and looked at me as if he were admiring new hubcaps on his car. He said he wanted to introduce me to someone and escorted me into the control room. Lights spilled onto a panel of switches and television monitors, and reels of film hung from pegs on the back wall. "This is Will." Chuck pointed to the man at the panel of switches. "This is our engineer. He wants to meet you."

Will spun around and clunked his head on a gooseneck lamp as he shot out of the chair. Whirling toward me, he thrust his right hand out to shake mine, decided against it, and jammed both hands into his pockets.

"Will wants to ask you out for his twenty-first birthday." Chuck grinned again.

Will shot Chuck an irritated look, swept his eyes over the panel, then along the floor before they finally landed on me. He extended his hand for a second try, and shaking mine this time said, "Hi," then quickly returned his damp palm to the safety of his pocket.

I had never seen a man with such a tangle of curls, each soft twist a temptation to be touched. My own hair, bedraggled by Mick Jagger, felt damp and clingy around my neck and I self-consciously anchored a strand behind one ear. Finally, he smiled. His light brown moustache outlined bright, crimson lips and the rising color of his cheeks. His eyes, now that I could see them, were the most intense blue I had ever seen and they unnerved me.

"So, how old are you, Danny?" Chuck wiped his nose with the back of his hand; a sorry nose, I thought, a purple mash of broken veins and blood vessels.

"Seventeen."

"She's legal," he laughed. "You're twenty-one, she's seventeen, it's perfect. So, why don't you two go out tonight?" Chuck smiled, showing yellow, crooked teeth.

Will nodded.

"Okay," I said, wondering why Will wouldn't speak up for himself, but I liked his boyish, shy good looks, and his fidgety twitches. And I was intrigued by a man who seemed more threatened and nervous than the girl who stood before him.

Winter starts early in Alaska and by October the immortal days of endless light slipped into the eternal nights of winter. Rivers froze, fog crystallized the air, and green mountain glades swelled white with snow. But I hardly noticed. The sub-zero temperatures and a drive-in movie seemed an odd combination for a date, but that was how we spent our first hours together. Fortunately, the drive-in provided plug-in heaters for the car engines and electric heaters for the passengers to keep both from freezing. Half an hour into the movie, Will lowered the convertible top of his Corvair and a blast of icy air swooped over us. He bumped our seats into a reclining position and pulled a couple of blankets from the back, bundling them around us. Above, against a black sky, the aurora borealis painted waves of shimmering colors. Bands of greens, blues, and reds swept across the stars in celestial silence, swirling like the hemlines of long dresses. Our romance began under the cosmic breeze of the northern lights, not looking forward at a movie screen, but gazing up at the impossible heavens.

Will had an edge that appealed to me. He rode motorcycles, raced an Austin-Healey, and wanted to learn to fly and skydive. When he taught me to race over winding roads at night, he'd shout, "No headlights coming. Make your corner straight. Don't hesitate on the curve. Use both lanes. Keep your speed." Into the curve he'd yell, "Down gear, now, and accelerate. Take the curves. Control your RPMs."

I may have learned to control the revolutions per minute of a sports car, but I had no idea how to control my passions. My feelings for Will were as new as snowflakes, but my father's curse still haunted me. I was a ruined woman. Ever since the birth of Paul, I wanted to tell every man I met that I had been raped, that I had a baby, that my father didn't want me anymore. It was as if I sought absolution, and they could forgive me, but I knew that was impossible. So I told no one. Until I told Will.

A month after our first date, we sat in the apartment he shared with a roommate who had gone to work for the day. "There's something you have to know." My chest throbbed. I felt like I'd eaten a bucket of nails. "I was raped," I said.

"Jeez, I'm sorry." He took my hand. Maybe it was the crush of his hand, or that I sensed he didn't judge me. Maybe it was the tone of his voice, but I felt I could tell him. In a gush of words and tears, I told him everything.

This is the nature of things: remembering fear, and a man's hands grabbing and groping and hurting. You want to push men away, to hide and never be touched. Never trust again. You think danger is a single jeopardy and, once subdued, will not return, and that life demands you pass through the eye of a needle only once, and no challenge will ever be as great.

But then comes another man whose slow hands are open and soothing. He doesn't rush and push, but hesitates and waits. You love the crisp starch of his shirt and the soapy scent of his skin. He makes you feel clean. His is not the suffocating breath of force but the sweet scent of spice, bringing a flush of heat that rises up from your chest and colors your cheeks. He is irresistible. His fingers fumble with belts and clasps and you say, "Let me help," and you don't cry, but giggle with excitement. You love how he's unsure, and how he pauses on your curves. He doesn't pin you down with his unbearable bulk, but lies beside you and jokes about forgetting how buttons work. The courtship of hands and bodies kindles a glowing fire that burns away fear. You want him. And you are not afraid.

After, when he pulls the damp hair from your face and asks if you're all right, all you can say is, "Yes." He whispers, "You are my first," and you whisper back, "You are mine." And all else fades away.

My life was finally clicking into place. *The Varsity Show* lit the way to my future in television. I began to believe I was worth something. And I believed the past never repeated itself. I was wrong.

I never talked about birth control with Will. Didn't know how. Maybe he didn't either. Like the nuns used to say, we just had to trust in God about these things. This time, I knew the signs: missed periods, morning sickness, dizzy spells. One year after Paul's birth and I had turned back the clock and revisited the scene of my first trauma.

Looking back now, I can see my subconscious mind at work: reprogramming the past, rewriting history, rewinding and editing the film. Making myself a better movie—maybe this time, the baby would be mine.

Will seemed delighted. "We'll get married! Right after the baby is born."

"Why after?"

"We need, you know, time." He suggested we move in together, saying, "It'll be fun. Honest."

I was three months pregnant when I graduated from high school. I couldn't bear to tell my mother. Will and I found a furnished, one-bedroom duplex on the outskirts of town advertised in the newspaper. We drove over and had a look. It wasn't much of a love nest. When I pulled back the dark-brown curtains that hid a small front window, the light spilled onto an orange shag carpet that smelled like dog pee. A rickety wooden side table stood next to a plaid couch with sagging cushions. I ran my fingertips along the grimy kitchen counter and wondered if I should learn to cook. Down the end of a dark hall, I spied the bedroom. The room hugged a stained, thin mattress sprawled on a metal bedframe.

"Whadaya think?" Will threw out his arms as if he were embracing a great find.

"It's super," I said, scratching my swelling tummy.

The next problem was how to leave my mother without telling her why. I had betrayed my father because I feared him, but now I was about to lie to Mom because I loved her. Another crisis and she might hate me, too. And she had sacrificed so much for me already. In a balance of contradictions, I kept my mother by deserting her first. My excuse to go came with an argument late one night when Mom came home from the hospital; the boys were already asleep. I still cringe with shame when I think about it.

"I'm thinking of moving in with Will." I tried sounding nonchalant.

"No you're not." Mom kicked off her shoes and headed for the kitchen.

"But I love him."

"Doesn't matter." She filled the teakettle and plunked it

on a burner. Turning to face me, she crossed her arms and leaned against the stove. "You're needed here."

She was right, of course, but this pregnancy was my problem, not hers, and I wasn't about to put her through it again.

"But we have a babysitter now. You even said when we hired her that I needed to live a normal life."

"I didn't mean *leave.*"

"But you said go out on dates. Meet people. Have fun. Well, I did."

"I didn't mean shack up with someone." She brushed past me and sat down on the couch with a sigh. I followed behind and stood in the middle of the small living room, strewn with baby toys. A pang of sadness and guilt struck me—knowing I would also be leaving Paul.

"I'm not shacking up. We're getting married."

"When?"

"Soon."

"Right."

"You don't understand." I felt frustrated, needing to explain, but unwilling to tell her anything. This wasn't going well.

"I understand perfectly." Mom rested her head on the back of the couch and closed her eyes.

"No, you don't! You don't understand anything. I have to go." Determined not to tell her, I grabbed a bag of clothes sitting in the corner and rushed out the door just as the kettle began to scream.

A year before, I'd hidden my pregnancy and lost half my family. Was I doing it again? I tried not to think, but night after night I couldn't outrun my dreams. Nuns in black hoods, pursuing, pushing, punishing.

Throughout the summer, Will and I played house. I put up new curtains, he wired the speakers for the stereo, and

I even tried my hand at cooking. We often played canasta with our neighbors, Frank and Terri. But by September, and seven months pregnant, I grew bored with banging around the apartment all day. I wanted out. Way out.

The rugged peaks of the Chugach Mountains dwarfed the city's skyline, and appeared to shoulder the whole sky on wide white prongs of snow. Ice fields glinted in the foothills, slivers of ice slashed into shadowy gullies. That's where I wanted to go. We drove to a campsite parking lot by the foothills and began the climb.

A steep slope led to a low patch of snow three hundred yards long, lining a narrow ravine. The snow had curdled like sour milk in the summer sun and wizened into grains of pellet-sized mush called corn snow. Spying a tuft of wild flowers on the other side of the gully, we traversed the ice field to set up a picnic blanket near them.

In the middle of the ice field I lost my footing and slipped. I laughed at first, bobsledding on my rear end down the sloppy snow, but I was soon careening out of control down the gully, feet first, like a bloated torpedo. Below me a mass of boulders blocked the end of the chute, and they were getting closer by the second. A sickly fear raced through me. I saw myself bashing against the rocks, exploding in a slurry of blood and baby. I screamed, digging my heels into the snow, and sprawled sideways. Despite clawing at the snow, I kept sliding towards the rocks. Snow gushed up my back and burned my raking hands as I tried in vain to stop my fall.

And the world gave way, as if time and space were impractical now. I seemed to slow to the speed of a cloud and drifted weightless overseeing a great sky—drifting with time to think. My son Paul would never know me. My mother would never find me here among the debris of rocks and blood. This baby within me would never become. I didn't want to die.

I screamed again and with one last thrust I dug in my heels, my legs buckling with the effort. Inches from the rocks, I came to a stop. I gasped for air. My knees trembled uncontrollably.

Will scrambled down the edge of the snow field, clutching at tufts of grass for balance, slipping in the mud. "Danny. My God." He knelt beside me, fluttering his hands as if he were shooing away flies.

"I'm all right, I think." I reached for him.

Will hefted me to my feet and brushed the snow from my back. We carefully slogged down the steep hill. By the time we reached the gravel parking lot, the sun slipped behind the mountain and the air turned cold.

"We shouldn't have come in the first place. It's not like we're free as birds anymore." Will opened the passenger door, "Get in." When I did, he slammed the door shut.

The Corvair rumbled over sinkholes and maneuvered around rocks that had fallen from the cliff above. The combination of the bumpy road and the near tragedy woke the baby up. "Baby kicked me," I said. "Got big feet." I reached for Will's hand. "Here, feel."

He wrenched his hand away. Perhaps we understood for the first time how slippery life had become, how things between us had changed. He tightened his fists around the steering wheel and said, "I'm sorry."

WILL'S PLAN

SUMMER DIMMED LIKE A DYING CANDLE. AS shards of winter slashed the air, I grappled with Will's dark moods and suffered through days of silence. Our love flickered in wisps of unspoken words mourning the loss of the gentle touch and the soft kiss.

The child I carried became my only friend and I confided in him, explaining who we were and where we came from: "We are from the long line of the House of Jasterowski and the Polish count who fought the Czar and escaped to the Carpathian Mountains. He changed his name to an anagram from his coat of arms. The wild boar, the lion, and the sword became our name, Rylko. Our name was conceived by a count and passed on through our grandfathers to us."

I took comfort in believing my baby heard me, that in the warm amniotic fluid of his unborn world, he curled safe and content with the sound of my voice.

One lonely day, Will shot into the house during his lunch break looking flushed, his eyes sparkling with excitement I hadn't seen in weeks. He pulled out a kitchen chair. Asked me to sit. I plunked into it like a dumpling slipping off a spoon. Yanking a manila envelope from his coat pocket, he grabbed a bunch of papers and shoved them towards me. He said he was too young to be a father. Can't do it. Wouldn't be a good father. He'd be a lousy father. Maybe even leave me and the baby. He's no good. Not as a father. He's not ready.

His blue eyes pleaded for understanding. I placed my hand on our baby and scanned the papers in the dim yellow light of the kitchen bulb.

HE DRAGGED HIS CHAIR ACROSS the peeling linoleum floor and sat closer. "Just listen, Danny. I've got a plan." My throat burned and I couldn't swallow as I listened to the torrent of words tumbling out in meaningless phrases. "The couple really wants a baby . . . they'd pay for the delivery . . . not like an orphanage or anything . . . a good family." He forced a smile and nodded.

My chest heaved and I gasped for air. I felt sick. When I didn't speak he threw back his chair and hollered, "I'm talking about farming the baby out." He paced to the kitchen sink and back to me, his hands on his hips.

My eyes swept over the white papers covered with black words. "You mean adoption? Give our baby away?" I shivered, disbelieving the words on my lips.

"It's the best I can do," he sighed. Then perking up, "The doctor says the couple is really nice."

"This isn't a puppy, Will. We can't just give him away." I wanted to grab onto something to steady myself.

"Look." He slammed his hand on the papers. "It's the baby or me. Your choice."

The same fingers that once touched my lips and swept back my hair now drummed relentlessly on the table. There it was, all these weeks of silence and neglect summed up in a single, profane mandate: *Give the baby up.* Will stared at the papers. I stared at Will. An unbearable loss stared back at me. He said the attorney was waiting. It's that or he leaves me. He pushed the papers back in the envelope. With tears rolling down my cheeks, I begged him not to do this, that I didn't have a job, or money, or a car. That I needed him. The baby needed him. Will's eyes were glacial blue and just as cold. "Let's go," was all he said.

Crying harder now, I climbed heavily into the car. The lawyer wore a light-blue suit, the jacket buttons strained across a rumpled shirt. He sat in a high-back leather chair behind a scuffed wooden desk strewn with papers. The stink of an uneaten pizza combined with the smell of his cigar made me nauseous. I didn't get his name. I couldn't stop sobbing.

He asked if I was making this decision of my own free will and waved his cigar in the air. I shook my head, *no*. But Will said yes, slashing his eyes in my direction.

"You understand these papers turn the baby over to my clients upon birth?"

I sobbed harder.

"Sign here, and here, and here." The cigar fingers pointed to spaces on the documents.

The papers blurred in front of me. Will shoved a pen at me. "Please. No." I pleaded, but Will hung his head and eyed the floor.

"Just sign the papers, Danny."

I signed each page, telling myself the contract meant nothing.

Will drove me home and went back to work, leaving me and our unborn child standing in the living room. I knelt on the floor and rolled onto my back, trying to understand what just happened. "Remember me," I whispered, and fell asleep on the orange shag carpet.

It was Halloween—goblins and witches and fairy princesses bundled in parkas and towed by parents with flashlights trundled up and down frosty streets with paper sacks, trick-or-treating. Only three days after meeting with the lawyer, the labor pains began. Will rushed me to the hospital, as anxious as any new father. There, between contractions, I signed more papers. When the pains increased, nurses wheeled me into another room. More nurses. Someone told me to stop pushing. I heard a baby cry.

"It's a boy," someone said.

"Shush, she isn't supposed to know," another voice answered.

A mask came down over my face and everything went black.

I feel groggy. Down a hospital corridor on a gurney, one tiny voice is crying in the distance. My baby? I lean up on an elbow to catch sight of him, but see only walls striped in long bars of lights and shadows. I'm in a room. Nurses come. Then a doctor.

No, you can't see the baby. No, we can't talk about him.

I cry, "My son is gone. My son is gone."

Will comes and goes. I hardly remember.

Time to leave.

Instead of a baby, I cradle flowers home.

THOUGH I NEVER TOUCHED HIM, I called my lost son Matthew.

Goodbye Again

THE DAY I ARRIVED HOME FROM THE HOSPITAL,
Frank and Terri from next door met us at the car. "So, let's
see the little bundle of joy." Frank's eyes scanned the flowers
in my arms.

"He died," I said, pushing past them into the house and
closing the door.

I brought two sons into the world, but they were not
mine, each belonged to someone else, each had another
mother. This thought nearly drove me insane. Matthew was
here, somewhere in Anchorage, close to me but hidden away
in someone else's home, in someone else's arms. Warm tears
trickled past my ears and my pillow soaked up nights of
anguish. Relentless dreams continued to torment me:

*I sit on a chairlift, high in the air. I hold a baby. He slips
from my arms. Fumbling, I can't grab him. The child plunges
into water below. I dive after him. He's flailing in the water. I
swim as hard as I can but I can't make up the distance between
us. He disappears below the surface. He dies. Dozens of people
surround me, but my baby is dead and gone.*

Months passed. Will tried to act jolly, pretending everything was all right, but walls of stone had fallen around us
and our apartment felt like a tomb. We had become strangers,
avoiding direct contact. Yet, I believed Will had to love me;
our sacrifice was too great to believe otherwise.

But dear God, my arms were too empty. I needed my baby.

Paul. He could still be held. He was just a phone call away. Only a few miles separated me from baby Paul's soft skin and sweet breath. And Michael, my beautiful little brother with the inquisitive eyes and the trusting spirit. And Mom, and unconditional love. I needed them all.

Mom sounded happy that I called. "Work is going well at the hospital," she said. "I've bought a used Ford, but it's as good as new." She said she planned on leaving for California. "The boys need sunshine. I'm thinking of San Francisco."

As usual, neither of us spoke of the past. She didn't ask about Will. I didn't tell her about Matthew. Neither of us referred to the argument that separated us—as though nothing had happened. I'd accepted those rules by now, the British stiff-upper-lip way of dealing with life. Move ahead. Ever forward. Never back. For a while, my mother's therapy seemed to work. My father's shadow, however, grew darker.

"The change will do you good." Will seemed encouraging when I mentioned driving with Mom down to California. He kissed me on the forehead. "I'll be right behind you. I've always wanted to go to California. I'll work two more months here, tie up some loose ends. And we'll get married in San Francisco. Why stick around this dump, when we could have California?"

Within a month, my mother, Paul, Michael, and I were back on our old friend, the Alcan Highway. For me, the motivation was the same, escaping pain. This time, however, the pain wasn't from my father, but from losing my son. Once before on this highway I ran because I had a child, now I was here because I didn't. Again we barreled towards an unknown address, not through the peril of ice but to the pledge of sun where people wore flowers in their hair. Rather than being driven by fury and fear, we drove with purpose, not to a frigid landscape of uncertainty, but to a warm destination of our choosing.

For a thousand miles, the unpaved Alcan evaporated in clouds of grit, reeling out the road between Matthew and me, scattering the miles like ashes. We climbed mountain passes into the sky and skirted summit lakes that looked like violets strewn across the landscape. Time collapsed behind me. The dreadful Canyon Creek Bridge that once held our lives on perilous planks of wood now had railings and cross boards. We didn't need to get out of the car to cross it, although the bridge still groaned under the effort.

I stayed glued to Paul, hugging him, holding him, hanging on. I delighted in the smell of his hair and searched his face to see parts of myself. It hardly seemed possible that within eighteen months I bore two sons. I loved Paul twice over and couldn't look at him without thinking of Matthew. My mother kept giving me concerned glances, perhaps puzzled by my silence, or worried about my lack of vitality, maybe she even guessed what happened to Will and me, but she didn't say anything. Neither did I.

We followed the same trail through the Yukon Territory as other intrepid adventurers, like Jack London and Wyatt Earp. I imagined Sergeant Preston of the Royal Canadian Mounted Police striding up on his horse looking for renegade trappers. I thought of George Carmack, Skookum Jim, and Dawson Charlie striking it rich in Bonanza Creek in the Klondike, creating the great Gold Rush stampede. More than a hundred years later, we were on the same beaten track in our own stampede for the golden hills of California and a magnificent Golden Gate.

For hundreds of gravelly miles, we drove with our headlights on. Dust powdered our faces and our ears ached with the endless churn of stones under the car banging like marbles in a clothes dryer. Paul was fidgety and irritable. Every time we stopped, white-legged black flies ripped at our skin, leaving vicious and swollen sores.

"It was easier in the wintertime," I said as we punched into massive potholes and rattled over sections of road corduroyed with rough logs. We bumped and ground our way to Dawson Creek, Mile 0 at the southern end of the Alcan, Mile 0 of my life to Matthew, and a thin stretched line from Will.

After ten days of gravel roads and grimy motels, the soft air of Seattle pressed like perfume on my skin. A glint of sophistication shimmered through the town: fancy restaurants, clothing stores sporting big picture windows, antique furniture shops displaying expensive chairs, red brocade couches, and glittery lamps. Here, people wore hiking boots but shopped at Nordstrom. Flower stands and outdoor fish markets intoxicated my starving senses. Shiny cars whizzed by on spotless streets.

"Look at that seagull, just as proud as you please," Mom said as she took us along a pier at Pike Place Market. The bird landed on a nearby post and cocked its head, staring at us as if it understood we were newcomers to this place. We had nothing to offer, so it ruffled its feathers and sailed off, catching an updraft, riding the thermals above us with effortless grace. "I could be a seagull." My mother faced the water, her eyes closed, inhaling the soft, salty smell of sea air.

I could see my mother as a seagull, an air traveler borne up by warm currents, a graceful, independent, and self-sufficient bird, a lover of water and bridges.

"What kind of bird am I?" I rocked Paul in my arms.

"You're an eagle." With her eyes still closed, she said, "Beautiful, strong, resilient."

I felt no kinship with eagles. More like a roadrunner, I thought, running away from everything.

That night, we stayed in a real hotel in downtown Seattle with clean crisp sheets, a warm bath, and soap that smelled like vanilla. But the comfort didn't stop my menacing dreams: *Three nuns in black habits pursue me. A river appears. I swim. Behind me nuns follow like killer whales. On the opposite bank more nuns wait for me. They hold a child. They point at me. I run again.*

Arriving in San Francisco, I felt like Alice in Wonderland, entranced by a peculiar world of odd people and strange colors. Mountains and glaciers had insulated me from the counterculture erupting in the Lower Forty-eight. In 1968, young people walked barefoot and wore beads and bell bottoms. Everyone had long hair. They flashed peace signs. They were my age and yet they seemed a different species. I didn't own anything in rainbow colors; I didn't possess a single bead. I barely survived the battles of life, much less shouldered opinions about Vietnam, or the military industrial complex. As for drugs, I knew the song about Alice and how the pills can make you taller or smaller. I just didn't understand the words.

The Pacific breeze provided a balmy contrast to the sharp-edged gales of Alaska. Here, the days were even with the nights, gardenias bloomed in the sun and jasmine scented the moonlight. From every corner and sidewalk, from every park and bench, music floated against a blue, forget-me-not sky. Groups with warm and whimsical names like the Mamas and the Papas, The Lovin' Spoonful, and The Beach Boys sang about The Age of Aquarius and California Girls. More like a festival than a city, San Francisco pulsed with anticipation. Something wonderful and new but still undefined permeated the air like fairy dust.

At the Golden Gate Bridge, I expected nothing less than pageantry. After all the primitive bridges of timbers and logs on the Alcan, I anticipated a heavenly gate made of gold, swinging wide as we entered. But the structure was neither golden nor a gate, just a big metal bridge painted orange. This bridge was not meant to be crept across by travelers quaking in horror at the watery peril below. People zipped across this archway at fifty-five miles an hour in their cars, neither with gratitude nor awe, but with an irreverence that comes with the presumption of safety.

My mother didn't share my view. "But it's a beautiful bridge. Look at the suspensions. Think of the engineering that went into designing it." Wonderful to my mother, the lover of bridges, but to me, the Golden Gate was just another disappointment in the center of a spinning universe where I didn't fit in.

We rented a duplex in San Rafael, and Mom again took a job as a nurse. I enrolled in Marin Junior College with free tuition and credits transferable to any university in the country; it was my first step towards a future my father swore I would never have.

Months went by. I wrote unanswered letters and made unreturned phone calls to Will, but I refused to believe he was gone. We had made a deal on the surrender of our son. Surely, he would keep his part of our terrible bargain. After two years I still waited, living a hybrid life of mother and sister, daughter and bride-to-be, bearing up, sometimes breaking down, but slowly moving forward.

During that time, I met Erik at a campus dance. He was a skyscraper of a man. Not gangly, basketball-player tall, but more like an old-growth tree. At six-foot-ten, he was long in the trunk and his limbs branched out in perfect proportions.

Olive skin, dark eyes, and curly hair, he whispered when he spoke and moved with the grace of a cat, compensating for his imposing height with a sublime delicacy. He was a towering love, big enough to save me, big enough to block some of the pain of Will and Daddy and Matthew.

My life gained balance. As French, Spanish, and writing classes went well at college, a wary confidence began to grow in me. A steady course with Erik developed. It was not a relationship in full bloom, as a portion of me was frozen in time awaiting Will's return, but I found myself surprisingly content with what we had.

During one of those optimistic days, as Blood Sweat and Tears sang about how love can make you so very happy on the radio, the doorbell rang. I finished singing the line about being glad you came into my life, then I opened the door. There stood Will. A self-conscious smile twisted across his face. In my shock, I managed to choke out a question like a stone caught in my throat, "Will! For God's sake, why?"

He shrugged, "Wasn't ready, I guess."

I wanted to hit him, to kiss him, to shake him; instead, I burst into tears.

He moved toward me. "I was wrong. I know that now. But I'm going to make it up to you, I promise." I let him in. We had coffee while he explained he wasn't ready to get married two years ago. "Had wild oats in me, I guess," he said.

We traded our baby for your freedom? "Sugar?"

"You know I like it sweet." He smiled and slid his coffee cup across the table.

Two years without a word. "I remember." I slipped a spoon into his coffee, stirred it, and slid the cup back towards him.

His lips touched the rim of the cup, his eyes avoiding mine. "Great coffee. Anyway, that's why I wanted to see you."

"You're staying?" *Please! Let me hear those words.*

"Yeah. Well, sort of. I'm on the road with a couple of guys. Going to Tijuana. I can't exactly bail out on them halfway through the trip. God, you're beautiful." He took my hand.

"You didn't come for me?" I pulled my hand away.

"What I'm saying is. . ." He took another sip of coffee. "I'm going to Mexico. For your wedding ring. Can you wait three weeks?"

What about Erik? Can't think right now. This is Matthew's father.

I should have felt unbounded joy, but instead my voice wavered a little as I said, "I can wait." Desperation cultivates that kind of hope. Desperation kills motion, denies facts, and fills idle moments with dreams chasing and condemning. Despair makes you clutch at strings when only ropes will do. You want to fill the cavity where your heart should have been, to stop the blur of a young life rushed to maturity. Desperation makes you do stupid things.

After twenty-one days, Will had not returned. My stomach cramped. Thirty-eight days, I no longer jumped when the phone rang. Forty-four days and his absence gnawed at me like a rat on a corpse. My vigil became an entombment of time, a separate measure apart from my three-dimensional life. In that ruptured reality I kept Matthew's bargain alive. I never stopped waiting for Will; I just stopped expecting him.

During the following year, I allowed my relationship with Erik to flower and my healing looked a lot like progress. Erik and I studied together, and my grades were good. Together, we earned our Water Safety Certificates and became swim instructors and lifeguards. We started a swim school teaching infants water survival skills. We plotted a book about water babies that I eventually published. Our collaboration became the first book endorsed by the Red Cross on teaching water survival to infants. In the back of my mind I thought Erik would make a wonderful father for Paul, even if Paul called him an uncle.

But such happiness seemed to cue Will back into my life. I was still living at home with Mom and the boys when he returned. This time, when he stood at the door of our rented house in San Rafael, there was no quirky smile. During the ensuing year of his disappearance, he had become haggard, older. He had grown a beard and his chest looked caved in, as though his heart had been scooped out. His blue eyes paled to a watery gray.

"I'm sorry. I messed up. All I could think of was you."

"Will, don't." I backed away from him.

"No, really. I wouldn't blame you if you just threw me out. I deserve it. But just hear me out, first." I paused this time before I let him in. I loved Erik. Will was a sore memory, an inflammation of my heart, an interminable wait. Whatever he had to say wouldn't work.

"I'm no good." He stood in the hallway, trying to avoid my eyes, scanning the walls, the floor.

"So?" I marshaled an attitude of indifference.

"I've given away the best thing that ever happened to me, you and Matthew." He looked straight at me for the first time.

Matthew. My resolve melted like butter. He must have seen my expression soften because his pace quickened and he stepped towards me.

"And so I thought, I just wanted to see you one more time. I love you. I know that now."

I walked into the living room. I had to sit down. I had to catch my breath.

He sat next to me on the couch. "Let's get married, today,

tomorrow, any time you say. And then let's go get him." He sat back against the sofa as though he'd just finished a good meal.

I snapped out of my muse. "Go get him?"

"Matthew. Let's go get him. I've been thinking it over. Nothing's more important than family and home. I was afraid before, but not now."

"You want to get Matthew?" How I longed to hear those words! Everything I ever wanted, Will and Matthew, together at last. We'd be a family. Matthew would be saved!

Matthew would be saved. What did that mean, saved? Saved from what, saved from whom? Something other than joy stabbed at me. My blood raced through my veins like runoff in a dry wash. Rage welled up in me from a storehouse of disappointments.

"After five years, you want to go and get him?" My teeth clenched as hard as my fists.

Will looked bewildered. "Yeah, I mean, I thought. . ."

"You let him go. You left us both. For years. And now you want to disrupt our lives *again?* You want to tear Matthew from the only family he's ever known because *you're* ready now?"

"Well, I just thought—"

"How could you be thinking?" I shook with anger and stood up. He jumped up and looked surprised. "It's too late." I grabbed Will's arms. "He has a family and a life. He's not ours to take back. Promise me. Promise me on your life that you won't do that to him."

Will looked shaken. "I promise. Okay." And then he perked up and said, "But that doesn't mean I can't find him and just watch him from across the street one day."

"Will, you mustn't. If you've never done a decent thing in your life, do this one thing. Leave him alone." My instinct to protect Matthew overwhelmed me. "You can't take back the past, Will. You can't change what's done."

Tears streamed down both our faces. Matthew would be all right, but we mourned for ourselves. We would never be all right. After several more halting rounds of attempted reconciliation, I never saw Will again.

FORFEIT

Dear Rick:

How you doing? How's school and life in Bellaire?

Everything is fine here. We live in California now, Marin County actually, in a house we're renting in San Rafael. There's lots of woods and water and especially sunshine.

Mom works at a hospital as a nurse.

I've just been accepted to the University of Colorado in Boulder. I have three different scholarships, three jobs, and a work-study program to help with tuition. I start in the fall. With credits from college here, I'll be graduating in two years.

In case you want to write to me, you can mail me letters straight to the dorm where I'll be staying. . .

I miss you.

Danny

I TREMBLED WHEN I SLIPPED THE LETTER INTO the mailbox. I knew my father would read it.

Colorado reminded me of Alaska and though the Rocky Mountain state was not immune from protests against the Vietnam War, it offered some relief from the intensity of San Francisco, where students at SF State threw typewriters out of windows and graduation ceremonies had been suspended.

I had all the tear gas I needed during the People's Park riots and sit-ins in Berkeley earlier that year and felt sheltered by the rocky familiarity and the clean, cold simplicity of Colorado's mountains.

In the meantime, Erik had just been accepted to the University of California at Berkeley and we agreed to marry after graduation. That commitment helped absorb the miles between us.

I had my work cut out for me majoring in both communications and philosophy. I would learn to express myself and keep from being misunderstood. Since I had to pay my own way, I worked as an activity director for emotionally disturbed children on alternate weekends, planning day trips to parks and museums. When not with the kids, I taught private ski lessons at a local resort. During lunchtime midweek, I served up Mulligan stews at McFee's Irish Pub and at night, I worked as a cocktail waitress. I managed to pay for groceries and books. Between disturbed children, Irish stews, ski lessons, and last calls for cocktails, I managed eighteen hours of classes each week.

In spite of my relentless schedule, I felt isolated and lonely. Erik's letters were becoming sporadic and they lacked emotional substance. Gone were sweet poems penciled during an idle muse in the library. Instead he sent functional letters filled with class schedules, his mother's health, and his brother's travels in Europe. So, one weekend I decided to visit him.

I drove twenty-four hours straight to the Bay Area one rare, free weekend to surprise him after his Friday class. Using a spare key, I let myself into his apartment. Someone else was already waiting for Erik in his apartment. She was a beauty. Everything I was not: five-foot-nine, chestnut hair that fell to her waist, a long black skirt, lace-up granny boots, and a black shawl draped over porcelain arms as if she were born with it. She glided toward me like a swan.

"Who the fuck are you?" she asked, flicking at her hair with a lanky white wrist.

"I'm Danny, Erik's fiancée. Who are you?"

"That's impossible," she sniffed, "I'm Molly. And *I'm* Erik's fiancée. And he's never mentioned any *Danny.*"

She said my name as if it were a cheap beer. Her name, on the other hand, sounded musical, melodic Molly, marvelous Molly.

All five-feet-three and one-quarter-inches of me shriveled. I felt the skin peeling off my nose, burned from bright ski slopes and thin mountain air. The square, athletic frame of a downhill skier seemed dumpy and squat next to a swan. Hiking boots and blue jeans, regular attire for Colorado, smacked of Hicksville to the vogue of granny boots in 1971 Berkeley. This ugly duckling withered next to a lanky swan named Molly.

Just then, Erik entered the apartment. We stood facing him like two question marks. Rather than saying anything, he quickly turned and bolted from the room. He ran down the street and vanished around the block.

"Erik! Wait!" I jogged after him, but my boots were too heavy for running so I walked back to the apartment and waited for him to run off whatever chased him.

"How long have you known him?" Molly watched for him from the window.

"Almost three years." I felt bewildered.

"Fuck." Molly closed her eyes and shook her glorious mane.

"Yeah." God, I thought, she can even swear and make it sound good.

When he stopped running, Erik came back to the apartment and collapsed into a fetal position in the corner of the room. My old-growth tree huddled into a little ball and cried.

"What the hell do you take me for?" Molly stood above him. "You two-timing son of a bitch." I thought she was going to kick him with those granny boots. "Fuck you." She flung her shawl across her shoulder and stomped out.

I stayed and knelt beside him as he cried for his Molly, hugging himself, shivering and calling for his swan.

For hours he sobbed, "I can't live without Molly." And I felt that I couldn't live without him.

After I left Erik that night, a dark and desperate voice tugged at me. *The Golden Gate Bridge. Stop at mid-span.* Life pushed too hard, had become too painful. *Jump off that orange suspension.* And then another voice warned me: *Don't go near the bridge. The bridge will kill you, like the men in your life are killing you.*

Maybe Dad was right after all. There was no one who will have me.

Later that night, at home with Mom and the boys, I said, "I'm thinking of quitting school. Leaving Colorado. Come back to California. Be with you, at home. Get a job."

Mom's eyes pierced me like a fork. "You have a job. Your job is school. That's why I'm taking care of the family, so that you can go to school. Now get your rear end back there."

She was right, of course; I had to finish school. I just didn't know how.

LIFELINES

LIFE WAS A FARCE, A PACK OF LIES, LOUSY PROM-
ises, and broken bargains. I had to be smart, watch out for
myself, and trust no one. I burrowed into myself, kept my
head down, and my heart locked. I gave up Matthew for Will
and Will for Erik in a bargain of love. But the man I chose
chose someone else. I gave up Will for nobody. And I lost
Matthew for nothing at all. This ate at me like groundwater
nibbling at the foundations of my emotional life, generating
little landslides of failures until my losses outweighed my
gains.

There was only one man now to live for, not out of love,
but out of revenge. I would stay in school, excel in everything, and make my father proud. No other men competed
with his shadow anymore. My father stood alone, the one
mountain to be conquered, and I would conquer every
vicious judgment he had of me. I tightened hard around
that thought.

Eventually, the demons that drove me demanded a hearing, forcing themselves on me with a phone call.

"Dee? This is Rick."

"Rick? Your voice. It's deeper."

"Yeah. Five years."

"Five years. God. Rick. How you doin'?"

"Good. Got your letter." He spoke haltingly, like a young
man bucking up, trying to be older.

I waited for him to say more. When he didn't, I said, again, "So, how've you been doin'?"

"Dad's been sick. Heart attack. Been in the hospital." He sighed. "Didn't think he'd make it. But he did." Rick's pared sentences, stripped of all emotional flesh, bequeathed a bony carcass of bare facts. How should I feel? I wasn't glad he was sick, but I couldn't pretend we were close. Only "Oh, gosh," came out.

"Here, someone wants to talk to you." There was a long pause, followed by a rustling on the phone line.

"Danuta, this is your father."

My God! That voice! The way he said my name, punctuating all three syllables in blunt, nimble tones. A voice I dreaded, a voice I fled, a voice I longed to hear. Shock took my breath. Heat flushed my face. I was three again, singing the sunshine song on his knees. I was six again, trembling as his belt whistled through the air. I was sixteen again, ducking his fists. A rabbit caught on a road. Run, but where?

Squeeze your eyes. Shut out the light and vanish. Keep him out and me in.

But I clutched the phone to my ear.

"Daddy?" My own voice sounded tiny and far away.

"Danuta, I want to ask for your forgiveness. Will you forgive me?"

I gulped. A word tumbled out too fast. It was a small word, one my mind could assemble and deliver to my lips. "Yes."

"I would like to come to see you, at your school. In a few months. At Easter."

"Yes." An easy word.

"So then, I'll see you, at Easter."

"Yes." A steady word. A pleasant word.

"Good. Good, then."

"Yes." A meaningless word.

"Easter. Good, Danuta." After a mortifying pause I heard a click. Did I hang up first or did he? No matter, thank God it was over. I opened my eyes and exhaled, but the call shook me.

After five years and two sons, after rape, rejection, and loss, my father crashed into my life with a chat. Fifty-two words. He asked for forgiveness, but didn't say what for. I said yes, but I didn't know why. What kind of forgiveness is that? Forgiveness takes time. It's a process, not a word. It took hours for the daze to wear off. I repeated the conversation over and over in my head. And then it hit me. My father wanted to see me! At Easter!

Though I hated to admit it, I found myself counting the days to Easter. Ninety days. I'd show him then—where I worked, the classes I took, the hills I skied. I'd show him how well I managed without him. How he misjudged me. Success would be my revenge. Sixty days. Hope was possible. We could make up for all the hurt. Our family could come back together again. Wrongs could be righted. Easter was coming. The resurrection of hope. Forty-five days, halfway to hope, six weeks closer to those unspoken promises. What if he's still mad? Am I still afraid? How do I say I'm sorry I lied, but I was afraid of you? I practiced scenes and dialogues with him a hundred times. Should I kiss him? Would he like me? Did he miss me? Would he think I changed? Thirty days to new beginnings. And I could almost touch him.

And then the phone call.

"Dee?"

An instant smile warms my face. "Hi Rick."

"It's Dad. Heart attack. Last night. He died."

Tight-fisted words strike like a sucker punch. I don't understand them.

"No. He's coming. At Easter."

Rick is crying.

His words skip over and over in my head.

Dad died.

I don't understand.

Dad died.

It's not true.

Dad's gone.

What about Easter?

Dead.

No! I scream, "He can't do that. That bastard. He promised me Easter."

Aided by several shots of tequila, I was sufficiently drunk to deal with the funeral. By the time the plane landed in Michigan, I wobbled and cried into my brother's arms. I don't remember much about the funeral except for the throng of my father's admirers filling the church to capacity, overflowing outside. I don't remember the service or the burial, Bellaire, or friends. But thirty-five years later, I still remember one moment—standing at my father's open casket, staring down at the cold and waxy face of a man I loved and feared.

His jaw was clenched and locked, just as in life. I could almost see the chisels in his hands. There we were at last, face to face, somewhere between life and death, I with only half a life and he just halfway to the gods. If he had any mercy at all he would abandon his journey, back away from the stars, and breathe again. His blue eyes would blink awake. He would sit up and be with me. He'd keep his promise.

You lie silent now, but you still rail against me, damning me forever while you lie sleeping as though silence was always your nature. Why do I tremble next to you, now that you are cold and absent from me? You are silenced from the pain you suffered, removed from the pain you inflicted, bound for a windless tomb. Yet I tremble that you may still awake and find me here, enraged with my young and troubled life. You promised me Easter, but you cheated me with death.

The facts regarding my father's death were simple. After his first heart attack, doctors had ordered him to stop skiing, but he would rather die than not ski. After a day on the slopes, he was having dinner at the home of a doctor friend. Someone said he was going to town. Anything he could get? My father stood, reached for his wallet, and said, "How about getting me another pack of cigarettes?"

Those were his last words. Not grand and mighty ideas, not noble thoughts or expressions of beauty, remorse, or regret, not words of affection. Not a fond memory or a last wish. Merely, ". . . another pack of cigarettes." And then he slumped to the floor. Despite the immediate efforts of the doctor at his side, the White Pole had died. He was fifty years old.

My brother told me Dad lived with the doctor's wife. The doctor drove to Bellaire from his practice in Detroit on weekends. To hear my brother tell it, the doctor was grateful to Dad for keeping the doctor's marriage together. The physician's beautiful wife had agreed to stay married to the physician if she could have my father the rest of the week. It was peculiar to think of my father as the third wheel in an open marriage. I found it curious that a man who exacted such high ethical standards on me would cheat on my mother all those years and end up in a tawdry sexual relationship of convenience. Set by his own standards, he sank to the moral level of his shoes.

Months later, I was back at school. But life for me was a blur of school and work, sleeping and waking, drifting from one campus classroom to another—all without seeming to consciously participate in any of it. I suffered a great loss with my father's death—so many unanswered questions—did he still love me, was he proud of me, why didn't he write to us in Alaska? The University of Colorado reminded me of the places I wanted to show him, the things I wanted us to do, and especially the talks I dreamed of us having. He will never know his grandson, or the bravery of my mother on the Alcan. He will never understand how much it hurt to read the divorce notice in the anonymous envelope, or how his rage affected us, and how crushed I was that he never made it to our Easter reunion. Most of all, he will never know that in spite of it all, I still loved him.

There was one strange day that finally broke the spell, but I cannot fathom how it happened. One moment I was on a campus path taking a shortcut to my dorm, and the next moment I awoke to find myself sprawled on the grass.

Did I fall? I close my eyes. I know the answer. The nuns from my nightmares have me. They stand over me, hunters with their kill. The hems of their long, black habits flap next to my ear. I open my eyes and watch the wind licking the pages of books flung open beside me. Pages flickering in the wind like flames in a fire, hands clapping, and applauding defeat. No more fear, just the wind and the pages and me in the grass under the sky. I close my eyes again. No feeling in my feet or my hands.

I hear the voices of blame and regret and petition them for mercy.

"You're Mrs. John Rylko."

"Yes. I wore my mother's ring."

"You're nothing but a whore."

"But I don't feel like a whore."

The hooded creatures bear down on me, nuns without faces,

only eyes burning with indictments, "Slut with a bastard."
"But he's a beautiful baby."
"It's the baby or me."
"Don't make me choose."

BUT I DID CHOOSE. WILL broke our covenant. Erik chose Molly. My son is my brother. Matthew is gone. My father died and Easter never came. I need my mother, but she's in California raising Michael and Paul.

She didn't go to the funeral, saying, "Who would take care of the boys? Where would I get the money for the flight? How could I afford the time off from work?" Between the lines I heard, *Why go?* Why publicly mourn a man who didn't want her? We didn't talk about it. We have never talked about it.

The wires in my head are as tangled as old Christmas lights, blinking off one at a time. Shutting down. Just then, a distant mantra crosses a sea of years, rustling the grasses and finding its way to me, the woman sinking into the earth, waiting for the rains, wanting oblivion. It finds me and murmurs into my ear:

"We are from the long line of the House of Jasterowski, the Polish count who fought the Czar and escaped to the Carpathian Mountains. He changed his name to an anagram from his coat of arms; the wild boar, the lion, and the sword became our name, Rylko. Our name was conceived by a count, and passed on through our grandfathers to us. Never forget."

I open my eyes and squint against the sun. Insects buzz the landscape above my face. I hear the drone of a plane thousands of leagues high. The earth is warm beneath my back. Sitting up, I close the pages around me. Either I overcome the shadows in my life or befriend them. Gathering up my books, I tuck them neatly, one by one, under my arm. Walking ahead, I am assured by a mantra, and if nothing else, I will lean upon the pride of that heritage.

PART TWO

THE BLACK, THE BLONDE, AND THE BAPTIST

Ben Kinchlow, Danuta, and Pat Robertson—the Black, the Blonde, and the Baptist—on the set of The 700 Club, *1984*

Born Again

IT WOULD TAKE YEARS TO FULLY REALIZE THE consequences of my conversion to Christian fundamentalism. But within two years of becoming "born again" I had become a spiritual drug dealer imbued with the halo of power and celebrity, associated with the brokers of money and politics. I was a television evangelist. And I am embarrassed by it all.

My college degree in communications led me to a career in broadcasting, not preaching. My first television job in 1972 cracked the glass ceiling for women in Phoenix, Arizona, when I became the station's first female camera operator. I paid my dues, worked hard, and scaled the career ladder as a radio reporter and then news anchor. Eventually, I cohosted the television show *SunUp San Diego*. At the time, I was single, lived in a condo overlooking the Pacific Ocean, drove a Porsche, and had friends who loved me and colleagues who respected me.

I had met Kai Soderman, a dreamy Sinatra-like Swede, in the elevator of the condominium building we shared. He was a regal-looking man, impeccably dressed, and carried a guitar at his side. He had been a popular recording artist in Sweden who had come to the United States hoping to hit the big time here as a singer. When his recording career failed, he delved into the insurance business, becoming one of the top salesmen for a national insurance company. The day we met in the elevator, I was carrying a mandolin I had just rented and was determined to teach myself to play it. When he asked me if I played the instrument I lied and said, "Yes." Our relationship blossomed from there: he discovered I couldn't play the mandolin, and I found him to be a friend I could always talk to.

Life was good. I was living the dream.

While my career was advancing, I was also seeking a long-lost spiritual connection. I had spent my life in a deliberate search for meaning and God in whatever form I could find Him. This quest grew from the disappointment years earlier of leaving the convent as a young girl and, later, manifested itself in my study of philosophy in college. I was fascinated by Immanuel Kant and his two worlds—one where we only know what our senses tell us and the other world as it really is. Kant argued that our experiences are structured by our minds; space and time, cause and effect, were not part of the real world. What we smell, see, touch, and hear is all subjective, and we have no direct experience of reality. Was God lingering behind the curtain of our senses? Or was He part of my subjectivity, too?

I studied Soren Kierkegaard, standing up for authenticity and, like Sartre, valuing man without labels, man as an existentialist—an essence in pure form without categorization, loving God with pure faith. The Danish philosopher wrote, "God . . . will help you to learn anew, so that you are weaned from the worldly point of view that insists on visible evidence."

But I wanted visible evidence. As an adult, it was not enough anymore to love an invisible God. I wanted to connect with the spiritual and give faith substance. So I shined the light within and turned to TM, Transcendental Meditation. I practiced for years to let go of my thoughts, of yesterday's regrets, and tomorrow's expectations; to still the chatter; to

Danuta became one of the first female camera operators at KTVK in Phoenix, Arizona, 1972

be here, in the Now, breathing and without desire. In the end, TM seemed contradictory to Kant's humanness, to the mind's own drive to structure and to define. Why should I press against what was natural to the mind? And how did this get me any closer to the what, who, or if of God?

While hosting *SunUp San Diego* I spent some of my off time pursuing these philosophical questions with a small

Danuta on set with Maya Angelou, 1977

group of like-minded thinkers. We called ourselves the Practical Cogitators, from the book of the same name, and wrestled with ideologies and philosophies. There were four of us, Ernie, Ron, Kai, and me. We met weekly in Old Town, drinking margaritas and discussing books we had read. Sometimes the discussion got personal—the meaning of our lives, the point of it all—and the conversation began to dig deeper into a dialogue of faith and science.

We became fascinated by quantum mechanics. This was a strange world where electrons could be in two places at once, where mere observation of a thing changed that thing's behavior, and where light was a particle and a wave. Talk of God in all of this seemed poetic and old-fashioned. I was poised to ground myself in the physical world, escaping the clutches of superstition, to turn to science instead of faith, to leap into the world of evidence.

But then we came across a book by C.S. Lewis called *Mere Christianity*, and a passage that had us puzzled.

A man who was merely a man and said the sort of things

Jesus said would not be a great moral teacher. He would either be a lunatic . . . or the Devil of Hell. You must make your choice. Either this man was, and is, the Son of God: or else a madman or something worse. You can shut him up for a fool, you can spit at Him and kill Him as a demon; or you can fall at His feet and call Him Lord and God. But let us not come with any patronizing nonsense about His being a great human teacher. He has not left that open to us. He did not intend to.

We wrestled with many challenging questions. Why has the concept of God played such a major role in human affairs? How does a practical, reasonable person reconcile the scientific, empirical world with a faith-based world? What part does God play in science? And was Jesus a lunatic?

Serendipitously, Kai met a man named Harald Bredesen who was some kind of authority on Jesus. Bredesen lived nearby and Kai thought the man might be willing to bring some clarity to our discussions. The Practical Cogitators jumped at the chance.

Kai arranged the meeting, and Bredesen invited us to meet at his home, a modest, ranch-style house bordered by an avocado orchard in Escondido, twenty minutes northeast of San Diego. There were four of us, including Kai.

It was a warm summer evening in 1981, and we sat around a wrought-iron table in Bredesen's backyard. The conversation started casually, Harald nodding and listening politely to our philosophical reasons for meeting him. Somehow, I became the designated speaker for the Cogitators and finally asked what I thought was an obvious question, "If Jesus is the Son of God, why not prove it in some irrefutable way and have everyone believe it? Why spend two thousand years of misery and wars getting everyone on the same page?"

Harald asked me, "Do you like to choose your own ice cream at 31 Flavors?"

That question threw me off. "Of course I like to choose my own ice cream," I muttered.

He went on. "God wants you to have a choice in the matter of your life," he said. "What kind of love would it be if you weren't free to choose to love Him?"

Harald had me on that one, so I tried a different tack. "Why doesn't God just forgive our sins and forego all the nasty business of crucifixions and suffering?"

Harald tossed another monkey wrench at me with a question out of the blue, "If you were caught speeding down the road and got a ticket, you'd have to go to court, right? And you'd stand before the judge and he would be obligated to fine you for breaking the law, right?" I liked his full, round, almost impish face and his ready, warm smile. I wasn't sure where this was going, but I nodded in agreement; the judge would be obligated to do his job. "Good, that's exactly the position God is in. We have broken His laws. The penalty is death. But He loves us and doesn't want us to die. So he sent his Son, Jesus, to accept the punishment instead."

"Yes," I said, "but why have the penalty at all?"

"What good is an unenforceable law?" Harald said.

And so the debate went on.

It turns out I was talking with one of the most highly regarded Pentecostal evangelists of his time. The singer Pat Boone, who had an encounter with Bredesen, wrote, "Abraham, Moses, Gideon, Elijah, I think I've known a man like these. His name is Harald Bredesen. Miracles trail him wherever he goes." Bredesen was a Lutheran minister but more significant, a charismatic or Pentecostal Christian, meaning

Harald Bredesen, the "Hound of Heaven" and best man at Danuta and Kai's wedding in 1984.

he believed in the spiritual experience of the Baptism in the Holy Spirit that some refer to as being born again. The experience is often accompanied by prophesies, "signs and wonders," and speaking in tongues. During the Camp David Peace Accord just several years earlier, President Jimmy Carter called upon Harald Bredesen to write a prayer that Christian, Arab, and Jew could all agree upon for peace in the Middle East. This man ministered to Arab heads of state. In some circles he was reverently addressed as the Hound of Heaven. I was having an encounter with the man often referred to as the father of the charismatic movement whose adherents numbered in the hundreds of millions.

I didn't have a snowball's chance.

By now the sun had set, but Bredesen had not turned on the patio lights and we all sat in the dark, Bredesen's cherubic cheeks gleaming in the moonlight. Late into the evening, he continued addressing me, the others in the group hunched over the table absorbing every word. We grappled with the nuances of C.S. Lewis's argument about the deity of Christ, which, as Harald forcefully and kindly presented it, soon had me cornered. "Danuta, think about it this way: if Jesus isn't the Son of God, then he'd be the world's biggest liar, wouldn't he?"

"I don't think Jesus was a liar, but is he God?" I wasn't ready to make that leap of faith.

Harald prodded on. "Yes. You see, if you agree that Jesus was not a liar, then he'd have to be insane to claim some of the things he said, right?"

"Right. I mean, no, I don't think he was insane."

"Well then," Harald scooted his chair closer, "if Jesus isn't a liar or a lunatic, that leaves us with only one other option. Jesus is really Christ, the Savior." He sat back, outside the spill of the moon and dissolved into a silhouette. "It's your choice."

"I never figured Jesus for a lunatic," I said, now speaking to the preacher's shadow. A Pacific wind rustled the leathery leaves of the orchard. The Cogitators sat silent as lambs, captivated by the debate. It was as if this was a high-stakes poker game—whoever won this hand would win the table. The salvation of our immortal souls was at stake, and the Hound of Heaven was about to pounce.

The preacher leaned into the moonlight once again. "Danuta, will you take Jesus Christ for your Savior, right now, tonight?"

When I was fourteen, I wanted to become a nun. It didn't work out. Now, at thirty-two, I had the opportunity to commit to God again. If not now, would I ever commit to anything, ever? Were any of my questions important? Would I always keep running—from men who wanted me, the gods who taunted me, nuns who haunted me? Maybe it was time to stop running.

"I do. I accept Jesus."

"You do?" Harald sounded surprised. He popped up in his chair, a fisherman with a catch in his net. He threw his arms in the air. "Hallelujah!" he said.

"Hooray!" I hollered.

We clasped hands around the table and with bowed heads followed Harald in a prayer of acknowledgment that Jesus was the Son of God, and invited the Lord to dwell within us. Amen and amen. We hugged each other, our eyes red with unexpected tears. Feeling self-conscious about this wonderful emotion, we tried to wipe them away, only to laugh at the awkwardness we all seemed to feel. Laughing and crying at the same time, we experienced what I can only express as sheer joy. There was a lightness to the air, a congratulatory feeling of having successfully crossed some great divide. We had no idea what it meant, but something was different.

We were saved—spared from a life of trial and error, for a life of straight and narrow, from ambiguity to righteousness, from ethical grays to black and white convictions. Destined for heaven, washed in blood, and born again! I was finally a Bride of Christ.

My philosophy group now became a Bible study group. We met every Tuesday night at our favorite Mexican restaurant, Casa de Bandini, in Old Town. The pastor of the Four Square Church I had attended, Coleman Phillips, agreed to lead our Bible study. While we gushed with enthusiasm over finding Jesus, we did not accept a single word in the Bible without a fight.

Years later Pastor Phillips told me he prayed every Tuesday for the strength to meet with us because our questions were so daunting—questions like, Now that we're saved, why go on living? Why not suicide and heaven, and skip this earthly part? And, where in the Bible does it say that suicide is illegal? Isn't that what Jesus did, volunteering for crucifixion? And, why did God suddenly change character from the vengeful, jealous, murderous God of the Old Testament to the gentle, loving, forgiving Christ of the New Testament? Did God grow in character? Did He learn how better to handle mankind? Does God learn? Why does the Son have a different character from the Father if they are one? Why did God test his most beloved servant Job so severely? Just to win a wager with Satan? Is God a gambler? During these Bible studies, we were probing and serious, heartfelt and pointed, not easily satisfied with pat answers, and deadly practical. Now that our hearts had been won by faith, our brains demanded intellectual satisfaction. We weren't easy on the good pastor. But it was through this biblical jousting that I was able to understand the scriptures enough to satisfy my curiosity.

In the meantime, I learned to navigate my new world through Pentecostal lenses, alert to coincidences signaling that the Lord may be speaking to me. I believed the Lord spoke to me through "signs and wonders" on several occasions. Once, while jogging on the beach in Coronado, a woman stopped me to say she recognized me from TV and that she had a dream about me: climbing a staircase to see her rabbi, she saw me at the top of the stairs, instead. "What does it mean?" she asked me, looking quite perplexed. "Are you a rabbi? A teacher?" I assured her I wasn't even Jewish and could not explain her dream. But I did not forget that encounter.

Another, even more remarkable instance was a chance meeting with Menachem Begin, then prime minister of Israel. On a trip to the Holy Land only months after I was saved, a mutual friend invited me to lunch with *Time* magazine's senior correspondent, David Aikman. During

An encounter with Menachem Begin in 1981

lunch, Aikman extended an invitation to accompany him to the prime minister's own Torah class in Begin's home that evening. I experienced a profound sense of clarity—the Lord was in this! It was both humbling and exhilarating to observe Begin's command of his faith as he and his group discussed Saul and David and the Jews' need for a King. Towards the end of the evening, as I made my way to the door, the prime minister stopped me and asked me my name. And then he said something extraordinary, "One day, young lady, you will be interviewing leaders around the world." And then he was swept away into the crowd waiting for him in the next room.

These two events signaled to me a future in which the Lord would use me for some extraordinary purpose. I was open to anything and everything that would show me the way.

TICKET TO JERUSALEM

TWO AND A HALF YEARS AFTER BECOMING BORN again, I became the cohost of *The 700 Club,* albeit through the back door. Thanks to Harald again. Without my knowledge, that charismatic minister sent a videotape of my television work to his friend Pat Robertson. Decades earlier Bredesen had led Pat into the Pentecostal experience. Pat went on to found the Christian Broadcast Network and Harald sat on the board of directors as a founding member and mentor to Pat. After receiving the tape, CBN enticed me with an offer to be news chief in their Jerusalem Bureau.

At the time, in early 1983, I had never watched the Christian Broadcasting Network, had never seen *The 700 Club,* and had never heard the name Pat Robertson. I was a California Christian, accustomed to Bible studies over margaritas with the sound of mariachis in the background. Southern Baptist preachers and evangelical television programs were not part of my world.

Nevertheless, I jumped at the offer to work in network news, and I didn't care what network wanted to hire me. I was on my way to being a foreign correspondent for Jesus, my dream job. I was thrilled to serve Christ as a journalist in Israel.

But apparently Jesus had other plans for me. I said goodbye to friends and family in San Diego, quit my radio and television jobs, sold my Porsche for a "sensible" Volvo, and drove to Virginia Beach, Virginia, the bastion of southern hospitality and conservative Christianity. At the time, I had no idea what I was getting myself into it.

I arrived on a Tuesday morning at CBN, where an impressive red brick Georgian mansion with tall white colonnades welcomed visitors on a grand, manicured expanse of green lawns. Similar stately buildings offset to each side served as offices and the broadcast studios. The new graduate school, CBN University—later renamed Regent University—defined the perimeter of the acreage, giving the estate a presentation of pure southern grace.

In a meeting with the executive producer I was told that I could pick up my airline ticket and go through the job briefing the following Monday. While awaiting these final details in preparation for my new life in the Middle East, the producer asked if I would "temporarily" serve as cohost on the network's flagship show, *The 700 Club*, named for the 700 contributors that were needed in the early days of CBN to keep the enterprise solvent. He said the program's female cohost had suddenly left; could I sit in on the show for the next couple of days until they found a replacement? I obliged, still without ever having seen the show, and for the next three days felt quite at ease with the two cohosts, Pat Robertson and Ben Kinchlow.

My duties were quite simple—occupy the third chair on the set, do a lot of smiling, read the teleprompter to introduce taped segments, and interview authors who had come on the show to pitch their books. It was like hosting *SunUp San Diego* but in a living room straight out of *Gone with the Wind*. The set featured three leather chairs, heavy and masculine. We sat around a low wooden coffee table which held a small bouquet of artificial flowers, behind us, a wood-paneled backdrop with a bookcase and a standing lamp. Pat's chair commanded the far right of the rectangular set, while Ben and I sat to his right. The studio featured several layers of bleachers along one side for a live audience. The room was dark except for the spotlights and backlights focused on the set, and it was air-conditioned to protect the cameras and lights from overheating. Three cameras pointed at us from the dark surrounds, their operators dwarfed behind them, while floor producers darted between the cameras and the set with updates and reminders. Pat, Ben, and I appeared comfortable with one another on camera, our exchanges were cordial and even at times breezy—not the easiest thing to communicate on television. I liked Ben right away and thought Pat Robertson was more like somebody's favorite uncle than the powerful and imposing man I would come to know.

I hardly slept the night before I was to fly to Jerusalem, and packed and repacked my bags in anticipation of this thrilling new adventure in the Holy Land. Monday morning, less than five hours before my departure, I drove to the stately campus of the Christian Broadcast Network and walked into the human resources department to pick up my ticket. By chance, I noticed a white flyer on a hallway bulletin board. Then I saw copies of the same flyer pinned to doors and cubicles everywhere. The flyer read, "Please welcome Danuta Rylko to the CBN family. We hope you make her feel at home as she assumes her new position as the permanent cohost of *The 700 Club with Pat Robertson*." Goodbye Jerusalem. Hello Virginia Beach.

I accepted the position for a number of reasons. I had quit my jobs in San Diego, given up my condo, and sold my furniture. There was no going back. I was offered an opportunity to be part of a worldwide cable network doing the Lord's work (even though at half the pay I made in San

Diego). And I was in the grip of "signs and wonders," following the Lord's will. When the position of cohost on *The 700 Club* was presented to me as a done deal, I believed that was the meaning of the stranger's dream on the beach. And I believed it was fulfillment of the prime minister's prophecy.

My position at *The 700 Club* may have been predestined, but I had a lot to learn. I got quite an education during my first official days at CBN. Terry Heaton, the show's producer, invited me to lunch the day I was hired.

Terry had ordered oatmeal. "Irritable bowel syndrome," he explained, rubbing his stomach. "Pleasing Pat is a full-time job." I ordered the chicken salad. And when the waitress asked if I wanted anything to drink, I ordered chardonnay.

"Tea," Terry said, carefully adjusting the napkin on his lap. When the waitress had left he added in a hushed voice, "It's grounds for dismissal, you know, drinking wine, or any alcohol for that matter."

"You're kidding," I said.

"Nope."

"But Jesus drank wine."

"Jesus didn't have the high standards of CBN," Terry chortled, and then coughed, and nervously covered his lips with his fingers. His pale, gentle face balanced a dark moustache and black-rimmed glasses. Terry was about thirty-five but the dark circles under his eyes made him look ten years older. "So, you drink wine?"

I splayed my hands open as if to say *So?*

He pursed his lips, his moustache wrinkling to half its size. "It's frowned on. May cause alcoholics to stumble." He twitched his left shoulder as though he had an itch he couldn't reach. "We are role models for the world."

"Yes, but Jesus' first miracle turned water into wine."

"It could have been grape juice."

"Grape juice?" I searched his face, hoping to find a joke in his helpless expression. He fiddled with his napkin.

Just then the waitress delivered the chardonnay and placed it before me. The golden liquid sat between us, a sweet temptation. It seemed to take up the whole table. My mind strained under the weight of it. Was it the apple offered by Eve, enticing but forbidden, or one of God's great gifts?

"But Terry, the whole history of love is tied to wine. Noah planted a vineyard and made wine. Wine was used in offerings to God and served at the Lord's Supper. And even in the Bible it says that wine gives happiness and that a little wine is good for the stomach, and it looks like yours could use some." I caught myself babbling. "I don't understand."

"It's really not what I think. It's what Pat thinks." He rubbed his hands as if he felt a chill.

"Pat thinks Jesus turned water into Kool-Aid?"

"All I can say is, no wine or alcohol of any kind is allowed, even in your house."

"Pat tells us what we can put in our own refrigerator?"

The chardonnay twinkled between Terry and me. All this sounded crazier by the minute, but many of CBN's formalities were strange and new to me. I needed to know what was expected of me, even if it did seem ridiculous.

Terry's shoulder went into a slight spasm. A glass of wine might fix that tic, I thought. I asked about Communion, the body and blood of Christ.

"I'm a Baptist, myself. We sip juice." Terry popped a couple of Rolaids into his mouth.

The body and grape juice of Christ? The glass of wine now seemed beyond my grasp, indicted and outlawed from the life of true Christians. Throughout our lunch on that first day at CBN, the wine remained untouched at the rim of my plate, abandoned but not forgotten. I did not drink that chardonnay, but I remember having had the strange feeling of a twitch settling in.

The Appearance of Appropriateness

I'D BEEN WORKING AT CBN FOR ABOUT A YEAR when Harald Bredesen called me from California one day and reminded me that I was his daughter "in the Lord." I knew he had something up his sleeve. He continued speaking over the phone in this round-about way, suggesting that "a woman of your age ought to be thinking of something more permanent." When I asked him if he was talking about the need for a will, he burst into laughter. "No, daughter," he said, "I'm not talking about death. I'm talking about marriage. A woman of your age ought to be married."

That cherub of Christ who kept popping up in my life, the impish evangelist powerful enough to persuade presidents and prime ministers to seek Jesus, the same one who led me to the Lord, the man who delivered a videotape of my work to CBN, this man was now suggesting that I marry. Apparently, given my position as a visible on-air face of CBN, Harald said marriage was the "appearance of appropriateness," and since I had been a very single woman, traveling at times alone with the very married Pat Robertson, it was time to be appropriate.

I didn't understand how it was inappropriate traveling on Pat's Boeing 727. The private jet, an Air Force One look-alike, was rumored to have been owned by country singer Kenny Rogers. Pat had the red velvet wallpaper removed and the plane remodeled for privacy with his own master suite and bedroom up front behind closed paneled doors, quite separate from the staff and other guests who sat in the back of the plane. I rarely saw him come out from his suite during the dozen times we flew on trips across the country to Christian conferences and conventions.

In my first few months at CBN, I learned that born again Christians perceived an unwed woman as a source of temptation but, if I were anchored to a man in marriage, I could move freely among men. Why a wedding ring reduced temptation or why an unwed man was not perceived as inappropriate was never made clear to me, but it was just another unfamiliar thread in this new fabric I agreed to wear in my early days as a Christian.

Not only had Harald counseled me about the need to marry, he had decided to play Cupid. He took the liberty of asking Kai how he felt about me. Harald then came back to me saying that since I was his daughter in the Lord, Kai would make a wonderful son-in-law and that Kai loved me and would I marry Kai if he proposed? There was silence on his end of the phone. He was waiting for an answer.

I was in a complete state of shock. But I had to say something, so I blubbered on about marriage being a very heavy thing, a serious deal, something one doesn't come to lightly, that marriage is for two people who are in love and that we were best friends, and I loved Kai like a brother, and that I couldn't marry Kai because I'd have to be in love with him, wouldn't I, and since I did love him, but wasn't sure about the *in love* part, with marriage being such a very serious business, it wouldn't be right, would it, and he got where I was going with this, right?

Marriage was disconcerting to me—something that happened to other people, a fairy tale that eluded me, and I was content to live without it. I felt quite comfortable as a single career woman. While I knew my Swedish troubadour had feelings for me, our relationship had been on and off for several years, including times when he moved back to Sweden. Kai had been married twice before and had eight children from those marriages, some who still lived with their mothers. Depression and alcoholism played a role in his life over the years, although he had assured me that he had come away from those experiences cured. Kai was ready to marry me, yet I wasn't sure I felt the same way about him.

Nevertheless, Harald and Kai met in a Taco Bell parking lot in San Diego where they roamed the pavement praying in tongues, praising the Lord, and talking about strategies for a Kai and Danuta union. A week later, Kai flew out to Virginia Beach to see me. I knew why he had come.

The day he arrived, we met in the studio after the show. I was as nervous as a cat in the rain, making a few jittery comments to the make-up crew, Olivia and Linda, that this visit from Kai was not casual, ducking into crowds, avoiding any opportunity that might find me alone with him. I chatted with members of the audience, consulted with producers, and talked with Ben. But I felt Kai watching me every moment, reading my fears like a book, gazing at me clear-eyed and steady, smiling patiently at every excuse to escape his charms, his arms, and the looming question he had come to ask me.

Kai followed me into the dressing room. Olivia and Linda had quietly disappeared. I was cornered, with no more evasions. "Darling," he whispered as I backed up. "Darling," he said again, and stepped towards me. He took my hands in his; there was no getting away this time. My heart leaped in my chest. This was it. He was going to ask me. He peered into my eyes and said, "It is only fair that you should know that I think you and I ought to be married."

I opened my mouth prepared to answer him, to let my best friend down easy, to tell him that marriage wasn't in my vocabulary, that I wasn't ready, but curiously, he didn't ask me the question. Before I could respond, he continued, "This isn't a proposal. I don't want your answer. I want the answer God gives you."

Danuta and Kai, 1986

Damn! This was not going to be easy. We prayed for guidance from the Lord and let the matter drop until dinner. At a romantic little restaurant later that evening, we talked practically about what marriage would be like and I drilled him on his finances, his future, and whether he wanted more children (he already had eight, but I thought I might like at least one). I explained I wouldn't be an ordinary wife, cooking and cleaning, that I would expect help around the house with chores like grocery shopping, that although I was tidy, housekeeping wasn't my priority, that I had a career.

He said he wasn't looking for ordinary, that he didn't want a wife, that he wanted *me*. He said all the right things. Kai left for California the next day saying he would wait for as long as it took for the Lord's answer.

Feeling immense pressure now to be married, and sensing this was too important to make such a big decision all on my own, flying by the seat of my pants, not trusting the budding emotions swelling in my heart, I decided to put out a fleece—to ask God for a sign. The idea comes from a scripture in which Gideon tests God's ear by putting a sheep's fleece out for the night. Whether the fleece was damp from dew one morning and dry the next gave Gideon the answer he needed. So I asked the Lord for an improbable sign—to make the wind chimes in my bedroom ring if I was supposed to marry Kai. It would be hard to mistake such a Godly affirmation. Several nights later, I bolted awake from the sound of clanging, thinking it was an earthquake. I waited for the swaying of the floor, an event all too common in southern California, except this was Virginia Beach. They didn't have earthquakes. As my head cleared from sleep, the bells fell still. Was it a dream? A draft from the window? Or the sign from God I had asked for? For years after that, I gave my testimony of faith, telling the story of marrying Kai and how the Lord rang my chimes. To this day, I still don't know how the wind chimes rang, or indeed, if they did at all, but I knew I was in love with Kai. We were married six months later in San Diego. Our pastor, Coleman Phillips, officiated, and Harald was best man. Kai adored me, and I felt safe and cared for with an older and wiser fifty-five year-old man. I believed I had finally found the love that had eluded me all my life.

Marriage was not the only requirement for my new position at CBN. Being appropriate also meant, as Terry had made so plain to me, not drinking alcohol—at least, not in public. That understanding was made crystal clear to me at a convention of Christians meeting at a large hotel in Dallas. I was to be the keynote speaker that evening, and while making my way to the conference hall, I stepped into the elevator with two waiters from the hotel. They were talking in hushed tones, but I overheard one say to the other how he loved Christian assemblies because he made more tips delivering room-service booze than during any other convention.

I quickly learned to discern the difference between a public persona and a personal life. Being appropriate meant that when I dined at a restaurant I felt compelled to ask the waitress to bring my dinner wine in a coffee cup so I wouldn't get caught disobeying corporate policy or offend attending Christian diners. I was "outed" several times for abusing the policy. Once, by my housekeeper who confided to a CBN secretary that she saw a bottle of wine in my refrigerator. Learning that I had a spy in my own home, I asked her to leave. And another time, a flight attendant who served me on one of my red-eye specials flying back from a speaking engagement told her mother who told a CBN official that I ordered a wine spritzer on the flight—white wine mixed with 7-Up. The flight attendant used my wine as an argument with her mother to have champagne at her wedding. Both times I was called on the carpet by a CBN executive for not presenting an appropriate appearance of Christian behavior. My consumption of wine at home did stop, but not because of CBN's admonishments. I stopped when I understood that Kai had a substance abuse problem (though my appreciation of good wine never diminished).

Being appropriate at CBN was just the tip of the iceberg.

Changes were coming my way in rapid succession. Within two short years, I had gained a new belief system, a new job, a new home, a husband, and his large family. I was in a whole new ballgame.

THE BLACK, THE BLONDE, AND THE BAPTIST

BY 1985, I WAS A TELEVISION EVANGELIST watched daily by millions around the world. Still, my role in saving souls baffled me. My growing understanding of the conservative Christian world of televangelism was causing me to question my own beliefs. In this world, Jesus was different. He didn't condone dancing, wine, or too much levity. Instead, He answered prayers for plunder—fortunes lifted from the misinformed.

The revelation of this dysfunctional deity came awkwardly to me, more slowly than it should have. Perhaps my thinking was clouded by celebrity and appearing closer to God than other mortals, a mantle bestowed upon me by our spiritually needy television viewers. People trusted me with a blind faith that I found deeply unnerving. They trusted me with their souls and their salvation. They wanted divine reassurance from an earthly source—someone they could touch and speak to personally about their deep and intimate fears: Does Jesus love me? Will He really forgive me? Will He keep me under His wing and protect me from the ugliness of the world? The spiritual confidence entrusted to me was the kind of faith that puts people on pedestals. In the eyes of the faithful, God listened to me because I was on television. I was chosen, almost an apostle, albeit a female one. The repeated assertions by the faithful that God had ordained me for this role made me responsible for carrying that weight. In spite of my own doubts, I felt I couldn't let people down. But the light of this folly eventually did dawn on me.

It was the time before everyone had cell phones, CDs, or PCs; the world was clearly defined by television and the people on it. On television, everything seemed so intoxicatingly simple. Hungry souls in sixty-three countries watched us daily on the Christian Broadcast Network's flagship show, *The 700 Club with Pat Robertson*. Miracles popped up everywhere, slickly documented by our crack team of producers in some of the best equipped broadcast studios in the world. Our viewers loved us. They prayed with us and sent us money. We were rock stars for Jesus, the ministers of joy, examples to the world of the Christian life. That was the simple story in front of the camera. But it was the hustle of reality behind the camera where simple answers broke down and the questions just kept on coming.

The collision of simplicity and complexity began in slow motion, picking up speed as the days and months progressed. It began in our home the day Kai's eyes were red and bloodshot, when he slopped his coffee over the floor and walked through the spill without noticing.

In the past few years, Kai's health had slumped along with his insurance career. He decided to start up his own financial consulting business. While he continued to make phone calls, traveled a good deal, and spent a lot of money on all the trappings of success (expensive clothes, a Cadillac, a personal secretary), his behavior had become erratic. He was moody and tired all the time. Kai was a tall, elegant Swedish man, twenty-two years my senior, but lately, I felt more like his mother than his wife, worrying about him and what he might do next. I was a whiz at saving souls on TV, but I seemed to be at a loss when it came to saving the man in my life.

That morning, the bloodshot eyes and slopped coffee raised red flags for me. I knew there was a problem; there were always problems. Whatever it was this time, I would fix it later. Right now I had to be off to work. I had a television show to do. Little did I realize how quickly life at home was spinning out of control.

In my CBN dressing room that morning, our invaluable team, Olivia and Linda, were busy blow-drying my hair and applying my make-up. Their support and cheerfulness each morning went a long way to bolstering my confidence in my new position at CBN and we had become good friends. Terry Heaton, the producer, walked in pinching back his shoulders as if to loosen the stiffness in his neck, his blue suit buckling around the collar. He handed me the show's format, a bundle of papers outlining the program minute by minute. "You introduce the first piece, about Marilyn Crow, an American Indian woman healed of breast cancer after she prayed with you and Pat last year. Then there's a satellite interview with Senator Orrin Hatch about prayer in schools, new legislation and all that, and then you interview Bonnie Malone who wrote this book on prosperity according to biblical principles." Terry plunked the book on my lap, jerked his shoulders again. "See you in Pat's dressing room in ten minutes?" He brandished a smile, trying to keep things light, but he left wringing his hands.

After Olivia and Linda finished prepping, dressing, styling, and powdering me, all three of us moved to Pat's dressing room down the hall. One wall was filled with mirrors, the other with pictures of celebrities who made their way to the show: Johnny Cash, Pat Boone, and Billy Graham, among many others. Three high-backed make-up chairs with red vinyl upholstery faced a single television monitor. I found a chair next to Ben's. Besides being the regular cohost on the show, he was vice-president of Operation Blessing, the charitable outreach program of the ministry. "Hi, Blondie," he said. Ben was a handsome six-foot-four African American who always wore cowboy boots, a vestige of his grounding in Uvalde, Texas. His bronze skin was dappled with freckles; his smoky Afro and moustache matched a ledge of thick eyebrows. A white make-up towel hung across his chest.

"Hi, Kinch. How's it going this morning?"

"Fantastic. You?"

"Super," I lied, not letting on my concerns at home.

"Tremendous," Ben gushed with a seemingly bottomless well of joy. "Seen the Baptist this morning?"

Just then Pat Robertson blew into the dressing room, a portly thundercloud in a dark gray suit. The very walls seemed to stand up straighter as the room snapped to attention.

"Speak of the devil. How you doin' this mornin', Pat?" Ben's easy charm broke the ice and you could almost feel the walls relax.

Pat slammed into his chair and tilted his face up for the make-up towel. "Just got our statements in from last year." He leaned forward as Linda chased his chin with a sponge, his eyes squinting with excitement. "Do you realize we took in close to $300 million last year?"

Ben blew a low whistle.

"*Three hundred million!*" Pat pumped a fist in the air.

Ben slapped his hands together. "That's amazin', man."

"God is blessing us, there's no doubt about it." Pat closed his eyes and settled back in the chair as Linda dabbed his ashen face to warm beige.

"Praise the Lord," Ben said. I wondered if beneath his overt delight, Ben was really all that enthusiastic about what was essentially Pat's empire. But then again, he would appreciate the funds since his Operation Blessing department helped deliver books and Bibles and built churches and schools around the world.

"Wow," I said, trying to wrap my brain around that kind of money.

"You see," Pat leaned past Olivia, missing the hairspray that lacquered the air where his head had been, "if we ask God for anything, the Bible says He'll answer." Pat wagged a finger pointing to heaven and silently mouthed the words, *Three hundred million.*

"You know a Gallup poll showed the number one problem among Christians is loneliness? Well, we cut right through that loneliness with the Word of God. And He's blessed us." Pat sat back under Olivia's hairbrush.

I thought of Detroit and Pittsburgh and the hundreds of other places I had preached and the lonely faces I saw there. I wondered if Christian TV hadn't fostered that isolation, giving a false sense of community without the human touch. But I didn't say that. I wondered if people who looked for God on TV grew accustomed to getting tidy answers to life's messy questions in sound bites. I wondered if God really wanted celebrities as Jesus stand-ins. And why did God answer CBN's prayers for money but not my father's wartime prayers for peace, or my alcoholic husband's prayers for peace of mind? But I didn't say that either. I didn't say anything.

There was no denying the fact that people seemed compelled to give to the television ministry. Every dollar was a vote of confidence. And millions of dollars poured in. Superficial answers to complex questions eliminated any shade of gray and gave comfort in an increasingly uncomfortable, complicated world. It was just good business. Why should people pay money to a ministry that doesn't deliver the goods?

Part of delivering the goods came with a cosmetic price tag—targeting the Jesus demographic, essentially white people between twenty-five and forty-five who found the Lord, improved their lives, and radiated health and wholeness. All CBN producers clearly understood that Christianity was to be synonymous with attractiveness. Their stories often concluded with a request for a donation to the ministry. The mantra "If you give, you will get" was a powerful motive to be a good Christian.

Terry came into the room carrying a pile of videocassettes for us to preview ahead of the day's program. He popped the first tape in the playback deck; it showed a couple who couldn't make their house payments, choosing instead to donate $100 to CBN. God returned the favor: the husband got a new job and the wife received a windfall inheritance. Soon, they owned their home.

Pat nodded. Terry sighed an audible relief.

"Next," Pat said, staring impatiently at the dark monitor as Terry slid in the next videocassette.

"This is the story of a woman who was healed by the Word of God. She was a paraplegic, but is now able to get around in a wheelchair—"

Pat leapt from his chair and tugged the towel out from under his collar. "Brother, I thought we talked about this. No wheelchairs! No crutches! No nothin'! God heals perfectly, every time. We can't show half-healings. That's half-faith." He threw the towel at the chair. Linda and Olivia quickly retreated from the room.

"But Pat, God can heal us a little bit at a time, too." Terry wrung his hands. "I mean, the woman couldn't move her arms and now—"

"No. No. And no. No wheelchairs. Period." Pat stood glaring at the monitor, waiting in judgment for Terry's next installment of divine healing. There was no room at the inn for anyone with a progressive illness, who was overweight, or who faced challenges that were too hard to overcome. There were no facial blemishes and no disabilities that could not be healed. I learned early on that it was bad television to have unhappy endings.

Terry ejected the videocassette from the recorder, exchanging it for another. "Okay, this next one is a woman who was completely healed through prayer several months ago on the show."

The video showed a woman in her sixties who said she had diabetes. She claimed a healing when Pat prayed on the show for a diabetic. She said she no longer has to take insulin. In gratitude, she sent a check to CBN to carry on its good work. Ben shot me a glance, put a hand to his mouth, and leaned back into his chair out of firing range. I took his cue and kept quiet.

"Terry, brother," Pat laughed, but it wasn't a good laugh. "I told you, no fat people." His voice squeaked in frustration. "No unattractive people. No one over fifty-five. That's not our audience. No one is going to relate to this person." Pat reached over to the VCR and pushed the pause button. "Look at her!" He pointed his pudgy finger at the image of a woman's face frozen on the screen.

Did it occur to him, I wondered, that he was over fifty-five and not in the slim blossom of youth? Producers worked for weeks, winnowing the telephone calls and letters from viewers who said they were healed by one of our "words of knowledge," and then passing them across to our volunteer team of nurses and a CBN doctor to verify an incident of possible healing. The producers then travelled across the country taping the stories and spent hours in the editing booth. These stories typically cost thousands of dollars to produce. But it was just money, and if Pat didn't like it, it was dead. Nevertheless, Terry fought for every one of them.

"Look Pat, God loves fat people too, and God healed her," Terry said.

Shaking his head, Pat chuckled and glanced at Ben and me for support. "Terry, it's not going to air and that's that. Let's go, we've got a show to do!"

We shot up like toy rockets and trailed Pat out the door.

Like Ben, Pat wore cowboy boots, though for the life of me, I didn't know why. I liked to think of those boots as Pat's human side, his connection to all that was natural and honest and good, the side of him that was not only tough as leather, but also as soft. Unfortunately that notion was like faith, "the substance of things hoped for, the evidence of things not seen." Pat took long strides and the heels of his boots pitched him forward, forcing his upper carriage into a slight tilt, giving the impression of a charge. We scurried behind him into the studio and television land, into the hearts and minds and souls waiting for the human touch from the Black, the Blonde, and the Baptist.

By the time I arrived home from work later that day dusk had settled over the Great Dismal Swamp, a huge and aptly named marshland that bordered our five-acre farmstead in Chesapeake, Virginia. The water moccasins, copperhead snakes, and snapping turtles had bedded down for the night, but the deer flies took a last shot at me for dinner. I ran between the car and the house swiping at the vampires, reminded once again that I wasn't in San Diego anymore. It had been a long day and I was glad to get back to the sanctuary of our home—a place Kai and I fondly referred to as the wild kingdom. The house was dark when I opened the door. I called for Kai, no response. I called for Mom, still no answer.

My mother moved in with us six months before. She had "held the fort" as she used to say, for the past seventeen years, raising the boys, keeping food on the table, paying the rent, allowing me time for school and a career. In the past few years I had been able to help support the family and even purchased them a home close to where I lived in San Diego. But Mom seemed wrapped in a perpetual loneliness. She never remarried, seldom socialized, and in rare moments of nostalgia, she would express a deep and abiding guilt for leaving Rick behind. (It didn't help that Rick never forgave her for abandoning him.) I believe that my father's rejection played no small part in causing her pain, and his death, though she never uttered a word about it, must have fixed a permanent wound within her. Michael had graduated from college and Paul was nearly twenty-one. Her intense focus on raising the boys seemed to have been replaced as they had grown older by fierce bouts of depression, as if all those years of looking forward, never back, finally caught up to her.

We thought she'd enjoy living with us permanently now without worrying about paying the bills. She could retire and spend time gardening and reading. To help her feel welcome we airlifted her pets across the country, including a sheep named Emma that we housed in the barn. Paul would be joining us in the fall to continue college nearby. (He and Michael were spending the summer kayaking in Puget Sound and climbing the Cascades.) But since moving in with us,

Mom had lapsed into long quiet spells and when she did speak, she complained about the tone of Kai's voice when he spoke to her, or some other perceived slight. Sometimes she went days without eating.

When there was no response to my calls, I checked Kai's office—papers were strewn across the floor. I felt a twinge of panic. Calling for him again, I ran upstairs. Just then, I heard a noise from the guestroom down the hall. Then a roar, "Get outta here! Get out!" Kai's voice was slurred and guttural.

I rattled the locked door. "Kai? Kai, open the door, it's me!"

"Watta you want? Go away! Get outta here!"

"Kai? What's happened?" I leaned into the wood, my hand clutching the doorknob.

"Goddamn fuckin' peepo . . . get outta here!"

"Kai? What's wrong? Open the door! Where's Mom? Kai?"

"I'm warnin' ya, get out! I'm gonna do it! I gotta gun. I'm through with it, through with everything! I'm gonna use this thing, and you and nobody is gonna stop me."

I tried to be calm, but fear was getting the better of me. I stroked the door in some meager attempt to comfort us both. "Kai, darling. Why don't you just open the door and we'll talk."

"Damn bitch . . . Fuckin' pepo . . . nobody gets . . . getta gun . . . fuckin . . ."

Almost thankful now for the door separating us, I called back at him, "Kai, you've been drinking. You don't know what you're saying. Don't do this!" I wanted to sound calm and firm, but my voice quivered. I hated that wedge that kept us apart, the odor of secret bars and stale air that crept between us, the bloated look of booze and pills, the frantic nights, the denials, the apologies, the acid pit in my stomach. I struck the door with both fists, rattled the knob again. "Kai!" I couldn't stop shaking.

He'd gone on binges before and just passed out, but nothing like this. I didn't know we owned a gun. And where was my mother? I leaned my head against the frame of the door. Tried to think what to do. Call the police? What if this was just another drunk episode—just more drama? A call to the police would blow the lid off, take it to a whole other level, create all sorts of havoc. Pat would be furious. Besides, we were born again, charismatic Christians with a personal relationship to Jesus. We could work this out. I needed to find my mother. She'd know what to do. I raced back down the stairs looking for her.

Out on the porch, I called for her again, scanning the grounds in the crepuscular light. And then I saw her, standing in front of the barn a hundred yards from the house. I figured she was probably feeding Emma. I ran to her, flung my arms around her, and between sobs choked out that something was wrong with Kai.

But instead of returning my embrace, her arms hung motionless at her sides. She didn't speak, but stared straight ahead looking at . . . nothing. I took a deep, wary breath and backed away to look at her. "Mom? What's wrong?" And then I saw it. Behind her, in the barn. A noose hanging from the rafters. It was thick, heavy, ugly, hanging there, gaping, wide and waiting. Who put it there? What did it mean?

When I touched her shoulder, she didn't move. Her eyes were fixed on a position beyond anything I could see. "Mom, what's going on?" I demanded. No answer.

Questions fired in my head like a rapid succession of bullets. Was she distressed about Kai? Did they have an argument? Did she loop that noose over the rafters? They were twenty-five-foot high beams; we had no ladder that could reach them; it was too high for her to climb. Kai is threatening to shoot himself. Did he mean to hang himself, instead? Was she in shock from the sight of the noose? What kind of a mind-bending game was this? What had I come home to?

Backing away from her, I turned and ran for the house—from one insanity to another. I ran to the man I married from the mother I loved, knowing it was beyond any power of mine to save either of them.

I pounded on Kai's door, begging him to help me with Mom. He didn't respond. I tried to swallow back the acid taste of panic. I tried to think logically. For the time being, Kai's locked in the room. If the noose is his, he probably won't come out now to hang himself. The noose is too high for Mom to reach. And besides, she's never threatened suicide before. I opened the bathroom window and looked out over the barn to search for a sign of my mother, but by now darkness had taken over, balling up the sky and the earth into one black humid night. Things were bound to look better tomorrow, in the daylight.

I stumbled into the bedroom, got into bed, and pulled up the blanket. I tried to pray. But the only words that came out were, "please . . . please . . . ." Without a prayer, I spent the night dreading the sound of a gunshot.

JESUS WITH A TWIST

THAT MORNING, AS DAWN ROSE OVER THE swamp and my stomach cramped with pain, I looked for my mother. To my great relief, the hangman's noose was empty, but she was missing. Kai snored in a drunken slumber behind the locked door. A few hours later, I was back on television to the world of love, light, and clarity. I hadn't slept. I hadn't eaten. I was tired and bone weary.

The night of Kai's suicide threat, my mother's frightening behavior, and the question of the noose found me without a spiritual anchor, gripped by emotional paralysis, and utterly useless in their time of need. Jesus was nowhere to be found. Did I lack sufficient faith? I didn't think so. Had I not given up my career in the secular world to spread the Gospel? Had I not moved my family from one coast to another to serve Him? Why wasn't the Lord holding up His end of the bargain? Perhaps I wasn't trying hard enough. Perhaps I wasn't strong enough. Perhaps I was missing something. I wrestled daily with these doubts, and my morning prayer was often, "Oh, Lord, please don't blow my cover." I reminded myself over and over that everything would work out because I was born again.

The born again proposition was that by accepting Christ in my life, through the Baptism of the Holy Spirit, I would have a wonderful bag of divine goodies. Not only was I guaranteed a place in heaven, but as a Pentecostal Christian there were bonuses: the Holy Spirit would dwell within me, empowering me with spiritual gifts such as divine healing, speaking in tongues, prophesies, and miracles. I would have a personal relationship with Jesus, a real, living, daily, spiritual, practical, evidentiary, ongoing experience. A symbiotic relationship with the divine Himself! The temptation was irresistible. A God I could talk to; and he'd respond, in symbols, dreams, situational outcomes, interpretations, and biblical quotations. This would be a God of evidence. Science was not to be abandoned, but incorporated with the Bible, the inerrant Word of God, to understand the mystery of life itself and the wonder of the Lord's creation. This was not just a declaration of faith; it was the annointment by the Holy Spirit Himself. For anyone in my position searching for a spiritual connection, this took the cake. And so I accepted the Savior's gifts.

Though I was anointed, I still had to learn how to maneuver through this new life. One of the primary lessons to be learned was that, as born again Christians, Satan hated us because the power and presence of God in our lives was so strong. Therefore, we were in a constant battle against spiritual enemies. Fortunately, the Holy Spirit had empowered us for this spiritual warfare. We could exercise our power of discernment, seek out divine direction from the Word of God, and in prayer, enlist the Holy Spirit to defend us.

Among the weapons in our spiritual arsenal was glossolalia, or speaking in tongues, a babbling of sounds and syllables supposed to be the Holy Spirit's way of communicating with us. Once a person felt compelled to gush out sounds in a congregation, another person might be compelled by the Holy Spirit to interpret those sounds. The interpretations were usually benign, starting with something like, "Thus sayeth the Lord, verily, verily, I say unto you . . ." and so on, encouraging the worship of the Lord, more study of the Bible, or obedience to His laws, and warning of certain kinds of doom if we failed. I always found it interesting that the interpretations were commonly longer than the message in tongues.

One of the most controversial Pentecostal gifts was the word of knowledge practiced on the set of *The 700 Club*. Essentially a word of knowledge is the ability to know what God is thinking or what He intends to do in the life of another person. It is usually a revelation that can be used as a prophecy or a healing, like Noah getting the word from the Lord to build an ark. I had never experienced this particular gift before joining CBN, and was taken aback the first time Pat, Ben, and I joined hands in prayer. With eyes closed, and whispering, "Dear Jesus . . ." Pat said someone had a tumor on their neck and the Lord was healing him. Ben squeezed my hand and said the Holy Spirit was restoring a man with lost hearing in his right ear. Then Pat said a woman was praying for her child and the Lord had heard her prayers, and that someone was asking the Lord for a million dollars and it would be granted to him. Then Ben said a woman named Nancy had gout and the Lord was raising her up out of her wheelchair. And on it went until Pat and Ben mutually ceased and the prayer was over.

Routinely, after words of knowledge, the show's script had Pat or Ben deliver an altar call, an invitation for the nonbelieving viewers to kneel or put their hands on the TV set and to join in prayer to be saved by the Lord. Next came the call to action. Once viewers were in the fold, they were asked to call CBN and tell us they had just been saved, or to claim a healing. And while they were calling that 800 number (at the time CBN was the largest user of the 800 number in America), to remember that the Lord blesses those who give, and told they could join *The 700 Club* at various membership levels, pledging a certain amount of money to CBN every month. CBN gleaned a huge database of names, addresses, and telephone numbers this way from our 16 million daily viewers. Calls poured into the CBN Counseling Center, a bank of employees and volunteers who worked the phones around the clock, counseling callers about their spiritual concerns, taking messages of healings, and logging pledges for donations.

For the first several weeks, I did not have a word of knowledge. I was a silent partner in prayer sitting quietly beside Pat and Ben day after day while healings were dispensed like tissues. And then one day it happened to me. In an unpremeditated moment during Pat and Ben's prayers, a burst of warmth bubbled up from my throat and blasted out, "There's a man in Jerusalem who cannot walk. The Lord has heard your prayers and your feet are healed." I didn't know what came over me. All I can say is that I felt an impulse and gave voice to it. Was it a supernatural insight, a divine conviction? Or was it a sense of duty to fulfill a role as cohost? Whatever, I was a little embarrassed. But from that time on, I belted out words of knowledge with the best of them. I never got a second glance from Pat or Ben. In fact, no one ever mentioned that I had stepped into the spiritual big league. It was just another day of miracles on *The 700 Club*.

A fascinating part of this spectacle was the response we got from viewers who claimed these "healings." While we fired spiritual buckshot from our lofty satellite pulpits, some of it hit willing targets, yearning for a word from God, thirsty for some affirmation, desperate for an answer to prayer. The "medical miracles" submitted to CBN were vetted by a team of nurses who had a group of doctors at their disposal for consultation. But the ratio of healing testimonies to stories we could actually produce ran about three hundred to one.

And of course, there was the cosmetic factor. The person receiving the miracle had to meet CBN's physical standards to overcome the stereotype that Christians were overweight, polyester-wearing Bible-thumpers. While we were careful to authenticate video healings, the "miracles" we read over the air from phone calls were not vetted at all. We took everything pretty much on faith.

Two years after my first word of knowledge, while shooting a series of *700 Club* shows in the Holy Land, a man rushed up to me clutching a pair of shoes. He said he had been bedridden and unable to walk for over a year. Watching *The 700 Club* one day, he heard me give a word of knowledge for a man in Jerusalem. He told me he believed God was talking to him. His legs shivered, his bones creaked, but he rose out of bed and for the first time, put on the shoes he now clutched in his hand. On the soles of his shoes he wrote the word, "Danuta." Who was I to deny his conviction?

Faith does strange and wonderful things for some people.

Ben, Danuta, and Pat in Jerusalem

Danuta and President Reagan, 1992

And for the many believers who have told me over the years that I had sustained them in one way or another, I am grateful to have been instrumental in offering them hope, healing, or inspiration. I have always wanted to make a difference. But I am convinced that it wasn't me who did the good works in these believers' lives. It was them. I was a placebo, a spiritual sugar pill used to bolster their own faith. This may come as a shock to some fundamentalists who insist otherwise.

Fundamentalists—whether Christian, Muslim, Mormon, or any other kind of deeply rooted believers—are normal people. They go shopping, have sex, raise kids, worry about the economy, and watch TV. Rich or poor, they live in cities or farms around the world. Just like everyone else, they may (or may not) love their neighbor, hate cats, and ride horses. But their belief in a very narrow and entrenched religious doctrine changes everything. They are *in* the world but not *of* the world, constantly challenged by the normal to justify the beliefs that make them abnormal. To the fundamentalist, rationality is masked as evil lurking around every corner. Reason must be suspended for faith, and knowledge surrendered to belief. They must wage spiritual warfare and jihad against the infidels of their belief, their faith growing fiercer with every perceived threat. They row against the tide of rationality; only God can save them. And if His servants are on TV, all the better—the TV preachers represent the substance of things hoped for.

My fundamentalist, born-again experience was like falling in love. I was no longer a Bride of Christ, I was a blushing Bride, completed, filled, and consumed. I embodied my belief and the heaviness of it. Ordained by a higher calling, I bore my faith upon the shoulders of hopers across the centuries who gazed at a cross. I carried that glow even after the love dimmed. Then I carried that glow by faith. And when faith wavered, I continued my relationship with Jesus as a memory of what used to be.

Looking back, I am persuaded that meeting Harald tore a decade from my life—time I would rather have led elsewhere. However, as in any relationship, there were moments and memories I wouldn't trade for anything. In this period, I met people I would come to love and friends I would have for a lifetime. My brother Michael met and married Christy, one of the producers of *The 700 Club*. I have three gorgeous nieces thanks to CBN.

In my relationship with the Lord at CBN, however, there were times that buoyed my faith and pauses that shattered it. And then there were blowouts—like moving a hurricane.

GLORIA

GLORIA BEGAN AS A SOFT BREEZE SKIMMING
the sands of the Sahara Desert on September 15, 1985.
Warmed by the deep heat of the African wasteland, the
breeze merged with the cooler air above the forests and the
ocean along the Gulf of Guinea coast. Now a tropical wave of
undulating warm and cool air masses, Gloria blew east to west.
The rays of the sun bore down on the equatorial waters of the
Atlantic Ocean forming vapors that rose up fast and high. The
warm, moist air spiraled counterclockwise. Twelve hours later,
the winds picked up speed. Just south of Cape Verde, Gloria
organized into a tropical depression with sustained winds of
thirty-eight miles per hour. Speeding along a subtropical highway of warm water, she strengthened, amassing more energy,
the vapors condensing to thunderstorms in her whirling gut.
Her whole system now began feeding on itself, using warm
ocean water as its fuel. She grew into Tropical Storm Gloria
on the seventeenth. Approaching the Lesser Antilles, Gloria
had become a hurricane. Six days later, spinning northeast
of the Bahamas, she went into high gear with wind speeds
kicking up to 145 miles per hour. The next day Gloria was
dubbed the "Hurricane of the Century" as she churned up
the North Atlantic, evacuating nearly four-hundred thousand
people from their homes, from North Carolina to Connecticut. And centered in the bull's-eye of that massive storm stood
Virginia Beach, Virginia, the headquarters of the Christian

DANUTA PFEIFFER

Broadcast Network.

A halo of light illuminated the living room set in an otherwise cold and dark television studio where Pat, Ben, and I sat stiff-backed in our leather chairs, live across America, beaming across the globe. The floor director flagged his arm, cuing Pat. "Thank you and welcome to *The 700 Club*." Pat's eyes bristled with excitement, his voice lowered to a serious tone. "Ladies and gentlemen, we are in a crisis in America. A crisis of faith. We need Jesus now, more than ever." He flashed a glance at Ben and me. We were poised for anything. We never knew what he was going to say. "We need to pray that Congress approves a plan for a stronger military and a stronger nuclear defense. We need those weapons. It's just got to happen." Pat turned to us, signaling our support for big guns and bigger bombs.

It was just another day proclaiming the love of Jesus at CBN.

Pat's reference for more guns sparked an image of Kai in the locked room threatening to shoot himself. I thought of my father during World War II in Poland, torn from his safe life, bombs falling on homes and families. Did Jesus really want more bombs in the world? There was no room for liberals at CBN and even less for Democrats. But no one ever asked me about my politics. I was converted by association from my liberal democratic feminism to conservative Republican fundamentalism. I felt like a wolf in sheep's clothing adapting somewhat awkwardly to becoming one of the sheep. Until now, and this particular call to arms.

A scalding nerve flared up in me and before I could stop the burn, it blasted out. "But Pat, Jesus is the Prince of Peace. Some people say He wouldn't call for more weapons of mass destruction. Some people think Jesus would tell us to love our enemies, and to pray for them, not to threaten with bombs and call for bigger armies. Why don't we pray for more peace in the world instead of bombs? How would you answer them?" I swallowed hard, barely believing that I had confronted Pat before his people. I felt my face flush red with the heat of my brazenness.

His eyes flickered, but only for an instant. He leaned back, and the cameras locked into a close-up. "Well, Jesus wants His people to be safe." Pat eased into a time-to-think chuckle. "This is a land He has blessed, no doubt about it. The sin would be to leave it to the wolves and not protect what the Lord has given us. We'll go to a break, and come right back."

During the break, Ben spiked his eyebrows at me in a sign of approval and then rolled his eyes to the ceiling and then down to check the condition of his boots. "Blondie," he whispered, "I swear."

I was afraid to look at Pat. What was I thinking?

"Danuta," Pat leaned toward me, whispering, "that was good. Do it again. You ask me questions and I'll answer them. It's perfect. It's great."

And so I slipped, as softly as sleep, into the third person, seen but not heard, speaking, but denying my own voice, feigning the opinion of others while expressing my own. I stumbled on an outlet for balance in my unbalanced world. But just when I thought my two feet were firmly planted on the ground, when I thought I understood what I was doing and why, there was another surprise waiting for me. I know Jesus said with faith the size of a mustard seed we could move mountains, but we were about to move a hurricane.

Terry rushed over to the set clutching a piece of paper and whispered in Pat's ear. When the camera came up Pat said, "Ladies and gentlemen, I've just been informed that there's an enormous hurricane off the coast of the Atlantic, Hurricane Gloria, and it's heading directly toward Virginia Beach. There are millions of people who could be hurt, not to mention devastation to our headquarters here. But Jesus is bigger than any hurricane. And the Bible says when two or more are gathered in his name, He is there. Now I want everyone listening to pray with us. Place your hand on the TV, gather around and join us in Jesus' name to rebuke this storm. Pray with me now." Pat took my hand and I took Ben's. Ben squeezed his eyes closed and gritted his teeth, as if by sheer facial power he could beseech the mighty hand of God.

I closed my eyes and felt Pat clench my hand. He began to pray, "Jesus, you said you are in our midst. We ask that you turn this mighty storm around. In the name of Jesus we command the winds away from the shore!"

"In the name of Jesus," I whispered, offering up my heart and soul to the invisible and mysterious ear of God.

Pat continued, "We pray against this storm and the fury of Satan. We command this hurricane to turn away from land! Protect our shores; protect our headquarters here at CBN. We rebuke this storm in the holy name of Jesus. Amen."

"Amen." I squeezed Pat's hand, confirming faith and the power of prayer.

"Amen and amen!" Ben shook his head with vigorous agreement.

That afternoon, Hurricane Gloria took an unusual twist. Rather than slamming into the shore at Virginia Beach, the storm swung back to sea and weakened significantly by the time it made landfall on the Outer Banks. She then followed the eastern seaboard north and made a second landfall on Long Island, New York, dumping up to nine inches of rain, but during a low tide, when the threat of flooding was diminished. And, after crossing the Long Island Sound, she made a third landfall in Connecticut. The hurricane caused almost $2 billion in damage (in 2014 terms), and was responsible for at least eight fatalities.

Pat rejoiced. "My stars," he exclaimed on the show the next morning, "God listened and He saved us."

"But Pat, people are asking, what about New York?" I thought it was a good question.

"Well, it's interesting, that termites don't build things, and the great builders of our nation, almost to a man, have been Christians. The people who have come into our institutions today are primarily termites. They are into destroying institutions that have been built by Christians whether it is universities, governments, or our own traditions. The termites are in charge now, and that is not the way it ought to be, and the time has arrived for a godly fumigation."

"You mean, God turned the hurricane toward New York City because they're termites?"

Pat shrugged, "All I can say is that maybe they didn't pray hard enough."

And the faithful listened. And they believed. How could they not? We rebuked mighty winds from shore and the winds obeyed. An aberration, a coincidence? Probably. It was hard to dispute the synchronicity of prayers with answers. As for the death of people, did they not pray hard enough for their lives? Did the Lord take them because they were termites, or nonbelievers? Or were they good solid Christians and the Lord just wanted to "take them home?" If the Lord wanted them because they were good, was being spared a punishment? Or did they die because, of all the people who were saved, they lacked God's mercy the most? I wish I had asked those questions.

But within that matrix of faith and froth, I continued to believe that Jesus needed me, even if it was to provide stealth questions I didn't admit were my own, and to stand for political positions I didn't publicly embrace. I experienced a growing sense of responsibility to my unique position in the CBN hierarchy. I inhabited an environment unaccustomed to women. The case for women's liberation made little headway in the Pentecostal world. Women were expected to be seen but not heard, to be instructed but not to instruct, to counsel one another but not counsel men and certainly not their husbands, to praise the Lord and pass the potatoes but not to preach, to submit to the counsel of the male elders of the church, and, most of all, to be married. There were no women on the board of directors, no women holding corporate offices, no women preaching from the CBN pulpit. Women were wives, secretaries, staff, or volunteers.

I was in an exclusive club—The Black, the Blonde, and the Baptist—a visible triumvirate that met each morning, held hands in prayer, whispered and advised each other during ninety minutes of quality time together every day. This was a luxury not afforded even vice presidents and department heads. I sat on the right hand of Pat as a conspicuous and very audible part of this fundamentalist universe, an exception to the seen-but-not-heard rule. This was an enviable position among the many other courtesans in the kingdom.

However, the woman who prayed to turn back a hurricane hadn't owned up to her own stormy life with an alcoholic husband and a severely depressed mother. Mom had chosen to live in the tack room of the barn, sometimes disappearing for days into town or into the swamp. Many times she refused to come out, and took food only when it was placed in front of the tack room door. I called in a counselor, thinking that a professional might help my mother, but the counselor left shaking her head and said there was nothing she could do if Mom wasn't willing to talk to her. My brave, courageous mother now struggled not against ice and snow, but an invisible enemy she insisted on fighting alone.

As for Kai, the irony didn't escape me that CBN had an enforced policy against alcohol in the home for exactly the reasons I was facing. But Kai's addictions had little respect for corporate policies. For two days after the incident with the gun, Kai snored in a restless sleep behind the locked door. I was shocked when I finally saw him—filthy, wrinkled clothes, a puffy face, red eyes cut like slits in a watermelon, a shuffling gait, and dangling, inanimate arms. He said nothing as he shambled past me down the hall. Then he paused, turned, and looked at me with what I can only describe as a thoroughly reptilian expression. Licking his lips from a half-open mouth, he slowly smiled and continued toward the kitchen. I had never seen that expression before, and I had the creepy sensation that a stranger inhabited my husband's body.

Peeking into Kai's room, I saw wadded papers, indecipherable notes, and twelve empty bottles of champagne littering the floor. I didn't see a gun. An hour later, Kai got into his car and drove away. He returned a week later with a carload of flowers and promises that it would never happen again.

The Gift

THE FREEWAY SIGN READ, "TOLEDO 20 MILES."
Kai said my birthday present had something to do with
driving to Toledo, Ohio, and a promise I'd made to my
father when I was ten years old. "'One day I will tell my story
and one day you will write it.' Your promise to your father,
remember?" Kai flashed a satisfied smile.

I shifted uneasily in my seat, swiping a side-glance at Kai
and his Nordic blond hair, big, white face, and cheeks so rosy
they made cosmetics blush. I thought how the Swedish tones
of his voice sounded so much like Dad's Polish accent. My
father had been dead for fourteen years and I had made that
promise years ago, to write the story of his life. Now those
stories were buried with him. What good was a promise you
can't keep?

"Best present I've ever given you." Kai wagged his finger
in the air.

I thought about the time Kai rented two horses and had
them delivered to the house for an afternoon's ride; the time
he had a hotel prepare my room with rose petals and candles
and a professional masseuse after my speaking engagement in
Dallas; the twelve dozen roses he had delivered in buckets to
the studio. Kai loved to surprise me. It was his way of taking
care of me. He thought big splashes of affection made up for
the dozens of times he let our marriage down, but I loved
him for trying, and he tried so hard. His highs were as steep

as his lows, but his romantic nature always endeavored to save the day. I just wasn't sure that romantic was enough for us anymore.

"This is big, Danuta," Kai chuckled, patting my knee with one hand while he steered with the other. "You'll never guess in a million years."

Kai always had highs and lows. He called it his "disease." I called it his excuse. But his alcoholism was part of the deal, for better or for worse, in sickness and in health. And in my twisted logic I saw his destructiveness as a pathway to healing, with every cry for forgiveness, every deep regret, every renewed vow of sobriety, pushing me toward hope that maybe this time things would get better. And so I hung on, trusting in apologies and demonstrations of remorse. He would do something magnanimous, whether or not we could afford it. And so we lived, from disappointments to broad displays of affection to forgiveness, stepping-stones between vodka bottles and amnesty.

I was as guilty as he was for the merry-go-round of a life; I held our marriage hostage to his big acts of contrition. As long as he was sorry. I trusted in the Lord, prayed for the best, and dreaded the worst that was sure to come.

Not far outside Toledo, the car phone rang. He pressed a button on the steering wheel and answered into a microphone in the sun visor. It was a colleague from Sweden talking about a big hotel deal in the Bahamas and how Kai could get in on it. Kai was at his best on the phone, busy, engaged, with a sense of forward motion. My husband was a big name in the insurance business, a member of the Million Dollar Round Table, written up in a book titled *Sell and Grow Rich*. But that was before. Now, he pursued the success he used to be, while missing the life he had. He was tenacious, I'll give him that, and proud. He led with his chin when he walked, like a king viewing his court, so obvious that some people called him King Kai. The trappings of success surrounded him—the Cadillac, custom-made suits, silk shirts, monthly manicures, and the latest gadgets.

He once gave me a plaque that read, "Do Something So Big It Is Bound to Fail Unless God Intervenes." That was a motto we had come to live by, except to Kai it meant, "Exaggerate the Positive and the Rest Is Bound to Follow." Yet, if he fell victim to exaggeration, I found it symptomatic of a greater good in him—a kind heart.

We turned off the highway and cruised into a tired suburb of single-story houses with brown lawns. After driving into the carport of what looked like a deserted house, Kai jumped out and had reached the porch before I opened the car door. A man named Walt came out of the house and extended his hand toward me, his fingertips greased with the jaundiced stains of the unfiltered Camels he carried poking out of the breast pocket of his shirt.

Walt invited us into his living room, a bare rectangle with blank walls and brittle window shades which had long ago lost the battle against the sun. It was a room without a woman's touch, where the air hung stale and brown and smelled of cigarettes and dust. A brown cloth couch with cigarette burns in the cushions lined a far wall. Walt motioned for me to sit down on the lumpy sofa as both men stood grinning at me. Kai took a deep breath. "Danuta, I have a present for you. I wanted to buy one of your father's statues and drop it down on the lawn by helicopter. Under spotlights. At night. But no one would sell me a statue. That's when I found Walt."

Walt said, "Your dad was my best friend." He choked out the words, grimacing against the kind of pain men aren't supposed to show. He walked over to a high stack of boxes on the floor and flattened the palms of his hands on them like a preacher preparing a eulogy, but Kai interrupted.

"So when I talked to him about finding a statue, Walt said he had something better."

"It's your dad's tapes," Walt said. "He left them with me."

The ground shifted beneath me as Walt explained they were recordings of Dad's life in Poland during the war. He cast his eyes down on the pizza-sized boxes in front of him. "Sorry it took so long getting them to you, but I just couldn't part with them until now. Like giving your father up, you know?" He wiped an eye with his finger, sniffed back his emotion, and said, "But I figured, it's time to pass them along to the family."

I stared at the boxes stacked before me like the vertebrae of a giant.

According to Walt, Dad recorded them in Michigan, finishing them just a few months before he died. Walt opened one of the box lids like a casket. It was a reel-to-reel tape. I reached in and touched the tail end of a ribbon, a tape my father touched months before he died. Those same months when he was thinking about Easter, thinking about me.

Walt hefted a bulky Wollensak tape recorder from the floor onto the table. "It's reels of tapes, stories of Dachau, the escape, you know, through Germany, North Africa. Normandy, the Nazis in Poland. Wanna hear one?"

I nodded and reached for Kai to sit with me as Walt threaded the machine. He spun the tape through the slots, attached it to the catch reel, and turned a knob. I held my breath and swallowed hard as the reel revolved on the spindle. The first sounds were garbled, as though the magnetic particles were deranged by isolation and inactivity, but then, suddenly a voice crackled through the speaker. A higher pitch than I remembered, a tenor's voice, not the thunderous baritone I expected. The voice was musical, like a bird, each sentence beginning on a high note, then winging down to a ledge for a pause, flying up with a phrase, and coasting towards the completion with a gentle flutter before landing.

His voice broke my heart. Tears flashed to my eyes. I strained toward every utterance, but his words were fireflies, darting through the air, too fast, too much, too soon. He was here, but not here, dead but not dead. What was he saying? Was it about me? If I stopped breathing I might hear what he was saying:

By Christmas Eve, a cease-fire had been agreed upon by both sides. We decorated a little Christmas tree and sang a few carols and wished each other a safe and quiet Christmas.

Oh God! My father was a tiptoe away, not lying in a dingy grave under a snowy field in Michigan. He was alive. I could almost touch him. *Daddy,* I wanted to say, *Daddy, it's me.* I leaned into the sound of him just as I had when I was a child, just as hundreds of others leaned into him when he told his stories. I listened for the nuances of his life, the pucker of his lips before he spoke, his chair scratch across the floor, the rustle of his trousers as he crossed his legs. I listened over the pounding in my head and chest.

We were spread out in three buildings, stationed behind the lines. Late that night, one of the boys from the first building got up, took his rifle, and went out to the latrine. Returning, he noticed the shape of a German helmet gleaming in the moonlight by the doorway. He took aim and fired. A man dropped to the ground. Everybody jumped out of their bunks and ran when they heard the shot. A German lay wounded in the doorway, shot through the shoulder.

Inside the room, thirty-eight men were dead, their throats cut. The German had the knife in his hand and blood on his uniform. The blood from our men.

I never heard that story before. It was one of those horrible things he never wanted to talk about, not with us, not with his kids. I heard him breathe. He inhaled a cigarette, probably a Camel. I felt eyes on me, Kai and Walt watching my reactions with a curious pleasure, but I only wanted to hear his voice.

The interrogation of the German was swift and severe. He answered every question we put to him. He was among eight German commando paratroopers who had crept in with knives and butchered our boys. We gleaned every bit of information from him: where their quarters were, how far away, how many of them, to the smallest detail.

With tears in our eyes, we buried our men on Christmas Day.

We buried the German, too, after we shot him.

Gasping for revenge that Christmas, seven of us who had commando training volunteered for a vicious night. No guns, no revolvers, no thoughts of a Christ Child's birth. Just knives for quiet work.

We crossed No Man's Land, running silently, four kilometers behind the line, between buildings, through fields, passing guards and sentries in the village. We found the place. Four sentries, eliminated, one by one, without a sound. Once inside the building, we tripled their kill. We had vowed it. Our revenge was merciless and savage. Those who survived wouldn't forget it.

Where are the big words? Where are our leaders? Where are the religions that say love thy enemy? Love thy neighbor! There are moments when you hate your neighbor and you have to kill.

So much rage, so much pain. How could he bear living with that when I could scarcely bear hearing it?

Who are the leaders of the world? They sit comfortably in chairs. They drink. They eat. And they send orders by pointing to maps. Young men are so cheap. They gather them like eggs. Men who have hardly started their lives, too young to vote, too young to understand politics, but old enough to die. If you mothers of the world understood the power you have over your sons you would stop it. You could bring order to this world!

It's just business. Yesterday's enemy is today's friend. Bloody business.

If you ask me today who I am, what party I belong to, my one answer is, nothing. Nothing. I am a big nothing. I don't belong to anything. I don't have a nationality. I am a displaced person. And any political party stinks to me. Politics is greed. I want to lead my life away from people, away from gatherings. Life is nasty. It was nasty and it will be nasty. What is a man? Am I a man? I am a domesticated animal. At any time, any moment a wild instinct may jump up in me. I am not a man. I am a beast. That is all. Ask any soldier.

A beast? Did he think life was nasty with us?

We slipped back as quietly as we came. It was a very quiet Christmas.

Walt snapped the machine off.

"Wait." I reached for the switch, to click my father back to life, to keep him breathing, to keep him alive, here, with me, but I caught myself in midmotion and drifted back to my seat. Walt drifted down to a wooden dining chair. There we sat, a still life of people, leached of vitality, as though my father was more alive in his grave than we who sat and barely breathed. My father's life was frozen in time, in a voice that never grows old, with breath that will never cease breathing. With the tapes, I now possessed a living piece of my dead father.

For fourteen years, his stories slept like dormant seeds in magnetic ribbons awaiting the rainy season of longing when, in the bits and pieces of him, I would find a bit of me. Touching the tapes. Touching his voice. Thirty-six reels in the same sorry shape as our relationship, corroded by time and neglect, some parts flimsy as gauze.

"I'm sorry," Walt said, "I just can't listen to these anymore. Here, take them, they're yours. And the Wollensak, take all of it." He had dubbed the reels to cassettes and numbered them and gave me a Walkman to listen to them on the way home.

I sunk into Kai's warm chest. "It's the best present ever." Kai's shoulders straightened, validated by another stepping-stone of love. I was a stepping-stone away from tears. "Walt, how long did it take him to record all this?"

Walt slumped on the couch, collapsing his lanky arms into his lap. "About six months. I sat for hours listening to him record these. I left Michigan after he died. Had no reason to stick around. Had family down here." Walt cast his eyes around his empty room.

"Did he record all day? Did he use notes?" I wanted every detail.

"No, no notes, and he could only sit for about an hour at a time. He'd get sort of caught up in it, if you know what I mean? So, he'd shut the machine off, grab a cigarette, and kind of circle around the recorder like a dog around a porcupine. Then he'd work his way back to the microphone again. Sometimes, I think he got up in the middle of the night and recorded when no one was around."

I imagined my father throwing off his covers, reaching back into the twilight of memory, reawakening the sleeping souvenirs of his life, grabbing another cigarette, and switching the microphone on. When I was little he'd get that faraway look in his eyes just as he launched into one of the battles, or an escape. But I had never heard all the stories in their entirety. And now I had them all—in a posthumous gift, my father's voice, his spirit pouring down on me, after fourteen years, compelling me to listen.

"I admired John, you know? Just something about him. He could walk into a ski lounge and sit in a corner and he was like some kind of magnet. In minutes he'd be surrounded by women." Walt made a low whistle. "Uncanny."

I didn't want to hear that part, how he squandered his love on other women while Mom and I and my brothers nearly perished from neglect. "Did he say anything about me?" The instant I asked that, I regretted it. I wanted to sound nonchalant but instead I heard the plaintive voice of a girl begging for acknowledgment.

"Some." Walt shrugged. "He said he missed Michael . . . was pretty upset, you know, about you and your mom leaving."

Nothing about me. I wanted to say, "But we were coming back." Instead, I bit my lip. I'd said enough already. We packed the tapes and the recorder into the car, said our farewells to Walt, and rode back to Detroit for a flight home to Virginia Beach.

Perhaps now, as an adult, the day had come to recognize my father as a man and not the person I feared. This could be the opportunity to connect to him, if not in his lifetime, maybe in mine. These tapes held the key, I was certain, to the father I wanted to discover. Beyond the belt, the rage, and the pain, here was the man and the stories he could not forget. Here, I might find the answers to questions I didn't yet know to ask. I might even come to terms with the disconnection in my own life.

On our flight home from Detroit, I stared out of the window of the airplane and wondered, just who was I? An evangelist out of her league? A journalist out of step with objectivity? A wife out of balance with her marriage? Would I recognize myself if I ever met the real me? I hoped my father's tapes would lead me to the answers.

ADRIFT

VIRGINIA'S LETHARGIC SUMMERS DEMANDED a deliberate calculation of extraneous movement and speech. The heat, sticky and suffocating, the Southern drawls and the weariness of time itself hung heavy in the air. Virginia was a memorial to the War between the States, a museum of historical sites annotated with bronze plaques: The Battle of Great Bridge and Fredericksburg. Road names like Battlefield Boulevard were constant reminders of blood spilled between brothers. This was the location of the beleaguered Jamestown Colony, the bastion of Puritan entrepreneurs seeking what they could not find—gold and a shortcut to the Orient. The images of starched collars, muddy boots, and wild turkeys had morphed into colonial buildings, rusting bridges, and dilapidated shacks fringed with the cadavers of abandoned cars, their open hoods gaping like the mouths of looted skulls. This was not a place for an outsider to call home.

For me, home meant the ease of California's Spanish missions and melodious street names like Junipero Serra and Avenida Del Mundo. I missed the outdoor restaurants renovated from old haciendas, blazing bougainvilleas trailing along the tops of walls, and the dry Santa Ana winds tingling the skin with desert air. But this was Virginia, home of poison-ous cottonmouth snakes that stalked their prey with an eerie cunning, snapping turtles the size of garbage can lids, and other varmints that slithered regularly onto our lawn from the neighboring Great Dismal Swamp.

The glow of light coming from the tack room in the barn reassured me of my mother's presence—still eating her meals alone, coming out of her seclusion only when we were gone. It was an arrangement we had come to accept but one that defied explanation.

Easing through a narrow hallway from the porch and into the kitchen, I browsed through the mail, mostly bills, stacked on the table. That stack of unpaid bills seemed to grow every month. I lit up when I saw Kai coming out of his office to greet me. He had been away on a business trip. It felt good to snuggle into his bear-hugging arms.

"You coming to bed?" he asked, stroking my hair.

My smile froze with the whiff of his breath suggesting mouthwash or medicine or that thing we don't talk about. I caught his reflection in the hall mirror, the startled look of a vanquished man, overwhelmed by forces he could not fight, clinging to me for life support. I wanted desperately to save him, but right now I wanted to be saved, myself.

The moon rises, casting the bedroom in cinder light. He pulls me to him, searching my body for comfort and confirmation. His skin smells sour from unprocessed alcohol rejected by overworked kidneys. I try to ignore the gassy odor of his breath on my face and the taste of mint on his lips from the Tic Tac he'd sucked to disguise his "disease." I am repulsed by the man I love, yet press against him and the unspoken divide between us, keenly aware of the sheet wrinkling under my back and the shadows in the corner of the ceiling. Finally, he is asleep and snoring with the satisfaction of a drunk. I kiss him on his forehead and slip from bed and the dull ache of my life there to roam the dark hallways of the house.

THOUGH I HADN'T CONSIDERED IT at the time, perhaps I married Kai because he was twenty-two years older and I felt safe, and he certainly loved me. Kai would provide the emotional shelter of a father figure that I lacked as a young adult. It would be the perfect parent/child relationship. What I didn't anticipate was that I would become the parent.

The child—my husband—was boozed up and asleep in our bed upstairs. And so, for another restless night, I sighed in the darkness of the house, feeling adrift, longing for the pulse and passion of an authentic life rooted in immediacy and meaning. My father's tapes came to mind.

I pulled one of the tapes from the stack of cassettes resting on the coffee table in the living room. Here was one thing I was certain of: the personal story of a Polish soldier on the battlefield against Hitler, told in his own words—a priceless historical document. My legacy. My life.

I slipped the cassette labeled Tape One into the tape player. With the press of a button, I heard a melodious voice, words picked as delicately as berries off a plate, whooshing and shushing Polish sounds made round and soft. My father's tone began light and conversational, but gradually took a dark turn.

He set the scene. It is September 1, 1939. German tanks had crossed the border. The pace of his story then slowed, his voice lowered, his words became halting, unattached, hypnotic. Tenses changed from past to present. Chaos *is* everywhere. His voice catches on a memory, horses sweat, men shout. His throat sounds constricted, his breathing, shallow. The fumes of heavy trucks fill the streets and tanks pound country roads. His machine clicks off. The next sound on the tape is another click and he was poised, calm, and back in the past tense. Left to my imagination were his struggles for composure between the clicks.

TELETHONS

A CAR HORN WOKE ME UP. I WANTED TO SLEEP. It blasted again. Seven o'clock—a.m. or p.m.? I flipped on the light. Was it still Tuesday? I pulled on some clothes and dashed out to the car waiting to take me back to the studio. We were halfway through our annual telethon, a red-eye, head-spinning, gut-wrenching ordeal for anyone's circadian clock. Two weeks, day and night, of tally boards and begging for money.

We drove past Witchduck Road, a glum reminder of a time in American religious history when hundreds of women, suspected as witches for healing with herbs, consorting with the devil, and practicing sorcery were tied up and dunked into mucky borrow pits and wells. Legend has it that if the poor woman lived, she was presumed guilty and sentenced to death. If she died, she was unfortunately innocent but safely in the hands of God. In that warped form of justice, the guilty were punished, the innocent pardoned, but the poor woman was dead just the same. Twenty minutes later I was in the make-up chair again, preparing for our own kind of fundraising sorcery.

"Your make-up held up from this morning," Linda said, reaching for a sponge. "Did you get any sleep this afternoon?"

"Hard to tell. My body doesn't do telethons."

I saw my tired face in the mirrors banked along the wall—blue eyes rimmed in black pencil and mascara, frosted blonde hair starched with spray, face powdered and perfected for the lights. I wondered what my real face looked like.

"Hang on girlfriend." Linda dabbed eye shadow on my lids. "Only nine more days to go."

"It never fails." Pat walked into the make-up room with Ben. "When you have a building go up, people send in money, but give them a concept, something they can't see, and the money stops. You always have to give people something tangible. Show them bricks, and they'll give you dollars." Pat never looked tired during these fundraising marathons; they seemed to energize him.

Glancing out the window, I spied halogen lights shining on a huge, half-constructed conference center—another building for the CBN complex. Something tangible.

In the studio, twenty-one telephone "counselors" sat behind long desks mounted on risers, three tiers deep. The phones rang in response to the video stories we played, and to the appeals Pat, Ben, and I delivered during live segments between video clips. Sometimes we "challenged" our audience to match funds from an anonymous donor within a prescribed time period. If our viewers gave, for example, $150,000 within twenty minutes, the anonymous donor would match the challenge dollar for dollar, thereby doubling the amount raised. If the time passed without the matching funds being met, theoretically we'd lose the challenge money. We never lost a challenge. As for the anonymous donor, I came to understand it was actually CBN, quietly setting the scene to prompt a sense of urgency for giving. Every time a phone rang, it meant another donation, another name and address added to a database of donors, a goldmine of givers who joined various levels or "clubs" of benefactors, depending on the depth of their pockets.

That afternoon, a few minutes into the telethon, Pat challenged our audience: "Ladies and gentlemen, if you give, God has to act. That's what He promised. If you're ready for a blessing, send in your donation right now. And if you really want to be blessed, reach for more. Join the Founder's Club at $2,500. Let's see what happened to John and Margaret Champion when they joined the Founder's Club." The broadcast cut away to the prerecorded story.

"We didn't know where our next dollar was coming from until we gave to CBN," John Champion said. Pat glared at the video on a studio monitor.

"Terry," Pat hollered, "this is terrible."

Terry rushed across the studio floor. "What's wrong?"

"Well, look at him. He's got a mole on his face. This isn't our audience. How old is he?"

"Well, he's in his mid-fifties, I guess," Terry said.

Slapping his hands for emphasis, Pat said, "He's older than that. I can tell a man's age. How many times have I told you, no one over fifty-five. Who wants to look at someone with a mole on his face? I mean, look at him." As if disciplining a child, Pat grabbed Terry by the shoulders and spun him around to face the monitor.

"Okay. Yeah, I see what you mean, Pat. I'll check into it."

"And tell those guys if they can't find more attractive people, we'll hire people who can." Pat stormed out of the studio and into his dressing room while a series of tapes portrayed beautiful people who had claimed a blessing from God just by sending in their dollars.

I gave Terry a little pat on the back. "You doin' okay?"

"Our producers have to look long and hard for those stories." Terry winced and rummaged through his pockets. "For every person that had some kind of windfall there are thousands of others who didn't. We're just trying to build a little faith here, you know?" He slammed several Tums into his mouth.

"By the way, congratulations on the *Washington Times* article," he said.

The floor director scurried up and crammed some papers into my hand. "Coming to you in three minutes," she said.

Terry went on, "They called you one of the most visible women in Christianity today."

"Me?"

"Yep, right next to God and everybody." Terry forced a smile and rubbed his raw, red hands.

"Good grief, you'd think there'd be other women, real ministers, who've been doing this sort of thing longer than me."

"Sure," Terry said, "tons of women, but they're not on *The 700 Club*—the most visible television ministry in the world. I gotta go find some miracles for Pat." Terry hurried across the studio floor into the dark rim beyond the splash of studio lights as the floor director, taking her position, counted down the seconds until I was on the air.

In my hands, I clutched dozens of prayer requests from viewers who promised to give CBN money in exchange for a blessing. Were we misleading these people or did they benefit from giving? I tried to convince myself that we presented an ideal. That was why we exaggerated the positive, and all those premiums, books, donations, clubs, and monetary challenges helped increase our viewers' level of faith. This was a necessary part of doing the Lord's business. Jesus said faith moves mountains, but at CBN you had to have money. Maybe I was just tired, but still I wondered, if I had lived two hundred years ago, would I have been drowned on Witchduck Road?

"Five, four, three, two, one." The most visible woman

in Christianity smiled into the camera and began hawking blessings for dollars on TV.

My learning curve as a sidekick-cohost evangelist looked like a hockey stick. Within weeks of joining the television ministry, I stumbled into the role of an unordained surrogate pastor to millions of people who asked for my prayers, requested guidance for their lives, and wanted my interpretation of scripture. Before I learned the words to "Amazing Grace," Christian organizations booked me for speaking engagements. Now, I held a five-day-a-week job on television, and in between traveled the red-eye specials to churches, cathedrals, and banquet halls across the country. While I was always good at public speaking, preaching was a whole new ball game.

At first, congregations only asked for my testimony, that is, the personal story of how I "found the Lord." But soon, my testimony was not enough, they wanted more—a healing, a message, a prophecy. The shock of this realization happened first in Detroit. I remember the labored hum of the air conditioner losing its battle against the humidity. Rivulets of sweat trickled down the small of my back as I waited in the wings of a convention hall to address a thousand Christian autoworkers, church members, and loyal viewers of *The 700 Club*. A middle-aged lady in a faded flower dress, clutching a bag, rushed up to me. Her disheveled gray hair was pulled back in a bun and her face looked wizened like an apricot, small and dry under the stress of a harsh life.

"Please, Danuta, you have to bless my oil," she begged as she pulled two bottles of what looked like olive oil from her bag.

"Bless your oil?" I wasn't sure what she was asking.

"To make it holy, for anointing with the power of the Lord," she said, holding the bottles higher.

The thought of my imparting the power of God into anything made me uncomfortable. "I'm sorry, but I have no special gifts to sanctify anything—" Before I could finish, the poor woman began to cry.

Danuta, preaching in 1985

"I'm so sorry, I want to help, but I don't have the power to do that."

The woman sobbed into her little bag of bottles, wisps of gray hair falling over her eyes.

I felt terrible. I had to do something. "Okay. You bless your own oil and I'll agree in prayer with you." I took her hand in mine and placed them on her bottles for a communal prayer.

"No! Only you can bless my oil." She tugged her hand away.

"But why me?"

Her answer floored me. "Because you're on TV!"

Just then, my introduction echoed from the front hall, and, with no time left to negotiate divine rights, I assumed the position of a spiritual authority—I winced my eyes shut, whispered, "Oil be made holy," and ended with "in Jesus' name, Amen." The woman's face flooded with a look of gratitude and relief as my introduction continued.

" . . . seen every day in over sixty countries across the globe on *The 700 Club with Pat Robertson,* Danuta Soderman!"

The audience sprang to their feet and the hall echoed with applause. I wound my way past dining tables draped in burgundy, the air hinting of boiled broccoli and weak coffee. Through the throngs of clapping, smiling people, all I could see was the woman with the flowered dress, holding two bottles of "holy oil."

The podium loomed above me as I found the steps to the stage. I clutched the stand for balance and peered out upon a sea of faces, still disturbed by the lady with the oil. Pushing my prepared notes aside, I began speaking as though I were apart from myself, as though I were both the speaker and the listener.

"I want you to think back to the day you first met Him. Do you remember? When your dreams were prophetic? Remember the look in your eyes, that something was different? Remember the joy? When every aspect of your life brimmed with meaning, when signs from God were everywhere? And the hope. That from now on things would be different? No more sorrow. No more pain. You were forgiven. And all your prayers were answered? Remember how you believed anything was possible? You had found your way after all. You weren't lost anymore. Jesus was a friend who would never leave you, who would always keep His promises, who would always love you. Do you remember? Do you?"

For just a moment I was unaware of anyone else in the room.

"I remember when I met Him, the rush of a fast pulse, like a first kiss, like falling in love. He understood me, the way I wanted to be understood all my life." I caught a face in the crowd. And another. Were they staring at me, or were they dreaming with me?

"If you believe Jesus when He said He is the way and the truth and the light, why do you need somebody on TV to pray for you? Perhaps you think God gets cable and hears my prayers first?" A giggle rippled through the audience.

"You have power in Christ. Don't come to TV people with your private matters and spiritual concerns. Television isn't real. Jesus is. Your prayers are powerful. Jesus is the real intercessor. Go to Him."

For an hour and a half they nodded and applauded and ended by giving me a standing ovation. They understood. We connected. Jesus was their shepherd. Their Lord. My message was loud and clear. But then, eight hundred people lined up around the hall three rows deep, each wanting a separate prayer from me. I fell hostage to their needs and couldn't turn them away. Jesus may have been our intercessor, but I was his handmaiden. So I stayed and prayed. What remains with me so clearly is how I managed to see them, to see through their troubles, and how I think I was able to help. Their faces look back at me even now:

The short, elderly man with a thick, business-sized envelope. "I've written all my problems and prayer requests in here. I thought, in your spare time, you could read them and pray about these issues for me." He thrust the envelope at me. "They're itemized, 1 through 207."

"Itemized." I hefted the envelope in the air. "You have all your problems numbered, listed, folded, and sealed in this envelope?"

"Uh-huh, thirty-seven pages."

I placed his hand on mine over the envelope. "Let's pray together believing that Jesus knows your troubles and that He will help you overcome each one. Do you believe that?"

"Yes, I do." He nodded eagerly.

"Good, then." With that, I tore the envelope into little pieces, and tossed the man's documented troubles into the air. He grappled for them as they floated like confetti to the ground.

I grabbed his flailing hands. "It's all right. You don't need to hold on to your 207 problems, nurturing them, counting them out like pennies, keeping them locked in a sealed envelope so they won't get away. Let Jesus take them."

I saw relief sweep over his face. "God bless you," he said, hugging me.

Then the lady in her eighties, nearly bent over double, leaning on a thick black cane, hobbled toward me. Walking was clearly a struggle.

"Pat Robertson prayed for my arthritis, Jimmy Swaggart prayed for my arthritis, Jim and Tammy Bakker prayed for my arthritis, and now I want you to pray for my arthritis," she said.

Danuta with then-Vice President George Bush, 1985

"Do you think my prayers will be any more effective than theirs?"

"Can't hurt." Her cane wobbled.

"Are you collecting spiritual autographs, or do you really want to be healed?"

"Whaddaya mean?" She looked like a pitiful spider, craning her head up from the level of her cane.

"All those people prayed for you. You still have problems. Maybe it's not the arthritis we should be praying about. Is there something else?"

"Nothing." She pounded her cane into the floor.

"You're at peace with everyone in your life?"

"Absolutely," she barked back at me. "Except for my daughter-in-law. That woman can rot in hell for all I care. Taking my boy away. Marrying without my consent. I'll never forgive her for that."

"But they have their own lives. Why not forgive, or it will consume you."

"I'd rather go on having arthritis than ever forgive that woman." The spider woman turned away and hobbled painfully out of the room, clutching her hate as tightly as she clung to her cane.

As the evening progressed, I realized I could read their needs before they spoke. An uncanny empathy occupied each want and understood every desire. A heightened knowing, a keenness of spirit, a soaring sense of purpose overcame me. I knew I was in the center of God's will. For the next five hours I ministered to pains and losses, hurts and wounds. Crying. Praying. Hugging. Sweat poured down my back, and my feet hurt, but the people kept coming—drug addicts, thieves, the lost and the lonely, the unemployed and the depressed, diabetics, cancer patients, the hard of hearing and the brokenhearted—pouring their needs on me. I sponged up every longing, soaked up every misery, and absorbed each distress as though it were my own. Each needy soul in that line took a little of God and a little of me away with them, and I hoped I delivered a bit of comfort or a ray of hope. And so it went, until three o'clock that morning when I hugged the last person in line.

My dress dripped with perspiration and spasms ricocheted up and down my back. I steadied myself against the wall. I could barely walk back to my room. Hundreds of believers passed through me that night, needing my prayers. And I passed through them, absorbing their wounds. I didn't know how to keep myself apart or even if I should. If I had kept a distance, would I have been able to help? But when I gave without reservation, that was when I really felt God with me.

These aches and pains gripped me every time I prayed for large numbers of people in settings like this. Perhaps ministers better equipped for such events somehow avoided the physical burdens of prayer and consolation, but in the most satisfying moments of my service to God, I felt each supplicant's pain and tried to give every one of them comfort.

And yet, my own questions continued raging inside me. Why did they trust me and not their faith? So many didn't understand *why* they believed at all. It seemed that people believed only what they were told and had been taught not to think for themselves. "My people have been lost sheep," Jeremiah lamented in the Old Testament, and Jesus referred to his followers as sheep. After all these centuries, why are the sheep still so lost? And why would the Lord choose me, just another lost sheep to point the way? This was the blind leading the blind.

My duties at CBN had become an odd mix of a job and a calling—a profession and a ministry, sometimes a journalist, sometimes a preacher. I was at ease interviewing senators, celebrities, presidents, and prime ministers, adept at using my expertise at political dialogue, analysis, and the direct question. But woven between those obligations at CBN was a far more precious covenant with a Higher Power.

Money, Sex, and Power

THIS WAS THE HEADY DECADE OF THE EIGHTIES, when televangelism reached its peak of popularity and profitability, and eventually collapsed. Many of these TV preachers fell into disgrace and ridicule by way of three insidious temptations: money, sex, and power. And I watched them fall like the walls of Jericho.

Early casualties were Jim and Tammy Faye Bakker. The couple had worked with Pat in the early days, helping establish *The 700 Club*. The Bakkers had a puppet and interview segment on *The 700 Club* that became so popular that Jim and Tammy branched out on their own. Eventually, they created the flashy Christian resort, Heritage USA, the third most popular theme park in the United States, paid for in part by their evangelical TV program *The PTL Club* (short for Praise the Lord) and in part by questionable fundraising tactics. Following the pattern established by CBN, the Bakkers had created their own satellite TV network—broadcasting twenty-four hours a day on 100 stations reaching about 12 million viewers.

On several occasions I was a guest on *The PTL Club* and the Bakkers put Kai and me up in their own suite at Heritage USA. The suite was filled with Tammy's stuffed animals and dolls, hundreds of them, small and large, lining the shelves, the couches, the bed, and the overstuffed chairs. We were constantly moving the dolls just to sit down. Motor-controlled drapery unveiled panoramic windows overlooking the theme park, a sprawling 2,300-acre vacation destination trailing only Walt Disney World and Disneyland in popularity. It attracted nearly 6 million visitors a year and employed 2,500 people.

Jim and Tammy had set themselves up as examples of the Prosperity Doctrine, the belief that the Lord gives money to those who give, and give generously. They lived lavishly under that endowed-by-God umbrella. While Jim held the position as preacher and planner for Heritage USA and masterminded the finances, Tammy was the color. Her persona became more and more exaggerated as she herself disappeared behind the heavy use of make-up which became the butt of jokes on comedy shows and late-night television. Tammy seemed to enjoy her celebrity as a target of ridicule with self-effacing segments on their show about her shopping habits, but behind it all was a fragile and frightened woman hiding her insecurities behind masks of mascara. Her frail nature revealed itself during an interview that Tammy and I shared with a mainstream news organization. Just before the cameras lit up, Tammy clutched my arm and whispered, "Danuta, don't let them hurt me." Since then I've always had a soft spot for Tammy and try to deflect criticisms lobbed at her for her husband's indiscretions.

Heritage USA was bankrolled in part by contributions from viewers at a rate of about $1 million a week. They aggressively sold "lifetime memberships" to the park's hotel facilities. In all, the park included TV network production studios, conference facilities, a 501-room Heritage Grand Hotel, a 400-unit campground, Main Street USA, an indoor shopping mall, the Heritage Village Church, the Jerusalem Amphitheater, a skating rink, prayer and counseling services, Bible and evangelism school, the Heritage Island water park and recreational facilities, visitor retreat housing, staff and volunteer housing, and timeshares.

Those timeshares, led by a sexual scandal, a cover-up, and a payoff, began the couple's slippery fall. Fellow evangelist Jimmy Swaggart, well known for his ranting against promiscuity and pornography, reportedly denounced Jim's affair with a secretary, Jessica Hahn, to the Assemblies of God Church officials. Jim had used a buddy of his who helped build Heritage USA, Roe Messner, to pay Hahn $279,000 for her silence. It was later learned the money came from *PTL's* "nonprofit" funds. To add to the Bakkers' problems, they were accused of selling more timeshares than they could accommodate, using much of the resulting money for their notoriously lavish lifestyle. That brought federal charges of fraud.

When Jim Bakker resigned from *PTL*, he turned over the enterprise to his friend and evangelical colleague Jerry Falwell. Bakker ended up with a five-year prison term. Tammy later divorced him and married Roe Messner. As for *PTL,* one can only imagine the Bakkers' surprise when Falwell later called Jim "a liar, an embezzler, a sexual deviant, and the greatest scab and cancer on the face of Christianity in two-thousand years of church history." The former friend never had any intentions of giving *PTL* back. The press loved it, and for good reason. It was a shabby story of sex, money, infidelity, hypocrisy, and fraud filled with unsympathetic characters who lived lavishly and fell spectacularly.

Back at home base, CBN never mentioned *PTL* or the Bakkers in public. But rumors about naked pool parties and homosexual behaviors spread like wildfire. None of it was substantiated, but the cat was out of the bag. With news accounts coming out every day about *PTL's* troubles, it was difficult to know what was true. One thing was certain, Pat was nervous. The Bakker affair put an ugly spotlight on television evangelism. And it couldn't have come at a worse time for Pat, who had his own political ambitions on the line. But there was more on the horizon.

Oral Roberts then came into view with his fundraising debacle. Roberts was an icon of evangelism who brought the Pentecostal version of Christianity out of the tent and into television where mainstream America was introduced to divine healings, speaking in tongues, and biblical prophesies. He was a master fundraiser, marketing "seed-faith," the "prosperity gospel," and eventually, "abundant life teachings." There is no doubt he influenced the preachers who climbed on the TV bandwagon he helped create. The wheels started to come off for Roberts in 1987 during a fundraising drive when he announced that God would "take him home" unless he raised $8 million by a certain date. Problem was, he said something similar to that the year before. Nevertheless, with the new deadline looming he was still $4.5 million short of his goal. His loyal viewers responded to his death threat and he raised $9.1 million. But he lost much more than that; he lost his reputation. Eventually he lost his homes in Beverly Hills and Palm Springs, his Mercedes cars, and the City of Faith Medical Center, which he had founded and which was one of the largest medical centers of its kind at the time.

Televangelism was becoming a bizarre world of soap opera proportions; the viewing public began turning a skeptical eye toward the Peddlers of Prosperity. And it didn't help that mainstream America confused Roberts with Robertson. As far as most Americans were being led to believe, they were all crooks.

It was Jimmy Swaggart's turn at bat. The evangelist, cousin to rock-and-roll icon Jerry Lee Lewis and country singer

Mickey Gilley, began his ministry on the back of a flatbed truck in the Fifties. He soon rivaled his cousins' success with his own unique style of performing for Jesus, holding the Bible high in the air, strutting across the stage, ranting against adultery and promiscuity, and preaching on 250 television stations across America, with hundreds of millions of viewers worldwide. He raked in close to $150 million a year. But it was Swaggart's notoriety in a sex scandal that really got everyone's attention, and the story read like pulp fiction.

In 1986, Swaggart, who was credited with outing Jim Bakker's affair, exposed another minister in the Assemblies of God Church, Marvin Gorman, for having adulterous sexual affairs. Subsequently, Gorman was defrocked and lost his ministry. But Gorman retaliated. Setting a camera up in a sleazy New Orleans motel, Gorman's agent photographed several men coming and going, establishing its use for prostitution. One of the men was Swaggart. The seedy story continued to unfold in the motel parking lot where, reportedly, Gorman's son Randy let the air out of Swaggart's tires, giving Gorman time to confront the evangelist on the prostitute's doorstep. They struck a deal. Gorman would not expose the photographs if Swaggart helped reinstate him in the Assemblies of God Church, apologize publicly, and say he lied about Gorman's indiscretions. A year went by and Swaggart had not kept his part of the deal. Gorman carried through on his threat and delivered the photographs to ministry elders in the church. Swaggart was suspended.

In the meantime, the prostitute failed several polygraph tests when questioned if she was paid by Gorman to set Swaggart up in the sting. But the damage was done. Swaggart's tearful confession—"I have sinned"—on national television was replayed hundreds of times. The Assemblies of God hierarchy defrocked him on grounds of immorality. Swaggart went independent and his Family Worship Center became nondenominational. Three years later, Swaggart was stopped by a police officer for driving on the wrong side of the road. He had a prostitute in the car. Now he tells his congregation, "The Lord told me it's flat none of your business." The Swaggart image was gutted but not dead. Currently, Swaggart and family have revived their ministry in another global television network, touting the purpose as "Spreading the Message of the Cross around the world."

Jimmy Swaggart's downfall was breathtaking. His penchant for throwing his ministerial colleagues under the bus for sexual misconduct seemed like the justice of Jesus as Swaggart's own sins rolled over him in a humiliating display of utter hypocrisy.

The tabloids must have thought these stories were manna from heaven. Late-night comedians had fodder for years. Televangelism had become a laughingstock. And while money and sex were knocking off other TV preachers, power took a swing at Pat Robertson.

THE SECOND COMING

"I BELIEVE THE LORD WANTS ME TO BE THE next president of the United States."

A gasp rustled through the small CBN contingent that had gathered for the annual weekend retreat in Pat's getaway lodge. Located in the Allegheny Mountain community of White Sulphur Springs, West Virginia, the lodge was only 250 miles west of Washington DC and within throwing distance of the prestigious Greenbrier resort. Greenbrier boasted itself as a destination and refuge for "kings, queens, presidents and politicians, luminaries and celebrities from all corners of the globe." Bearing an uncanny resemblance to the White House, the posh resort offered activities befitting the upper class: golf, tennis, croquet, and, for the more adventurous, falconry classes.

It seemed fitting for such an announcement that we would be assembled near Greenbrier, in Pat Robertson's version of Camp David. His casual retreat was deliberately simple in its décor and furnishings—comfortably worn chairs and sofas, a toss of cushions, crocheted blankets, unadorned walls—a change of pace from the benefits of living large. Discreetly set back from the Greenbrier golf course, the provincially chic, unpolished environment spoke of money.

Pat was as casual as I had ever seen him, at ease in a big maplewood chair, sitting not straight forward like Lincoln in his memorial statue, but leaning back, cowboy boots poking out from under pressed jeans, hands clasped gently in his lap, dress shirt sleeves rolled up. A cool diluted light filtered through the windows in the large front room where an inner circle of department heads and vice presidents were assembled around him. While I held no corporate position, Pat always included me in these assemblies, as though "cohost" had its own unique jurisdiction, a privilege few women were granted in these enclaves of male authorities. Although it was the height of summer, the room had a clammy, heat-neglected feel to it, like an unused church. Late afternoon shadows crept across the plain wood floor, over the muted expensive rug, but no one moved to turn on the lights.

Pat spoke in a measured cadence, every nuance to be tasted, every subtlety to be seized, his voice so soft we had to lean in to be privy to his reflections. With the slightest tilt of his chin, he imparted his wisdom, spooning it out to us through the gritty smile of a Southern gentleman. Resurrecting a phrase I had heard him use many times before, he said, "It's a matter of *noblesse oblige*, a French phrase meaning the obligation of the noble to serve the people. I like to think of it as living up to the expectations of one's position." He paused, holding the best for last, then, with the leisure of a man familiar with holding court, said, "I believe the Lord may want me, as president, to usher in the Second Coming of Jesus."

For a moment, I was caught up in the suspension of reality. Though I had expected Pat to run for president since his formation of a political action committee, I never imagined associating it with the glory of Christ's return. And in my lifetime! More observer than participant, I watched the group, silent as stones, absorb the immensity of Pat's words. Suddenly, one man wept into his hands, another fell to his knees. Behind me a murmur, "Praise Jesus." In the corner, a department head prayed in tongues. "Praise the Lord," whispered from the back. A producer clapped his hands three times and raised his arms in worship. Pat dropped his head in humbleness to the Lord.

It was a holy moment. I saw a bird sing outside the window, then flutter to a low rocking branch. Slowly, my suspension gave way to epiphany. God was in this. I began to see it—telethons and television were the cost of doing God's business in a modern world. Of course God would choose television's most powerful religious personality. Pat Robertson would *have* to become president. He was positioned to be the second John the Baptist.

In the midst of our murmurs, Pat left the room, leaving us to whisper and wonder. As if fearing our own voices would break the spell, we confided in sighs, embracing in exultation, sharing in prayer, worshiping the Lord, marveling at His plan. We all understood it. Each of us had been chosen, each a vital part of the divine plan. We were disciples, a chosen few who would spread the good news of the Second Coming.

I regretted my earlier doubts and felt shame for questioning my role as a religious celebrity. Christ was in this. The money, the politics, the programming of only beautiful people really was God's plan. Pat would be president. Dazed and prayerful, we were anointed apostles, called to be something greater than ourselves, to follow a higher calling than any of us could have imagined. Witnesses to history, we would see Christ's return. We were on the inside track to the Lord Himself.

Grasping the nuance of effect, Pat reemerged and appeared to us now, not just speaking for the Lord, but anointed by Him. Charlton Heston could not have played the part better. As he passed through the room, we paid him homage, lowering our heads, and stepping aside.

Pat Robertson, the trumpet for the Messiah.

Several months later, after the official launch of Pat's presidential campaign, that trumpet began sounding more like a foghorn. I realized early on what the motto "journalism with a different spirit" meant at CBN. We reported news from an obviously Christian, conservative perspective, without the veneer of objectivity offered by traditional news outlets. But though Pat dealt from a subjective deck, he still had a few cards up his sleeve. As his plan to run for president gathered steam, there was an unstated spin to the lessons he taught his flock.

During one particular *700 Club* broadcast Pat turned to the camera and said, "When I'm president, I will bring only Christians and Jews into my administration."

"Really?" Ben said. "What about Hindus and Muslims and other kinds of Americans, like atheists? I mean, you're not saying only Christians and Jews are qualified to govern America?" Ben laughed, assuming he had misunderstood.

"That's what I'm saying." Pat smiled. "This country was founded on Judeo-Christian values and I believe that's how the Founding Fathers meant this nation to be governed."

"But isn't that against the Constitution or something?" Ben laughed again nervously.

"The Constitution of the United States is a marvelous document for self-government by Christian people. But the minute you turn the document into the hands of non-Christians and atheists they can use it to destroy the very foundation of our society. And that's what's been happening."

Ben raised his eyebrows in surprise. I was speechless, never hearing this spin on the Constitution before. But Pat was on a roll. After the break he served up another hardball during a discussion of family values. "Fifty percent of marriages end in divorce," he said, wincing into a smile. "We need to take back this country from the Democrats and the atheists and the godless of this nation who make it too easy for women to divorce their husbands and families, women who go on to become witches and lesbians."

Was he serious? This was unedited, live television, beamed to sixty-three countries via satellite. I imagined that statement slipping through the gaping mouth of the camera, digesting through the atmosphere like a lump through the belly of a python, making its way to a worldwide audience who silently, blindly, absorbed it into their souls. I thought of my parents, the fights, the fists, the infidelities, and their roar in my ears. I couldn't let it go.

"But Pat, what about people who say divorce is the right thing if the family is abused? You don't mean women and children should stay in dangerous situations, do you?" I felt my face flush as I confronted Pat live, in color, before his people.

"Well," he said, "of course not, that's different. The health of the family always comes first."

My heart pounded, urging me on. "And surely you don't mean *all* women who divorce become witches and lesbians? Statistically, that would mean half the married women in the country, including my mother."

Pat fell back into his chair and held his hands up. "Well," he showed his teeth and smiled. "I wasn't talking about *all* divorced women, Danuta." Then he laughed. "And I certainly wasn't talking about your mother." Everyone laughed now, but in a sobering afterthought he said, "But it's a risk and we need to be aware of it."

Point scored. Pat took no hit on the ego-meter, and an absurdity had been cancelled.

But I found myself wrestling with confusion. If I was part of God's plan to change the world, why did it sound like a place I didn't like? Jesus said blessed are the peacemakers, but Pat wanted more nuclear arms. Jesus said blessed are the meek, but Pat courted only the wealthy and powerful. Jesus said blessed are the merciful, but Pat supported the death penalty. Jesus said love your enemies, but Pat called them termites. The spiritual contortions roared on—for Pat, the devil was around every corner, sin tempted every moment. Democrats were lumped in with godless creatures. Gays and lesbians were ruining families. Christmas was under attack. Our schools were run by the godless homosexual agenda. Democracy itself was teetering on the edge.

I hoped these troubling aspects of Pat's views, like the money and the telethons, were the rough edges common with all new beginnings, and that inevitably Truth would emerge, shaping and conforming us all to the will of Christ. It would take time for this sacred undertaking would mold us and train us. Patience would be required. More than I ever imagined.

The Liability

THE DAY I BECAME A POLITICAL LIABILITY, PAT called me into his office. His voice squeaked when he was impassioned, like a choirboy who's lost his ability to sing. He was squeaking now, and smiling at the same time.

"A reporter has been coming around asking me questions about your brother Paul. He asked me something I find impossible to believe. He asked me if he's your son, not your brother. I just didn't know what to tell him." Pat's eyes sliced through me.

A sick, empty pang struck my stomach, like a dream of falling when your guts haven't caught up with the rest of you. I felt sucker punched and couldn't breathe. I didn't know where to look. My legs began to wobble and I needed to go to the bathroom. The most visible Christian woman on television shivered with fear before her father again.

I focused on a black speck on the carpet and watched Pat's cowboy boots come creaking out from behind his desk.

"What's the story?" he said.

"Yes," I nodded at the speck, incapable of reacting to this lightning out of the blue.

The boots stopped. "You're telling me your brother is your son?"

I nodded, still standing and staring at the floor.

Then I heard the sound of my father's belt buckle. Gasping, I winced my eyes shut and raised my arm to protect my face. When nothing happened, I opened my eyes to see Pat standing in front of me, retrieving a pen from the gleaming, uncluttered surface of his desk. He seemed surprised at my reaction, but then said, "You've got to know that this could get out to the papers." He shook the pen at me. "They're looking for anything. If they got a hold of this . . ."

He went back behind his desk. There was a strain in his voice, the squeaking was higher, and the smile completely gone.

"Well, what's the story?" he asked again, sitting in his leather chair.

Pat Robertson and Paul, 1987

Though I wasn't invited to, I slipped into a chair, sitting on the edge of the seat, afraid of falling, or falling apart. It all came screaming back at me. I struggled to keep my composure as I tried to explain—the car skidding across the road. Lurching into a ditch. I strike the passenger door. My arm twists under me. My head jams against the window. My neck hurts. He's on top of me. I can't breathe. My tears, his sweat, the steam of his breath smearing my face. The baby at home. My father's anger. Our escape to Alaska. The secret my mother and I kept for twenty-one years. This truth held sacred all these years, had now spilled out here, in Pat's office.

Pat tinkered absentmindedly with the pen. "We've got to settle this. If the papers think they've got a story, it could be embarrassing to me. My cohost having an illegitimate child raised as her brother." He tossed the pen aside.

I understood. I was part of the team. Protecting Pat's pursuit of the presidency and protecting Paul's identity loomed over me like a monstrous shadow.

"It could be disastrous for Paul," I said. "He doesn't know."

"Disastrous."

"I don't want Paul to find out about this in the papers."

"Can't let it leak to the papers." Pat sat back. "Resolve this. Right now. Tell Paul today." It was an order.

"Today?"

"We can say its old news. Papers won't have anything to expose." He stood up.

I stood as well. "Paul has to hear it from me first." My head reeled. "Won't be a lie anymore."

"That too. It's for his own good. So, when will you tell him the good news?" he asked.

Fumbling under his scrutiny, with no time to breathe, no time to think, I said, "It's his twenty-first birthday today, maybe at dinner . . . tonight." My sour stomach began to ache. I wanted Paul to know, but should it be on his birthday? This was all too sudden, too soon.

"Perfect." Coming from behind his desk, Pat put his arm on my shoulder, maneuvering me smoothly to the door. "This is the Lord's timing. You'll never regret it," he said, closing the door behind me.

Later that afternoon, my daze had not yet worn off from the meeting with Pat.

"You're drowning it."

"What?"

"The lettuce. You've been washing the lettuce for ten minutes."

I looked up to see Kai, pitched against the kitchen doorway, comfortable in his burgundy velour sweat suit, an impeccable outfit that had never seen a bead of sweat. At that moment, I wanted to believe Kai held the whole house up in that doorway, and me with it. I wanted him to protect me from my tremors. He was older and wiser, like a parent, someone I should be able to depend on. But a second glance told the truth. He clutched his appointment book crammed with notes to himself, as if the book would one day be filled with business meetings and executive decisions. But for now it merely served as a journal for his patched thoughts, a penciled life he couldn't seem to master. I realized that the doorframe held him up, not the other way around. I would not find comfort there.

Staring at the bruised romaine in the sink, I thought about Mom, the one person I needed to talk to. She should know about this. Paul was her son, too. What would she think? Would she approve? Why didn't we ever talk about this? By now, she had moved to a rental house in Virginia Beach, a vast improvement over the past few months of living in the barn, and our relationship was on the mend—that is, I sent her flowers and cards and she received them. I never fully understood what broke our relationship in the first place, but suspect that Mom and Kai fought while I was at work. With Kai's drinking and Mom's mental state, I left a ticking time bomb in the house each day. I think Paul may have helped roust her from her depression, having returned from his summer in Seattle with Michael and living with her now while he attended school.

There was no time to talk to her now, anyway. Pat made it very clear, ready or not, the responsibility to tell Paul the truth fell on me and me alone. I was the parent now, and payment for years of no parenting came due tonight.

"It's time he knew," Kai said, moving next to me. "If you want, I'll leave you two alone when you tell him. It's going to be all right."

I nodded, but no one knew the impact the truth would have on Paul. At the time, I recognized intellectually that this information would be disruptive, but I didn't understand the depth of it, that identity is your roof and your foundation. I wouldn't know how it felt to have those securities shattered until years later, when it happened to me, when I would lose my own identity. Only then would I understand how precariously we walk the tightrope of trust—a thin wire of confidence. Balance is an art form that requires sure footing and focus, maturity, flexibility, and an ability to waiver without falling. These things I would learn when my time came.

For now, I could only wonder how the truth would affect Paul.

His young life was still locked into the security most of us take for granted—his identity and place in the world. I remembered how Paul pored over pictures of my father, as I used to do, wondering aloud if he, too, had the gifts of an athlete, the flair of an artist, the heart of a lion. Unknown to him, it was his grandfather he admired, not his father. How would I tell him his real father forced himself on a girl half his size, ignoring her pleas to stop? I felt sick at heart remembering the scene, feeling the half-moon cuts of my nails sinking into my palms. The word "rape" had no place in my child's heart. He still seemed so young, so vulnerable.

Which would cause him the least pain, the truth or the lie? Rehearsing the scene I was about to play out, I convinced myself that this was for the best and that it was no longer a question of if, but when, and who would tell him. I would take responsibility and make good on the big lie. In this race for honesty, I had to get to Paul first—to destroy his foundations with love before the newspapers destroyed them for politics.

Just then the doorbell rang and Paul burst into the room.

"Happy birthday, Paul." Kai and I painted smiles on our faces.

While I served the salad and Paul's favorite Thousand Island dressing, we talked about the community college he attended and his classes. As the spaghetti steamed on the platter, he gushed about the VW van we bought for him, and how he wanted to fix it up for camping trips. We talked about soccer and surfing and how he missed California. Since moving to Virginia with Mom, he said it was good to be with family, but he missed his friends in San Diego. While he piled on the Parmesan cheese, my stomach churned and I left my food cold and untouched. Kai poured the wine. "Your first legal drink," he said, and Paul's dark, blue eyes lit up the room. I couldn't stop staring at him, praying he'd understand. As he tore into the long stem of sourdough bread, I thought, here was my beautiful son, lean and strong, who seemed as if he never knew a bad day. I was about to take his innocence away forever. Would he love me? Hate me? Ever forgive me?

He dug into the spaghetti for a second helping as Kai disappeared into his study. I scratched the table with my thumb, digging into the seams of the wood. I gulped down several false starts, my voice breaking with each attempt to speak.

"I have a gift for you, Paul."

"Cool." Licking his fingers, he planted his fork firmly into his mountain of pasta, relishing his food like a boy who could never be filled.

"It is a gift of truth and identity." I picked at each word.

"Cool," he said again, slurping the spaghetti off his plate, wiping his mouth with his napkin, smiling with anticipation.

"Once upon a time, there was a girl who was only sixteen," I began. "She was dating a boy, but something happened. She was raped. And then she was pregnant."

Paul stopped eating. "And she had an abortion," he said, adding to the storyline.

"No," I paused, and taking one last deep breath, "I had you."

The silence of ice is deafening. Stilled and stunned, movement is suspended in a tundra of waiting.

In this airless, breathless vacuum, Paul digested the words. And just as suddenly, the ice broke and life gushed again. Slamming his back against the chair, nearly tipping over, he said, "Whoa." He wrinkled his face and peered into me. "What?"

"I had you." I whispered the words like a prayer.

"You had me. What do you mean you *had* me?"

"I'm your mother." *Oh dear God, I said it.*

"You're my mother." His fork hit the plate.

"Yes. You were born in Michigan, just before we left for Alaska."

"But Mom is my mother." He shook his head, shook the senselessness away, the absurdity.

"Yeah, Mom raised you. You see, when I had you, I was still in school and Mom decided she would raise us both. And you would be my brother."

"Oh, man." Paul closed his eyes, still shaking his head. And then, in a flash, he opened his eyes and stared at me, as if seeing me for the first time. I froze while his blue eyes scanned mine, like a blind man reaching for the Braille of recognition, the curve of my nose, the shape of my face, cellular acknowledgments, familiarities, and finally knowing, he gave out a nervous laugh.

"What? You were raped?" He turned somber for a second and then lit up again with expressions of someone on a roller coaster. "Then, that means, that Mom's my . . ."

"Grandmother," I said.

"And Rick and Mike are not my brothers . . ."

"They're your uncles."

"That means," he said, trying to follow the new logic, "that you're my mom. And I'm . . ."

"You're my son." The sound of those words strung together felt odd and beautiful.

"Wow. This is just like the movies."

In spite of the tension, I had to laugh.

"Then, you're my mom," he repeated. He searched my face again and I searched his. How handsome. His eyes puddled deep and wide, full of marvel, brimming with life.

"That's why I have blue eyes. And why my nose is like yours! I always wondered about that."

"You did?"

"Yeah, like Mom's eyes are brown and her nose is smaller. Yeah," he said, "cool. So, you're my mom." He leapt from his chair and hugged me. How relieved and grateful I felt, that he took to all this so well. We talked about how he was named after Paul McCartney, and then I asked him if he wanted a picture of his father.

Paul's face turned somber again. "No. I don't want to see him. I'm not like him."

"Of course, you're not," I said, and quickly changed the subject.

"Paul, one thing you have to know. Nothing about our relationships has really changed. Your brothers will always be your brothers. And Mom will always be Mom. I'll be your other mother, is all. You get two of us."

He fidgeted in his chair, trying to fit into his new identity, like trying on a new pair of pants. "Who can I tell?" he asked after a few long seconds. "I mean, is it a secret? Does Michael know? Does Rick?"

"Michael doesn't know. He was too little. Rick knows. He was there. You can tell anyone, everyone. It's not a secret anymore." With those words, the air tasted cooler and sweeter and I tingled as if I'd been scrubbed with a brush.

I hoped Paul understood we were free to be who we really were, to know our connections, to see ourselves in each other, to put all the missing pieces together and build on them. It seemed so rational, so logical to connect the dots and move on. But years later I would learn what a monstrous task I had asked of him, connecting threads in a fragile weave. At the time, Paul seemed to accept it all, asking few questions, with little curiosity about his biological father, or why we left Michigan, or how Mom and I made it through those hard, early years. Those questions would come eventually, I thought, and we'd handle them then, one by one.

He left later that evening, waving from his VW van, "Bye, Mom. I love you."

I stood in the middle of the driveway and cried.

He called me Mom. And I saved Pat from embarrassment.

POWER

IN 1987, AS PAT'S PRIMARY CAMPAIGN AGAINST George Bush for the Republican nomination heated up, Pat nurtured a huge political army of conservative Christians in a grassroots campaign to get them involved in the political process. Before he stepped down from the show, he used *The 700 Club* to interpret the social and political events of the day, unchallenged against the backdrop of the Almighty. "If I couldn't move a hurricane, I couldn't move a nation," Pat said, referring to our prayer against Hurricane Gloria. Now Star Wars military technologies, welfare reform, and balancing the budget became major moral issues to be supported by concerned Christians. While these discussions did little to elevate the souls of CBN viewers, they went a long way to elevating Robertson's status as a presidential candidate. Pat's conservative platform included a ban on pornography, a reform of the education system, the elimination of the Department of Education and the Department of Energy, overturning Roe v. Wade—criminalizing abortion, and pursuing prayer in schools.

Pat flexed his international skills for the media during the Contra-Sandinista conflict. CBN News ran a piece on *The 700 Club* showing Robertson walking into a Contra camp in the jungles of Nicaragua, shaking hands with camp commanders and being mobbed by adoring children. These same children, with guns slung over their shoulders, lined up like the Vienna Boys Choir and sang Christian songs for him. Robertson spent just the few minutes it took to tape the scene before flying out of the camp. The story ran that the U.S.-backed Contras were being unfairly represented by the "mainstream press" and that Robertson was invited deep into the jungle to see them for himself. He commented on the show that the Contras were simply Christian children fighting the good fight.

What viewers weren't told was that the camp was a prop set up by the Contras for Robertson's visit, hurriedly prepared on the edge of a landing field. The children were recruited and rehearsed for the taping by savvy Contra propagandists who out-spun the spinner at his own game. Nevertheless, Robertson portrayed himself as an intrepid diplomat who dared to go where angels and other journalists feared to tread. In so doing, he had aligned himself with Reagan's hard line on Nicaragua and positioned himself as a stalwart Republican spokesman.

Meanwhile, church organizations and human rights groups documented that thousands of civilians were killed by the Contras. Journalists and congressional committees also found that the Contras were involved in drug trafficking. Robertson never stood up, owned up, 'fessed up, or offered a journalistic mea culpa. It didn't matter that he had grossly misrepresented the Contras as peacemakers. What did matter was image.

His image sometimes flustered him. During a break on the set Pat confided to me that his wife, Dede, was going to the hospital that day for a biopsy on a lump that was found in her breast. If the lump was found malignant she would immediately go into surgery for a mastectomy. "The problem is," he said, "I have a speaking engagement and rally right after the show. What do you think I should do, go to the rally or stay with Dede?"

I stared at him in disbelief. "You've got to be kidding," I said. "Let's put it this way, how would it look if the press found out you left your wife on the operating table so that you could make a speech?" The point hit home. "You're right," he said, "I should stay with Dede, then."

It was Pat's concern for his image that forced me to disclose Paul's identity; in response, I began to resent the political motivation that manipulated my personal life and to question my beliefs. My mere presence on the set of *The 700 Club* made me an accessory to a progressively wilder and more extreme view of Christianity. Worse, I was helping leverage a campaign to make Pat the most powerful man in the world. I tried justifying my position with the argument that politics and faith are intertwined; both require judgments based on morality. But deep down inside, I was still a journalist insisting on documentation.

There was no documentation when Robertson suggested that feminism taught women to divorce their husbands, kill their children, practice witchcraft, and become lesbians. Instead, he came up with the Old Testament stoning solution. My head spun with questions. Why rely on the Old Testament's ruthless judgments of an angry deity when the Gospel of Jesus was supposed to have changed our relationship with God? Pat was more comfortable when judgment was quick, often lethal, and the problem eliminated. Simplify. Shades of gray were far too cloudy for viewers who have come to expect a Pat answer.

His answers reduced social and political issues to harsh and often bloody terms. During a news conference, Robertson supported the use of government assassination squads to eliminate terrorists. According to Pat, we didn't need science to figure out why we have global warming—it's simply the beginning of the end of the world. AIDS was a punishment from God for homosexuality. Adolph Hitler, Satanists, and homosexuals "seem to go together." Fires and floods in California were signs of God's displeasure with godless people. Separation of church and state was a lie of the Left. Planned Parenthood teaches kids to fornicate and masturbate. Episcopalians, Presbyterians, Methodists, Hindus, some Catholics, and Democrats have the spirit of the antichrist. To follow Robertson's lead, I had to ignore his contradictions. His denunciations were often made extemporaneously, shot from the hip, often using unsubstantiated or undocumented "facts" and figures.

Long after I had left the show Pat continued with his weird statements. During the Mars Pathfinder success, Robertson dismissed efforts by NASA to explore the universe, saying that anyone who believed in extraterrestrial life essentially believed in demons, and, according to the Old Testament way of dealing with things, such believers ought to be stoned to death. He also once said that there was nothing in the universe to explore, other than dying and exploding suns. It seemed we should discredit the entire field of astrophysics and to pick up fist-sized rocks to throw at astro-sinners. It was up to God to know how Robertson explained his belief in the celestial existence of angels, or the extraterrestrial existence of God Himself!

I couldn't believe my ears when Pat explained his plan to murder Libya's Colonel Kaddafi. I was on the set when he said, "The problem with kicking a mad dog is that the mad dog will bite you. Especially if he's got rabies. He might hurt you and he might infect you badly. So you don't go out and kick a mad dog. If you have a mad dog with rabies you take a gun and shoot him. I mean, that's the only thing you can do, mercifully, to keep yourself . . ." He began to laugh and the live audience clapped their hands in approval.

But I wasn't sure what I was hearing. "Wait, now, let's wait now. Back up just a step or two," I said as the audience laughed. "Are you saying that we should go in there and . . ."

Pat tuned in, "Danuta, there's an old saying, that you don't strike the king unless you kill him. You don't strike a king, just hit him in the face and walk away from him, because he'll turn around and do something terrible to you. And the only way to get rid of him is to do the thing that the old maxim says: if you're gonna strike him, you need to kill him."

Thus sayeth the Lord. The love of Jesus was beyond all understanding, especially when it came to Pat's answers.

By now, Pat was frequently absent from the show, making political fundraising speeches, forming political action committees and meeting with campaign advisors. The hosting of the daily show was left to Ben and to me. During one such absence, the program broke one of the most damaging and long-running spy sagas in the history of the United States. I interviewed Laura Walker when she disclosed that her father, John Walker, and her brother had been involved in twenty years of espionage for the Soviet Union. The interview, which first exposed the "Walker spy family," was taped when Robertson was out of town.

Apparently upset that he was left out of the loop of a breaking news story, Robertson discredited the interview and wanted the piece canceled. Previewing the tape before the show, he insisted that he could tell that Laura Walker was lying "just by looking at her eyes," and that the story was bogus. The producer and I prevailed with research substantiating the story, and the piece was shown. It was later learned that Walker had convinced her mother that week to turn over her husband and son to the FBI. In subsequent interviews with her, Robertson took the credit for helping break her story to the press and the authorities.

By now, the calamity of scandals associated with television evangelism was beginning to have a negative effect on Pat's campaign. He bristled when the press referred to him as an evangelist and insisted he was just a moral businessman who served as a "news analyst" on television. He distanced himself from his evangelical roots, resigned as a Southern Baptist minister, and later in the campaign, cut ties with CBN and *The 700 Club*. He was forced to admit that he had exaggerated his military service and his educational background, that he had failed the bar exam, and that he had altered the date of his marriage because his first child had been conceived out of wedlock. And I thought I was a liability.

During Pat's run for president, he was buoyed by his second-place finish in the Iowa caucuses, ahead of George Bush. He still thought he had God on his side. But his luck ran out in the New Hampshire primary and beyond. The writing was on the wall. He ended his campaign before the primaries were over. During the 1988 Republican National Convention, he threw his support to Bush, who went on to win the election. And Pat went back to being an evangelist.

But the damage was done. The dollars had begun to dwindle. Telethon pledges were drying up. CBN cut people from its payroll and slashed millions in spending to balance the budget. Contributions dropped so much that the ministry contemplated closing its satellite counseling centers across the country, and reducing its charitable outreach program,

Operation Blessing, which was Ben's department.

To add to the misery, the IRS showed up. There was speculation at the time that some tax-exempt monies had fueled Pat's political agenda. The agency spent so much time poring over CBN's finances that they set up what was, in essence, a permanent office on the ministry's campus. Twelve years later the IRS would revoke the organization's tax-exempt status for 1986 and 1987. Apparently CBN had provided $8.5 million in grants and unpaid loans to the Freedom Council and the National Freedom Institute—formed to encourage Christians to become politically active—but largely responsible for backing Robertson's political war chest. CBN would agree to make a "significant" undisclosed payment to the IRS, promising to get on with its Christian ministry and to stay out of politics.

Scandals would continue to haunt Pat long into the future. By 1994, after the Rwandan Genocide, Pat solicited donations from viewers to provide medical supplies to Zaire. What viewers were not told was that allegedly, Robertson was in cahoots with that country's ruthless dictator, Mobutu Sese Seko, seeking favor with the leader in order to negotiate a contract for a diamond mine. The airplane pilots for Operation Blessing reported that their main job was to haul diamond-mining equipment to Robertson's mines, not relief supplies to refugees.

But Pat's dabblings with dictators didn't stop there. According to newspaper reports in 1999, Pat negotiated a multimillion-dollar contract for gold-mining operations in Liberia. Robertson's contract with Liberian president Charles Taylor came under fire when the United States Congress offered a $2 million reward for Taylor's capture for alleged crimes against humanity. What's more, Taylor was harboring Al Qaeda operatives involved with illegal diamond trading. It didn't help that during Taylor's war crimes trial in The Hague the dictator proclaimed Robertson as his main political ally in the U.S. Pat would make the case that he was simply doing business the way most American companies operated in Africa at the time.

The Second Coming of Christ would have to wait for another John the Baptist.

THE WILL OF GOD

I NEEDED A BREAK. DURING PAT'S CAMPAIGN, I felt useless, a fixture on a political show pieced together at the last minute on Robertson's whims. For months, Pat disregarded the preparations of the show's producers, running into the studio at the last minute, haranguing the audience with thirty-minute off-the-cuff speeches, while Ben and I sat silently nodding and smiling, trying to look interested.

When I expressed my concerns, Terry understood. "I know it's frustrating, Danuta. I'm the one tossing out schedules and rearranging formats. I don't even know what the show is, and I'm the producer." He shrugged his shoulders back and readjusted his tie.

I told Terry that I believed my tenure at CBN had run its course and that Kai and I were thinking of moving back to California. He looked alarmed. "Don't make any hasty plans," he said. "All you need is some time off. You're tired. Take a break, go to the beach. You'll feel better when you get back. But promise me you won't make any sudden decisions."

With the promise made, Kai and I took a week off to rest and relax and to evaluate my role at CBN. We booked a hotel at Fort Myers Beach, Florida.

THE WATER LICKED AT MY toes. The turquoise Gulf of Mexico reminded me of the color of the glacial ice my mom and I traveled through on the Alcan twenty-one years before.

Kai snoozed in the sand next to me, caramelized with suntan lotion that smelled like coconuts. Would I be disobeying the Lord if we returned to San Diego? Kai could work anywhere he had a phone. I was sure the Lord would give me a sign.

I filtered the sugar-white sand through my fingers and sank into the silica oozing with the warmth of the sun. My thoughts wandered to the infinity of sand grains and stars, to the insignificance of man in the wilderness of space, if not for the love of God. I drifted into a sun-wrapped sleep.

"Praise the Lord," said a voice above me.

"Harald?" I heard Kai say.

"Harald?" I lost my grasp on infinity.

"Surprise!" said another voice that sounded a lot like Terry.

Terry Heaton and Harald Bredesen stood above us, blocking the sun.

"Thought you might like some company," Terry said, sitting uncomfortably in the sand in his suit.

"Ah, the Lord is good!" Harald beamed at me. "Hello daughter. Let's pray. Oh, praise you Lord, praise you Jesus." Harald lifted his hands in prayer. The sand and the turquoise water evaporated from my vacation.

"But what are you doing here?" I pulled a shirt over my bathing suit.

"For company, like I said," replied Terry, squinting at the water.

Harald rolled up his trousers and kicked off his shoes. "Let's walk, shall we?" He took my arm in his and propelled me down the beach praising the Lord. Finally he said, "Daughter, I brought you to the Lord and He has put you in a mighty position in His kingdom on earth, wouldn't you agree? And wouldn't it be a miscarriage of my duties as your spiritual father on earth if I didn't keep you from making a big mistake by leaving this ministry?"

"Well, I hadn't really made up my mind."

"We're going to pray and ask the Lord to give us direction." Harald stopped walking. "Jesus, oh God, we need your intervention. Show us the way."

He reattached his arm to mine and hiked us down the coastline. I explained that when I joined CBN no one asked me about my politics, that I was a Democrat, a feminist, a liberal; I drank wine and loved Jesus. But by association I was considered a conservative Republican supporting Robertson for president. Finally I said, "And Jesus isn't even part of the show anymore. It's hard to be someone I'm not."

Harald went quiet on me.

"I'm not a messenger of hope, I'm a political mouthpiece for right-wing issues. I'm very uncomfortable with that, Harald. I feel misplaced."

"Jesus, my Lord, my God." We stopped walking as Harald prayed again and then stopped abruptly and said, "Let's see what the Word has to say about it, shall we?"

Later that afternoon, in our room, Harald and Terry and Kai and I closed ranks in a small hand-holding circle, soliciting God and His Word for His comfort and guidance.

"God has placed you at CBN for a reason," Harald said, flipping pages in his Bible. "It says here in Psalm 50, verse 23, that 'whoever offers praise glorifies Me.' That means you are at CBN to help praise God. That's your mission."

"And," Terry said, pointing to the previous verse, "'Ye that forgets God, is torn in pieces and there be none to deliver.'"

And so it went, for three days. Morning, noon, and night the four of us prayed and read the scriptures, seeking the guidance of God. Terry and Harald had gone to a lot of trouble to convince me that "my sincerity was needed," as they put it. Besides, Terry said, what journalist wouldn't give her eyeteeth to be on the inside track of a presidential run? I was letting my emotions rule my head. Harald said I had to "put my ego aside and let God decide." Exhausted and tired of the debates, I was delivered of my doubts. I would obey God and stay at CBN.

Kai and I followed Terry and Harald back to CBN three days later. We didn't have tans, but we were certain in our future. I felt relief from having made the right decision to stay, and so did Kai. It all seemed so right, so settled.

The day I returned to CBN, Pat's son, Tim, had assumed the lead position on the show. Pat, I was told, stepped out of the show permanently due to equal time campaign laws. Any airtime given one candidate by a network must be given to candidates with opposing points of view. Pat would hardly give airtime on his network to George Bush. Besides, we were a nonprofit, tax-exempt ministry prohibited by law from engaging in political campaigns. Now, Ben and I would be the cohosts to his son, who appeared awkward and uncomfortable in his new role.

My first day back, Harald asked to meet for lunch at a local restaurant.

"Daughter, dear," he said, taking my arm in the restaurant lobby. "Mind if we walk a bit?" We strolled outside and walked around the building. "Daughter, are you aware that your position at CBN is hanging by a thread?"

I burst into laughter. "Sure, Harald, very funny."

"But it's no joke, Danuta. Your job is hanging by a thread."

I stopped laughing. "What thread? What are you talking about?"

"It's a warning. They may be taking you off the show." Harald looked worried.

"That's impossible. It's not God's will. You just convinced me of that three days ago on the beach."

Harald said nothing, but kept his head bowed and we circled the restaurant for the third time.

"Let's just pray and see what happens," Harald said.

I was certain Harald was mistaken. The Lord had the last word on the matter in Florida. I was needed here. Back at my office, there was a message from Terry asking to meet me after work in the parking lot. An odd request, but then everything was odd around here.

The lot was nearly empty when I got to my car. My briefcase bulged with the next day's notes and several books to review. As I fumbled with the keys, I saw Terry wringing his raw, red hands, walking towards me.

"Mind if I sit in for a sec?" he asked.

"Sure. What's up?" I scooted behind the steering wheel. The car felt hot and sticky, so I rolled down the window.

"It's *The 700 Club*." Terry laughed nervously, jerking his neck out of the bounds of his collar as if he were being strangled. "As you know, Tim is sitting in for Pat, now."

I nodded.

"And, it's been decided by the powers that be that since Tim is Pat's son, and since he's new at this job and inexperienced, your presence on the show makes him look less, how could I say this, um, authoritative. And that's a problem, because you're so good."

I nodded, trying to track with his reasoning.

"And so, and so you're off the show."

I kept nodding until his silence caught up to me.

"What did you say?"

"You're off the show. I know it's kind of sudden." Terry popped some antacids into his mouth and chewed them tenaciously while staring out the front window of the car as if we were going somewhere.

"I'm fired?"

"No, not exactly. See, you're so good—"

"You're telling me I'm fired because I'm so good?"

"Not fired, exactly . . ."

"You're firing me three days after telling me I'd be ripped to pieces by God if I leave?" I was shouting. The car was stifling.

"I know it's kind of sudden."

"Sudden? How is this possible? We prayed about this. You said it was God's will I stay. Now, it's God's will I go? I don't get it, Terry." I flicked on the ignition and turned on the air conditioner.

"I know. I know." Terry had his hands up in defeat. "It stinks, but I'm just a pawn in all of this. It was all decided while we were in Florida."

"Who decided?"

Terry just looked at me. I knew the answer.

"I want to talk to him."

"Sure, I would," he said, getting out of the car. "Call Pat's office and make an appointment."

"So what do I do now?" I asked Terry, now standing at the driver's window.

"Come to work. Answer your mail. You're off the show, but not out of CBN. We'll have a new job for you soon, maybe your own interview show. It'll be okay." He walked away holding his stomach as if his guts were spilling out. I knew just how he felt.

Pat wouldn't see me.

My absence on the show went unannounced. Viewers started calling and writing CBN by the hundreds, and Ben told me later that inquiries came in by the thousands asking, "*What happened to Danuta?*" The correspondence department at the network had been advised to avoid answering the question. Besides, no one had answers, not even me. At work, people stopped talking to me, as though I had a contagious disease. No one came by my cubicle to see me. Isolated and alone, I felt oddly ashamed, but I didn't know why. My disappearance became a mystery and the subject of conjecture. Rumors began and no effort was made to stop them. Some people said I must have had an extramarital affair. Others whispered that maybe Kai had embezzled money. Some speculated that my recent book, *A Passion for Living*, embarrassed the southern-bred Robertson because I discussed a relationship with an African American man during college. My book had been removed from the CBN bookstores. While Christian memoirs of child pornographers, murderers, and rapists who had turned their lives to Jesus were sold through the bookstore and over the air, the mention of a biracial relationship quietly slipped my book off the shelves and into boxes under the counter.

Ben Kinchlow, my Black compatriot and cohost, was also disenfranchised. Although he was vice president in charge of Operation Blessing, a senior Christian evangelist who had been with CBN off and on for seventeen years, he was overlooked when it came time to pass the mantle of hosting the show in Pat's absence. Tim Robertson was inexperienced as an interviewer, uncomfortable on television, untested as a spiritual leader, and relatively unknown to the millions who flocked to the program each day. Ben's authority on the show now had to pay obeisance to the boy. It was after all, a Robertson dynasty, and no Black preacher or blonde journalist was going to usurp the order of succession in the kingdom.

To make matters worse, no one told Ben I was off the show.

Ben called me two weeks after the parking lot ordeal with Terry. He sounded shocked and dismayed. Over lunch, I poured my heart out to him, pleading for some explanation or some spiritual relevance. This wasn't just a job, it was a calling. This bewildered me. How had God changed His mind from one week to the next? And why the humiliation of dismissing me in a parking lot, as if I brought shame to the walls and windows of the Christian Broadcast Network? What kind of a God had I been serving all this time? Ben listened with great sympathy and didn't pretend to have answers, but just shook his head in disbelief. When I asked why Pat was so cold, he thumped the table with his knuckles and said, "He can be hard. Compassion isn't Pat's strong suit."

Six months later, Ben resigned, saying he was "going home to seek the Lord." Fortunately, he was permitted a farewell on the program in which he told viewers he needed time searching for the Lord's direction. With CBN's finances in shambles, Operation Blessing facing cutbacks, and Tim Robertson trying to fill Pat's shoes, Ben probably felt that he was no longer needed. The dynamic days of the Black, the Blonde, and the Baptist were over.

After several months of not knowing quite where I stood, I realized there were no special assignments and no new show for me on the horizon. It was clear, I was fired. Eventually, I cut my days at the office to hours and then I just didn't show up at all. But I was not forgotten. CBN "elders" (ministers of God and various department heads) made regular visits to the house. They came, they said, to *pray with me*, to *help me understand God's will*, to *help me reveal my sin*. I felt like a scene out of the Book of Job where his friends came to console the wretched man and tried to reckon with him why God was displeased. "Job's friends" also consoled me.

"Perhaps you never knew the Lord," one counseled.

Even Harald had some advice one day, "Throw your face to the floor and ask the Lord to crush you under His heel to reveal your direction," he suggested.

"Could it be you didn't attend church often enough?" said another.

Let Him reveal the source of your shame to you, they said. Beg for mercy, they said, and you will be restored to God. They tried everything to explain the dismissal.

I felt sick and confused. It was one thing to leave the show voluntarily as I had previously considered; it would have been on my terms, with a predetermined future and prior notice, with a farewell to my colleagues and confidence that God was in the decision. But not like this. My dismissal came with the same unprofessional awkwardness as my hiring. I was hired in a memo and fired in a parking lot. And not only did I lose my job without cause, but I felt I lost my Lord as well.

What about all those scriptures and the will of God? Was the Lord with us in Florida, but gone elsewhere once we were back in Virginia Beach? Was He here or there? How could God be so erratic, so undivine? Was He only a ploy, a money-raising tool? I felt like a manipulated fool, used and discarded. In the course of a few days, I was embraced by the Lord and then soundly abandoned by Him. Just like a father.

I spent three months in prayers and tears and confusion before Pat finally consented to see me. But his explanation only made things worse. "The real reason you were removed from the cohosting role," Pat said, coming around from his desk and handing me an official letter of explanation, "is that Kai has previously been married and divorced, twice. In the eyes of the Lord, he is an adulterer." Pat stood before me and offered me the letter, but in my shock, I didn't have the strength to take it from him.

"An adulterer? But I've been married to Kai for five years. You met him before we were married. You were invited to the wedding. His former marriages were never an issue before."

"Well, it has been an issue and we just didn't act on it until now. It's a problem."

I took the letter from Pat with a feeble hand.

"But why is it a problem?"

"You are married to an adulterer who had two other wives. And God does not look kindly on divorce. You need to remedy this."

"Remedy this? What are you saying, that I should divorce Kai?"

"I'm not telling you what to do. But the Bible makes it very clear. You can't legally marry an adulterer."

"But I am married."

Pat threw up his hands and closed them together again. He had nothing more to say.

"So that's the reason I'm off the show. Not because of Paul, not because I've done something wrong, not because I'm too good, not because of my book, but because in your eyes, Kai was divorced and so he's an adulterer?"

"That's it," Pat said, going back to his desk.

As if on cue, his secretary, Barbara, poked her head into the room and told him he had a call.

Pat reached for the phone.

I stood up, feeling lightheaded. I wasn't sure if I should wait, or if the meeting was over.

"Hello, Senator!" Pat said and waved me off with not so much as a goodbye.

LAST DATE WITH JESUS

DURING THOSE LAST AGONIZING DAYS IN VIR-
ginia Beach, Ben convinced CBN that the hundreds of
questions regarding my absence coming into the Counseling
Center each week would best be handled by a straightforward
interview with me. We met Ben and the film crew at the
house and I garbled my way through it, saying it was true I
wasn't coming back to *The 700 Club,* that I was leaving for
California, and that I was hoping to develop a talk show of
my own. With no appetite and little sleep over the past few
months, I had also lost about thirty pounds and I made the
comment that half of me was missing. The segment took the
heat off CBN for dodging the question and, thanks to Ben, I
had an opportunity to leave with some dignity.

The rest of the year went badly. Due in part to my depression, and Kai's substance abuse, not only with alcohol but also
with pills now, we lost our home and belongings in Virginia
to creditors and bankers. Paul stayed with us while Mom
moved to Oregon, with Michael's help, to live near Rick and
his wife. While Mom's relationship with Rick started off well,
it deteriorated over time, infected by Rick's resentment and
inability to talk about it.

As for my career, mainstream broadcasting wouldn't touch
me. My work was affiliated with television evangelism. My
credibility was shot. I pruned away our possessions in garage
sales, selling my clothes and even our bed to gather enough

money to move us back home to San Diego.

I believed that sooner or later God would comfort me, and that with a little faith on my part, He would help me find work and peace. But in the year that had gone by since we'd moved back to San Diego, the strain of losing what felt like everything took its emotional and spiritual toll.

I remember quite clearly the night I resigned from Christianity. I was speaking to a Christian group in the high desert community of Ridgecrest, located on the northern edge of the Mojave Desert in California. Standing on the stage ready to deliver my usual testimonial, lined with the edification of the Church and the glorification of Jesus, the pain hit. I stood on the stage, the microphone in my hand, with tears rolling down my face, losing Jesus and my composure at the same time. All I wanted to do was run. "Excuse me," I said, "but I can't do this anymore." The audience was dead still and I began to walk off the stage.

"No," someone shouted, "don't go."

"Don't go," someone else yelled.

"Talk to us," another called.

"What do you want from me?" The microphone picked up a low, sad voice that didn't sound like mine.

"Tell it like it is," someone called out, and the crowd applauded.

"You want to know how it is? I don't know how to tell you." My mind felt like an empty bucket. "I lost Him. It's not like *I* misplaced God. It's that *He's* left *me*."

The lights obscured the audience as my voice echoed into the darkness.

"Maybe I didn't lose Him. Maybe I never had Him at all."

The silence of the desert filled the hall.

"I can't see Him. I can't feel Him. I don't hear Him. He's

gone. How is that possible? How could He just let me go?" I stared at the scuffed stage floor. "And so, I have nothing to give you. I have nothing to tell you. And right now, the last place I want to be is around a group of Christians. You remind me only of pain."

Rushing up from the side of the stage, a woman wrapped her arms around me. "I'm so sorry," she said. The lights came on in the hall. Some people applauded. I don't know why. Perhaps there were others who felt the same way. Dozens hugged me and wished me well. Some cried with me. It was my going-away party, my spiritual meltdown, my last night as a born-again Christian.

KAI SANK DEEPER AND DEEPER into depression and prescription drugs and booze; they made him even more remote and uncommunicative. I couldn't help him anymore. We were caught in a collapsing world of loss—our home and possessions, our income, and our future.

The only things that gave me focus anymore were my father's tapes. They served as a connection, a posthumous link to an unconquerable life. They suspended the buckling walls around me and took me away from my enfeebled existence to a time when a man was master of his life.

I wore an earphone attached to my Walkman and played the tapes all night long. I played them during the day.

I spent nine months in Tobruk, living like an insect in ditches, feeding the rats that lived with us, wagering on rat races in the trenches. It was 140 degrees in the tanks. The heat slowed down our reactions, our vision blurred, our lips glued together for lack of water. We used our own urine to unseal our lips, but even then, our tongues stuck to the roof of our mouths, and we still couldn't talk.

During one violent storm at the women's camp, tents were ripped apart, clothing, tools, and supplies were strewn across the desert. The women were lost in the storm. We searched for them in jeeps through the spitting grit, headlights bouncing in the black night. We found them scattered across the desert floor, huddled together, or alone, covering their nude bodies with their hands and screaming. In this biting, gritty, black blizzard, under the glare of the headlights, they looked like mermaids in the sand.

I had been stuck, out of my element, paralyzed for too long, but now my father was with me. Slowly, I began to write his stories. I had a promise to keep.

PART THREE
THE WHITE POLE

The White Pole, executing a midair turn

Codependent

THE SWAT TEAM SURROUNDED THE HOUSE. Coronado, with its seaside cottages and drowsy, gardenia-perfumed streets seemed the wrong setting for the black-dressed, rifle-clicking men standing in the flowerbeds. They asked where he was.

"He won't shoot you," I said.

"Just answer the question, where's your husband?"

"The back room by the garden." I pointed.

"We'll take it from here," they said. Two officers bolted through the front door, guns drawn. Others followed. Our golden retriever started barking. Someone shouted to call off the dog or he gets it! I screamed for the dog.

I screamed for Kai. Why did I have to call the police? I've made things worse. I should have let it go. I hear, "Put down the gun! Put it down!" Everything dead quiet.

"It's not loaded," someone hollered.

Despite my panic, I was furious at Kai. This farce nearly got us all killed over an unloaded gun. His substance abuse had escalated into bouts of hospitalizations, recovery programs, suicide attempts, and remissions followed by relapses. I felt like a bird battered under cat's paws, reacting to life as if it were a threat, scrambling, hiding, and hurting every day. Kai and I played our parts in the addiction game with clinical precision. While Kai feigned success, piling up hundreds of dollars in phone bills and taking first-class business trips to Sweden on borrowed money, I haggled with bill collectors, made excuses to his boss, and worried my stomach to ulcers. When Kai spent his office hours killing himself with prescription drugs and alcohol, I called the ambulances. While he recuperated in the hospital, I ran errands for him. Our lives revolved around the high drama of saving Kai.

My husband hated normalcy and craved intensity. He couldn't feel the beat of pleasant days and tender nights. Pleasantness numbed. He could only feel the sharp, wild swings of life-threatening drama. And he created them every day. And I, the perfect enabler, protected him from the falls, while he bathed in the cool waters of self-absorption.

The SWAT team stood down and the ambulance whisked Kai away to yet another private hospital ward where recovering substance abuse patients are protected from the glare of humiliation and the public eye. I called Kai's boss at the money management office and explained he'd had a mild heart attack. He would be hospitalized for a few days. No, there was no crisis; he just needed rest. No, no visitors allowed. I fought rush-hour traffic to the hospital, wound around the parking garage for fifteen minutes looking for a space, and checked in at the new patient desk. I found Kai in a private room, propped against pillows in bed, eating a meatloaf and mashed potato dinner. Eyeing the green beans on his plate, I realized I hadn't eaten all day.

He slugged down his milk and wiped his mouth with a napkin. "Sorry about all this," he said, as he stabbed another morsel of meat and plunked it in his mouth. He seemed pale and disheveled but remarkably upbeat. A nurse came in, took his temperature and pulse and examined the duffel bag I brought for him. She took out the aftershave lotion, his shaving kit, and the Listerine. No alcohol. No razors. Suicide risk. She handed them back to me in a plastic bag.

"Bring my electric shaver, tomorrow," Kai said. "I've got group therapy later, so I need to get some rest." With a casual flick of a switch he reclined his hospital bed like it was an easy chair. "Been a helluva day, hasn't it? Sorry about the gun business. That was stupid. Don't know what came over me."

I was too drained to plow into anger, too numb to talk about responsibility, too weary to forgive him.

"By the way," he said, "bring my warm-up suit, the purple velvet one, and my jacket, the Brooks Brothers, and a pair of pants, the gray stripes. Don't forget my briefcase and Day-Timer."

"Anything else?"

He turned on his side and fluffed his pillow.

"Did you call my work?"

"Yes."

"You didn't tell them?"

"No, of course not."

"Think I'll get some rest." He closed his eyes.

The doctor said Kai would need time and patience and would probably get a lot of help with the therapy group there. Help was exactly what I could use, I thought.

Two days later, against doctor's orders, Kai checked himself out of recovery and took a taxi home. He later explained he didn't have time for hospitals or to waste in therapy groups with a bunch of losers. He stretched out on the couch just as the telephone rang. It was the landlord. We were two months late on the rent. After I hung up, and without opening his eyes, Kai said it was just a cash-flow problem. When I persisted, he said not to push him, that he was working on it.

"But Kai, the rent's not paid, your doctor bills alone are huge, the car payment's due, and the phone bills are over a thousand dollars."

He flicked open his eyes.

Rising from the couch and poking his finger in my face, he scowled, "Why are you always pushing me? If it wasn't for you, I'd be able to get some work done, but you drain me. You provoke me." His face grew hot and red but his eyes were languid and watery.

I pressed my hands together, half pleading and half praying. "I don't mean to push, but you're so secretive about money."

"You don't trust me," he hollered. Beads of sweat formed on his face, giving him the complexion of a hot tomato. "You've never trusted me." He snapped up his car keys. My stomach muscles tightened.

Kai roared at me, his voice almost shaking the windows. "I have friends, though. My AA buddies, they understand me."

I was queasy. He was leaving again.

"I get more respect from them than I get from my own wife."

An alligator played slice and dice on the lining of my stomach. It was happening again. He was going to leave me.

"If we're not paying the bills, it's your fault," he fumed, grabbing up his duffel bag, still packed from the hospital.

I tried to swallow, but the bitter taste wouldn't go away. "What's my fault? What did I do? Kai, tell me." Panic set in. I started to cry. I felt dizzy.

Looking bloated as a Macy's parade balloon, he grabbed papers off his desk. "You just don't know when to quit," he bellowed, jabbing his finger at my face.

Hugging his appointment book to his chest, he bolted out the door. "You're sick, you crazy bitch," he cursed at me over his shoulder as he slid into his Cadillac. "I'm finished.

With you. With life. With everything." And he drove away.

Chaos to crisis, my life ricocheted like a ping-pong ball. Kai held all the checks, all the credit cards. His name was on the bank account. No cash in the house. Rent overdue. Bills piled up. And Kai was gone again. Threatening suicide again. I played the argument over and over: Why did I have to ask about the rent? I shouldn't have provoked him. Next time, I'll keep quiet. Next time, I'll be better.

I rested my head on the dining room table and fell asleep. When the sun came up the next morning, I found myself still at the table, studying the marbling in the wood—the tight knots, the deep whorls bleeding into currents of troubles, rivers of misery forming eddies and puddles, breaking into channels and disappearing into an endless clutter of disconnections.

The night settled in again and still I sat, staring into the dark. If he doesn't come back this time what will I do? Where will I go? No energy to think, to get up, to eat, to walk. None at all. I tried to pray, but I had stopped loving God. What was He to me—the corruptible God of preachers, the God who betrays, heartless as stone. The God who abandons. The slick, glib God of politicians. The God who manipulates. I wanted nothing to do with that God. I wanted to be unborn, not born again. I wanted to be unmarried, not married to a drunk.

It had been more than twelve hours since Kai drove away, leaving me with the mess of our lives. My father's tapes, strewn across my desk, reminded me of life, his life, living apart from my own, his voice undeterred by the present. We were soldiers, my father and I, fighting battles in losing wars. It all looked so hopeless.

I was tired, wearied to the muscles of my heart, and my thoughts turned dark: the Coronado Bridge. I would stop the car in mid-span, careful that no one was coming in either direction. It would be night. I'd walk to the edge and scoot over the barrier. I'd sit on the barricade and watch the water mesmerize me from below, beckoning an end, promising relief. There would be no sound but the wind licking at my face and hair. I wouldn't be afraid. It would be an easy little slip off the ledge, a simple movement, quite graceful really, so subtle yet immensely powerful, letting go of mighty earth. Effortless farewell. In one sweet fluid moment, arms outstretched like one of my father's statues, I'd fly away. Weightless. Floating. Wind rushing. Release. Would I regret it? In my last second of consciousness, would I struggle? In the final instant, would I clutch at the air to undo that little slip from the edge? Would I grapple for the ledge so far above me, the ledge where earth and life were linked? Or would I fall . . . and in one shattering flash of obscurity . . . be free.

My mother came to mind. And Paul. How to explain that I gave up, couldn't take it, lost my nerve. That life got too tough. That I couldn't keep my marriage together. That I let Christians push me over the edge. What about my father? He sank into freezing snow but kept moving. He endured scorching heat and insane thirst and lived. How could I be part of his blood and guts and be such a coward? The moment passed and the vision of ending my life faded.

I may have lost God, but I still had Kai. I had to believe in him. When he lied about money and the big deals he was making, I wanted to feel assured. When he lied about the pills and the booze, I wanted to disbelieve my eyes. When he raged at me, shaking the very foundations, I wanted him to love me. When he left me, I wanted him back. It had to be my fault, or I'd see the truth and it would mean the end of us. I didn't want the truth.

I just had to be better.

I found solace in my father's stories by playing his tapes in the background of my long days and nights. His tapes charred the edges of my unhappiness into feelings of guilt over my self-pity. My struggles were trivialized against his suffering. Even in death, his life loomed larger than my own. For every bit of my pain, he endured a thousand times more. For every one of my miseries, his tapes reminded me how little I knew of true suffering. His descriptions of Dachau tormented me, the rancid odors of the chimneys assaulted my senses, and the terrible man called the Butcher waited for me in the dark:

The burning point of metal under my thumb held my body up. For a split second, I didn't feel anything, sort of numb, as though my body tried to understand what was happening. Then adrenaline blasted through me. I lost my breath. And then, pain, intense, fiery pain!

"Would you like to talk now?" The Butcher lifted up on the locked pliers and slowly peeled back the nail from my thumb.

Every wretchedness in my father's past minimized my own in equal measure. Blinded from my own needs, the force of his life roared in my ears. With little else to do, I was compelled to write down his stories.

I am still in Dachau. I am in the Nazis' hands.

Sticky . . . blood over my face . . . sticky over my mouth. Blood running out of my nose. Bruises all over my body. Dizzy. I remember now, the beating…But why am I here in this small place? The bitter cold woke me up.

As I tried to move, I realized my body was frozen to the concrete floor. Little by little, using my hands and fingers, I tried to peel my skin off the floor, to make some movement, little by little, I stripped my flesh from the floor. Skin was cold. No heat in my body, none at all. No muscles in me. Only bones and skin after these months of starvation. Nothing left of me. Only my brain, shrinking, or was I losing my mind?

Gradually, bit by agonizing bit, I peeled myself from the floor. With gigantic efforts I tore my skin off the cement . . . Bleeding again. Drops of water coming from above. Freezes on the ground. Struggle to my feet. Shivering. Dizziness overwhelming me. Head full of noise. Strained to look around in the dark. Fumbling against walls . . . narrow little chamber, about three feet square or less. To my horror, I realized this was in the death chamber. Only dead bodies go out of here!

I could only write in short spurts; the stories were too brutal and my energy too weak. But between bouts with Kai, I worked on my father's book, transcribing the tapes, digging into research. I wrote to the Polish Olympic Committee, to get the exact records of my father's accomplishments in 1936. Finally, a letter arrived, but it brought only disappointment, reading in part, ". . . the files of our Committee say nothing about Mr. Rylko's participation in the Winter Olympic Games in 1936." I concluded they had incomplete information, lost files during the war. Everything burned and destroyed. I would have to write to Stockholm, Sweden, and get the full record of 1936 from the International Olympic Committee.

Each night I transcribed his story, fulfilling the promise we made to each other those many years ago. "One day I will tell my story and one day you will write it." This became our bond, a joint effort of genetics, but this time I was the sculptor and he the stone. He supplied the fiber and grit; I crafted the form. Through long days and late nights, I chiseled his words into chapters and carved out the sinews of his book. Forgetting my pities, I lost myself in the merciless world of my father and the power of his life.

As long as there is a bit of strength in me, I will fight. As long as there is the slightest chance to fight or escape, I will. I won't give in! To give in was stupid, that was my theory. God gave us brains and free will. You can die, but if you want to live, fight for it.

ANGELS

SOMETIMES, IN GOD'S SILENCE, THERE COME angels. Two angels in my case and not easy to see because they came while I was clouded by despair, but they persevered. The first angel came disguised as a cashier at Safeway, when hunger finally claimed me.

Suzanne, the friendly checkout lady, smiled. Everyone in the San Diego area knew me from my years on radio and television before CBN, and I had just been featured on the cover of *San Diego Woman* magazine, proclaiming "Danuta's Back in Town!"

"You okay?" she asked, putting the bread in a paper bag.

"Yes. Fine." I grabbed my purchases and fled the store.

That afternoon, the sudden sound of the doorbell echoed through the empty house. Resentful and suspicious of life's imposition on my long wake, I opened the door and sunshine flooded in. It was Suzanne.

"Hi," she said. "I thought you might want to go for a walk on the beach." In her forties, she still wore her hair in a ponytail that pumped up and down as she spoke. Her neatly creased white shorts seemed sharp enough to cut meat and her spotless sneakers glowed in contrast to her tanned legs. I had nothing in common with this woman. Go for a walk? Was she kidding? I was too busy to prattle on with someone in crispy white shorts and gleaming skin. I told her I was busy. She said she'd come by tomorrow instead. I nodded, just to make her go away.

Later that night, a police car crawled by the house, slowing by the front door, blinking blood-red brake lights, signaling danger, warning of doom. Solomon, our golden retriever, nuzzled my hand. *Please don't stop at my door! Don't tell me Kai is dead!* I sat on the floor, watching the car. The dog licked my face as the patrol rolled by. The angel of death passed over my house.

I fell asleep next to the dog.

The next afternoon, the doorbell rang again. Suzanne was back with a bag of oranges and bananas and grapes. She plopped the bag in my arms. "So, how about that walk?"

When I told her I couldn't find my shoes, she said she could help me find them and pushed past me into the house, returning with a pair of sandals she found in the kitchen.

Leading me by the arm and into her car, she had me walking along Coronado Beach within minutes. It was a gloomy June day in San Diego. A gray plasma of fog hugged the land and sea. Suzanne started jogging down the beach. So I jogged. I didn't like it. I was tired. But I wasn't going to be the first one to stop.

"So," she puffed easily between strides, "how you doing?"

"Okay," I said, determined to keep up with her.

"I guess I'm asking because you seem so sad." She was ahead of me a bit and her hair swung in the easy rhythm of her gait. She was so damn cheerful, so chirpy, so pulled together. What was I doing pounding flatfooted on a foggy beach with someone like her?

"I'm fine," I grunted.

She stopped and turned. "You're not okay," she said.

I lugged to a stop, breathless, out of shape, dragging the whole world behind me. "No. I'm not okay. I'm not okay. Is that what you want me to say? Are you satisfied now?" I was half screaming, half crying, and totally lost. Suzanne threw her arms around me. My isolation ended there, sobbing in the arms of an angel wrapped around me in the fog.

As days went by, Suzanne became a trusted friend, confiding about the struggles she endured as a young girl with an addicted parent. Every day, Suzanne showed up at my house, and we jogged on the beach together. I talked. She listened. I was able to move again and breathe fresh air; I felt rejuvenated.

And I played the tapes again with my father's stories.

My father didn't have mundane worries. He befriended the mountains and the cold in his life. In one of the tapes he described how he and his brother had just escaped from a labor camp. It was 1941 and Dad was only twenty-four when they crossed the Pyrenees, freezing, hungry, and lost:

> *The Pyrenees were beautiful, and terrifying. To understand mountains, you must take them as they are. No matter how much you love them, you have to give them respect. Don't expect too much from them, and they will cooperate with you, in their way.*
>
> *We started up the mountain, in rough, deep snow, climbing from one peak to another. The first night, we dug a hole in the snow against a cliff. Tree branches made a shelter from the wind. Food would last two days, enough to take us to our next safehouse.*
>
> *On our second day of waist-deep snow, there was still no house. The climbing became steeper. And exhausting. That night, under the shelter of tree branches, we built a small fire to warm our hands, still confident we would find the house. A snowstorm came up, blowing and twisting around us, forcing us to dig out our hole several times during the night.*

The storm continued into the third day and we tried clearing it by climbing higher, but after two hours, the weather grew worse. We decided to stay put and made another shelter. There was no point in fighting nature.

The morning of the fourth day we ate the last of our sandwiches, sitting in our hole, watching for a break in the sky. The storm sounded like a tornado, roaring through the trees, blasting between the cliffs, dark, bleak, and terrifying. We tied scarves around our necks and ears, protecting the circulation of blood to the brain. It was old mountain wisdom. Our faces could be frostbitten, but that wouldn't kill us.

By the morning of the fifth day, we climbed again, but by noon we knew we were lost. Mountains! How much I love them! How much I hated them now! Our stomachs ached for food. My brother half-joked, "John, it looks like we'll be eating bark soon."

"You know, Stephen, you joke now, but by morning, I'm making you breakfast."

The bark from trees is sort of nourishing: not too sweet, somewhat mild, and sometimes bitter. In the morning of our sixth day, I cut the bark from a spruce tree with my pocket knife, and scratched at the softer, cambium layer, rolled it into small balls, and baked them like marshmallows on a stick. They sizzled and boiled and gave the stomach something to do.

That day we scrambled, and climbed, sinking in the snow up to our waist, with no end in sight, getting weaker. Crawling on our knees and elbows. If only we could find a road, we could follow it deep into Spain! We lived on those hopes, weak, cold, and disoriented, stumbling and pulling each other along in the snow.

I thank God for the ordinary, little spruce tree. We baked it, we chewed it, we sucked it, and it helped us live. Sometimes we cut off small bits of a bush, like a deer, sucking the juice out of it, spitting out the hard parts. We ate snow for water. But we were starving, and getting colder. And we lost track of the days.

Finally, we staggered onto a narrow road. Limping downhill, we saw two soldiers ahead. One pointed his rifle at us and yelled "Alto." Standing in the snow with our hands in the air, we laughed. "Spain, John," Stephen sighed. "We made it."

Two weeks later, Kai came home with flowers, never mentioning the argument, or his suicide threats. I didn't say anything about it either. He said he spent the time in Las Vegas, hoping to win big money in a poker game. I didn't say we couldn't afford to gamble. Or worse, how much did you lose? I didn't tell him how I endured the terrifying long days and nights waiting to learn of his death. And although I felt angry, I apologized for making him mad.

My second angel found her way into my life through every objection and obstacle I could throw at her. Though we hadn't met back in Virginia Beach, Tilly had been a student at CBN University, graduating with a master's in theology, the same time I was on *The 700 Club*. She introduced herself to us at a restaurant in San Diego and told us her mother had a dream that she and I would one day be great friends. Oh brother, I thought, just what I need, a Christian fan with a mother's dream for a best friend.

Tilly was a perfect size 6 and had blonde hair that fell like a waterfall to her waist. Though she was stunning, she seemed unaffected by her beauty, wearing no make-up, and tossing her hair from her face as if her beauty bothered her. She said she worked with a gold jeweler in town and talked breezily with Kai about bracelets and chains. I brushed her off as a gushing young woman probably steeped in religious dogma. When Kai gave her our address and telephone number, I grumbled that I wanted no starry-eyed theology student who might question me about why I left *The 700 Club* and how I felt about Jesus today. Nevertheless, at Kai's invitation, she dropped by the house half a dozen times, trying to make friends.

But I didn't have time for friends. Crisis strung out my life and wired me with worry: keeping Kai sober, hiding from bill collectors, and fixing on the next disaster. But the day came when Tilly and I came to terms during my umpteenth attempt at saving Kai.

I found him unconscious. Unable to wake him, I searched the house, frantic for clues. I found the empty bottle of antidepressants under his desk. A Big Gulp cup half-filled with Coke. The empty vodka bottle on the floor. I called an ambulance and his AA sponsor, a woman named Joyce, who joined me two hours later at his bedside in the detox ward.

Seeing us together, Kai said, "Two beautiful women standing over me. How lucky can a guy get?"

Was I angry, frustrated, tired, scared? I couldn't identify any emotion at this point, so I smiled.

"You've been a shit, Kai," Joyce scowled.

Another call to Kai's boss at work, another lie about his heart. Deferring visitors to save his reputation. Once more, I lied my way through the entire ordeal. But that didn't stop Tilly. She wove her way through my pretenses and ducked my deceits and stood there in the substance abuse ward clutching balloons and flowers. Ragged from nervous energy and lack of sleep, I exploded. "How dare you. I told you on the phone he was not supposed to have visitors."

She tried to apologize, saying she didn't know he was an addict, that she only wanted to help, that she brought flowers. She gulped down tears and said, "Why won't you let me be your friend?"

"I don't need friends. I have this." I pointed to Kai, fast asleep in his room. "That's all I can handle right now, okay?"

The sunny bouquet of daisies in her hand was a sad antithesis to her tear-streaked face. A contrast of hope and despair, she seemed locked in a conflict she neither deserved nor anticipated. I tried justifying my frustration. "It's just that it's hard and it's personal. I'm trying to protect him, protect us."

She nodded, tears now dripping off her chin.

I felt as miserable as she looked and plunked her flowers in Kai's water pitcher. Here was someone who wanted only to give, and there was Kai, who was always taking. Why was I angry with her? This wasn't her fault.

"You want to go get something to eat?" she asked, wiping tears with the back of her hand.

"You don't quit, do you?" At this point, I almost felt like laughing. "Come to think of it, I haven't eaten since yesterday."

"Then let's go make some pasta," Tilly said, flashing a radiant smile.

I felt as hungry for companionship at that moment as I did for food.

In God's silence there come angels, breaking down walls of isolation, opening windows to air and light, waking me from my comatose life.

A change was coming on.

THE RAPTURE

I DID NOT PLAN MY METAMORPHOSIS. IT evolved in me, as naturally as a seed becomes a flower. Without effort or intention, I was becoming that which I already was. Like a fist unfolding to an open palm, I released my life to its own care. Now, buffered by friendship and absorbed in writing my father's life, I turned to my own life. In spite of the battles with Kai's alcoholism, balance and calm resumed their lease with me and the sun felt warm again against my skin.

The change began innocently enough, the way all obsessions do. Tilly and I started riding bicycles. We rode around town for exercise and fresh air, enjoying our comradery, and at times, our competitiveness. One mile led to another. Bicycling made us feel strong and able. My depression lifted with each invigorating outing. Tilly also enjoyed her newfound strength, and soon bicycling became something we had to do.

Within a few weeks we were riding thirty and forty miles, all over the county. We were biking demons, who didn't know diddly about biking. We didn't wear gloves, and I rode with the toe clips upside down, scratching the road with every rotation of the pedal. I didn't like the idea of locking my feet into pedals. And those cycling outfits! The helmets were dorky, and the pants were padded in strange places. We didn't carry food, water, or tools. Didn't know how to change a flat. Our arms cramped from single-position handle bars, our hands were calloused, our feet went numb, and our bottoms were killing us. We wore little sun tops and we got burned and blistered. We loved every minute of it. Besides, biking took me away from my troubles with Kai.

Eventually our bodies and our bikes taught us everything we needed to know. Gloves relieved the numbness in our hands; toe clips improved our efficiency using the pedals. Our legs taught us that peddling faster in a low gear was less fatiguing than a slow cadence in a high gear. Padding made all the difference in all the right places. We discovered oranges and nuts made us queasy and Fig Newtons and bananas gave us energy.

On any day we could be found at bike shops, covered with road grime, lugging flat tires and crooked handlebars and asking endless questions about bikes, brakes, and tool kits. We learned how to change our own tires, how to straddle the seats, not sit on them, to spin the pedals, not push them, and to ride in a straight, predictable line. Our enthusiasm spiked with every new bike trail and book; we talked incessantly about longer and longer rides. We biked with a gritty, lung-burning, muscle-aching intensity.

Biking brought deliberateness to my life and a ripening spiritual curiosity. My thoughts rambled as I rode. Why, I wondered, could brain surgeons create a spiritual experience in a patient by stimulating a certain fold in the brain? Did that mean God was all in my head? Or was that brain fold there for a reason? I thought about Joseph Campbell, the great mythologist who said the meaning of life was the *experience* of being alive. That rang so true with me; I felt that rapture when I rode my bicycle. I had discovered the simple joys of being alive. That's when the idea of a long-distance tour took root.

In a bike shop one day, we ran across a book called *Bicycle the Pacific Coast*, outlining a ride from Canada to Mexico, over two thousand miles, the entire length of Highway 101. The maps showed how to ferry across Puget Sound, circle the Sunshine Coast of British Columbia and Vancouver Island, ferry and bike through the San Juan Islands, and back to Washington, along the Hood Canal to Highway 101 and then south, along the coast of Oregon and California, through San Francisco, Monterey, Big Sur, San Diego, and finally cross the border into Mexico. Forty days and forty nights of camping along the Pacific Ocean. We bought the book.

We devised a campaign to raise money for Coronado schools by getting pledges for every mile we biked. Within two months, the bike tour came alive. Businesses in town donated equipment, new bikes, and even a flight to Washington. As my enthusiasm grew for the trip, Kai seemed to get better, too, with no relapses, regular AA meetings, and a consistent work schedule. Perhaps he was relieved that I no longer focused on his problems, no longer asked him about money or the rent, or monitored his sobriety. We made a bargain. I'd let go of my "stranglehold" on him, and he'd stay sober.

"You'll see," he said. "When you come back from the bike trip, I'll have everything under control."

The night before our journey Tilly and I arranged the personal items for our trip into two piles, our Want Pile and our Need Pile. The Want Pile was huge: a hair dryer, shampoo and conditioner, twelve pairs of socks, a dress, sandals, pantyhose, dress shirts, make-up kits, books, four pairs of riding pants, four t-shirts, hiking boots, underwear, earrings, sweaters, silverware, a camera, a gas lantern, a radio, a big knife, and a big pillow.

What we needed, and in fact ended up with, were two pairs of socks, two riding outfits, a light wind jacket, one small bar of soap, a toothbrush, half a tube of toothpaste, one can of Mace, Maybelline dark-brown, waterproof mascara, and one slim, paperback book, Carlos Castaneda's *The Teachings of Don Juan: A Yaqui Way of Knowledge*. All of it fit into gallon-sized Ziploc bags.

We packed our tent, sleeping bags, first aid kit, ground cover, mattress pads, one cooking pot, and a small butane stove on our bicycles. We each carried forty-five pounds, an amazing show of how little we needed to live. But I would have been a bit happier with the big pillow I reluctantly tossed aside.

By the second week in September the Pacific Northwest still clung to the last remnants of summer. The days were warm, and the nights were cool. My brother Michael, living in Seattle with his wife, Christy, took us to our first campsite along the Olympic Peninsula, just a few yards from a bluff and the Straits of Juan de Fuca. Tilly and I erected our tent with the knack of two girls at a pajama party. My brother watched as the pup tent popped up on its wire mounts.

When my brother asked about the tent—a bit too casually, I thought—I told him we bought it from the Junior Department of Sears, the lightest tent they had, weighing only 3.2 pounds. At the time, weight meant more to us than function. That would become a problem down the road.

"And what's this?" Michael pinched the cap on top of the tent.

"It's the rainfly," I said. "It keeps rain from coming in through the air vent at the top." Mike knew what a rainfly was—he was an experienced camper and hiker, a water scientist for the Environmental Protection Agency, had been around the woods and waters most of his career. Why was he laughing?

"Danuta," he said, barely containing his giggles, "they call this the great Pacific Northwest for a reason. You have to have respect. And this," he tugged the baseball-cap-sized rainfly, "this, is not respect." He sat on a log, fully involved in his laughter and giggles. Christy howled with laughter as well. I looked at the rainfly, the size of a doily. It would hardly keep the tent dry in the event of rain.

"Well," I said, "it doesn't rain in California."

More laughter.

"You bought a backyard toy," Michael teased.

Before they left us to our own defenses, Mike and Christy loaned us a large blue tarp from their van. They showed us how to hoist it over the tent and secure it to nearby tree trunks with bungee cords.

"The definition of rain in the great Pacific Northwest is when raindrops bounce when they hit the ground. Good luck," Michael said, just before they drove off.

That night, Michael's tarp saved our butts. The rain not only bounced, it ricocheted against our little tent, puddling against our sleeping bags and dripping on our heads. By 4 a.m. we were sleepless, wet, and cold as a blustery wind blew off the Pacific. It was still so dark I held a penlight in my teeth to go potty behind a bush. Since I wore a one-piece riding outfit, I had to strip completely naked. It was hard to pee with a wet wind licking at my back.

When we finally broke camp and rolled down the road on our bikes, Tilly hollered behind me above the whine of the storm, "Your bags are on backwards."

I wondered why my pedals were catching on the panniers with each go-round.

"Now we're going to be late for the ferry," Tilly complained as we stopped.

"Well, go on ahead then. Don't wait for me, damnit!" I yelled back, as I unloaded and reloaded the bags on my bike.

"Don't holler at me," Tilly said. "It's not my fault that we didn't buy a bigger tent."

We rode furiously for twenty miles to Port Angeles hungry, cold, wet, and tired. So much for our first day. Our sour moods turned sweeter, however, on the ferry for Victoria. So much oxygen and sunshine. Islands, trees, and mountains clustered around us in picture postcard scenes. We had espresso and scrambled eggs in the dining room and napped on the deck in the warm sunshine.

Our emotions swung wildly from minute to minute. Just as we traveled with minimal personal gear, we traveled with minimal pretenses. With so much physical and psychic energy expended in getting from one place to another, there was no energy for resentments, no time for manipulation, no space for pouting. If we were angry we yelled, if we were happy we laughed. Every emotion floated upon the surface to be acknowledged and handled.

We used our energy for the hills. In British Columbia, we rode from a little native Indian town called Sechelt to the ferry at Earls Cove. Between those two points rose forty-one miles of narrow winding roads and hills that seemed as steep as pyramids, obstacles as big as the problems I left behind. After hours of grinding up those inclines I noticed a particular pattern to the obstacles we encountered: just before the rise, the pace slows and the world stills. The bike creaks and breath comes hard. Inches creep by under my wheels. Halfway up, I want to stop. Think I can't make it. The bike wobbles. Then I hear my father: *And inside me, I felt something rioting, No! Not yet! As long as I am alive . . . as long as I can move . . . I tried to refuse to die.*

My father never quit. No! Not yet! Can't quit. Dig deeper. And I keep going. And with the effort comes transcendence, when body and soul sing the same song: "Press into the slope. Feel the heat. Suck the air. Listen to your lungs. Forget the sweat that stings your eyes. Patience, patience. Don't push the pedals, spin. Relax your grip, loosen your shoulders. Lean into the grade. Sink into the mass. Feel the pulse of your wheels. Breathe." And I roll uphill until the mountain benevolently gives way, shouldering me on its summit.

On the other side of every effort comes a little grace, the gift of completion, when the difficulty is done and the task eases into nonresistance and the mountain shifts to a downhill stretch of elegance. I fly with effortless speed. In a respite of windy minutes I sail the zephyrs. I am wind. I am sister to Mariah. I am the blustery wet Chinook and the hot dry Santa Ana. I am God's breath.

Would all obstacles in my life roll out to such exquisite moments if I stopped straining to overcome them? Could my difficult marriage, my search for God, and the approval of my father be easier to gain if I stopped trying so hard? Over the ridges of this world, I learned to merge with the hurdles in my life and to seek the effortless graces of their downhill sides.

Two hundred miles into our trip, I bonded with our little leaky tent and enjoyed starting campfires with no paper. I felt like a little girl again, living in a tent in Michigan, watching the campfire spit and sizzle red sparks into the black sky. How petty and complex I had made my life since then, how filled up with so many nonessentials. I didn't need to live an evaporated life in a bad marriage. In the wilderness of British Columbia I lived a big life. Trivialities blew away on the wind between the islands and the ferries. Air, sky, and water took the place of worry, grief, and concern. I peddled toward meaningfulness.

Killer whales, flashing their black and white patches in the sun, breached alongside our ferry boats. On San Juan Island, a crash of crows robbed us of our breakfast of Cornish pasties while we showered nearby. Then thousands of wasps descended on the crumbs that the crows left behind. In a matter of minutes, a bunch of birds and insects devoured our spread of baked goods. Nature wasted nothing. And while I loved the killer whales, I hated the nuisance of those crows and wasps, but after battling them for days we simply learned to accept them. In an odd turn, when we stopped fighting them, they stopped pestering us.

Before long, I felt connected to everything. I shared the same air and the same life as the birds and beasts. Prowling for a campsite in twilight, howling at the moon, feeling mud between my toes, I was part wolf—a wolf woman. Whales, wasps, or wolves, we all shared a pulse of electrons and orbits of atoms, the same double helix of DNA, the same dust. And in the dust, God was there and there was God in all things. All, experiencing the rapture of being alive.

THE RIDE

THE EXPERIENCES OF SWEAT AND SMELLS, OF sights and sounds cleansed me from the inside out. Not only did my body breathe and cool with the sweat of my brow, but the toxic portions of my life lathered out of me as well. Whatever chemicals produced withdrawal and fear, rejection and paralysis, dissolved within me and were creating something new. And if I was becoming a new creation now, what was I before?

In the world but not of it, that was the admonition of my born again past, to separate body from soul. But that dismemberment leached me of a vital kinship to the wonders around me. Sweeping down the coastline on a bicycle, in the eye of nature, I honed a new relationship between the world and me. I was not just in the world, I was part of it, flesh and spirit welded together in wholeness. Little comforts completed me: hot showers, dry socks, the crackle of the campfire on cold nights, the blue companion of the ocean, the blackberries tantalizing us along country roads. Wild as the wasps, and as strong as the mountains we climbed, it was not surprising that Tilly and I wanted an outward symbol of our transformation.

In the Castaneda book we brought with us, the old Indian shaman, Don Juan, taught that all things have meaning and purpose, and nothing should be taken for granted. Peace and patience would reveal the spirits around us and the powers hidden there, even in feathers. When we found two large eagle feathers lying side-by-side on the ground at a campsite on Orcas Island, we knew it was a sign.

I remembered a story my father told of the Tartars blazing across Poland on horses. The small but ferocious warriors wore feathers in their hair to panic their opposition. Though frequently outnumbered, the flapping and rattling of a Tartar charge terrified men and horses until defending forces broke ranks and ran. No army could withstand the power of a thousand feathers.

Tilly and Danuta, flying down the coast.

Now, we had earned the gift of the eagle, power and protection. From that day on we wore the eagle feathers. They captured the power of the wind and made great flying, flapping, Tartar sounds on the downhill glides. Now, we were wolves and warriors.

How was it possible that this world was here, all the time, available, livable, doable, breathable, while at home I perished in a dark world between four walls? How could I, the wolf-woman flying down the sloping vistas of the Pacific Coast wearing feathers in her hair, be the same woman who fantasized about flying off the Coronado Bridge?

While my reconstruction was well underway, Tilly experienced her own transformations. It was hard to believe the woman who pedaled with me was the same clouded girl she showed me in an early picture of her family. The color photograph, taken twenty-one years before, portrayed a pallid family, standing on their front porch in Spartanburg, South Carolina. Her mother stands grim and square as though she is prepared to repel any onslaught, her hair packed in tight curls, her lips as thin as wires. Tilly's father scowls at the camera giving the appearance of a man who is hard to please and seldom approves of anything. Tilly is nine years old. Her ponytail is so severe it seems to ache. Her ashen skin blends with her pale cotton dress. Dark circles target her eyes, making them appear like two bruises in her head. Her smile is terrifying. It is an unnatural light in the dark gathering; it plows across her face like a ditch, unreal, unworldly, wishing. Her smile is a lie.

There was nothing to smile about. Tilly's father was wretchedly depressed. He would not allow laughter or light in the house. "Shhh," her mother used to say. "Be quiet, your father's sick." The shades were always drawn as he lay on the couch, agonized by headaches and sleep that never refreshed him. "A dancin' foot and a praying foot don't grow on the same leg," he would say, and she was forbidden to play, or dance, or sing. "Knees are for praying, not for showing," he scolded when she wore a pair of shorts on a hot and humid Carolina day. And so, Tilly grew up, a flower in waiting, waiting for her spring, and the soft rains of freedom. Waiting, for this bike ride.

On Orcas Island we found a resort with a steaming hot tub sheltered in the trees, high on the cliffs overlooking a sheltered bay. A dozen other hikers and climbers were enjoying the water under a full moon the night Tilly and I showed up. It took no time at all for me to zip off my clothes and jump in. Tilly stood staring at the bathers in the water. Then, slowly, she unstrapped her riding suit and let it fall to the ground. She disrobed as if casting off old skin. Naked and new, she slipped into the water.

"I've never been nude in front of strangers before," she whispered. "And now I'm buck naked in front of fifteen people all at once." Tilly's smile was radiant.

Food was a huge factor on this journey. We ate with impunity. Our tanks were always empty. We ate for energy and metabolized every calorie. The more we ate, the faster we rode. Food drove our bodies like jet engines into a forward thrust, powering us up unbelievable slopes, propelling us to our next destination. Food was always on our mind.

One morning, Tilly and I pulled into a café outside a small Canadian harbor town where fishing boats bobbed in a tiny marina and men in orange waders hauled nets and cargo back and forth. The café was empty except for one man in the corner, smoking a pipe. Tilly and I ordered breakfast: a large bowl of oatmeal with a stack of pancakes, a stack of toast, coffee, a three-egg Spanish omelet with home fries, with another tall stack of pancakes, another order of toast, more coffee, a slice of lingonberry pie with ice cream, still more coffee, and one last stack of toast. Each.

The man who had been sitting in the corner sidled up to us and took the pipe out of his mouth. "I've never seen anybody eat that much food in all my days," he said. "Who *are* you girls?"

We never really understood how important food was to us until we pushed our limits one day and rode ninety miles without eating. The experience was brutal. After riding fifty miles, we pulled into the little town of Montesano, Washington. A sign there read "Westport 30 Miles." We felt good and decided to push on to Westport. Big mistake. We hadn't eaten enough. After seven solid hours of riding, I bonked—a funny word that cyclists use to describe hitting the wall, but a devastating phenomenon. Carbohydrates no longer powered my muscles. Having used up its reserves, my body started feeding on itself.

Although the road signs said the town was thirty miles down the road, it meant the town limits. The *real* town, with pasta and pie, was another ten miles beyond. Headwinds from the ocean pushed against us, and the road began sloping uphill. I drank some water and my stomach cramped. Eight miles to go. Collagen in my body faded. Three more miles to go, but it might as well have been three hundred. I couldn't think. Cell walls began to collapse. Two miles. I began to cry. Muscle structures gave way to mere muscle memory. My legs went on automatic pilot. I was riding, but didn't know where. I was pedaling, but couldn't feel my feet. One mile. I was literally starving. My hands went numb. Crying, wobbling down the road, blind with pain, I couldn't stop pedaling. Robotic.

Nerve endings fired desperate signals to my body to keep going, keep going or die. I remembered my father's words, "You think about nothing, you think about everything."

I rode right through Westport, past the café, past the stores. I couldn't stop, had to keep going. Tilly rushed after me and pulled me off the bike. "Food, Danuta, it's food, right over there." She helped me walk my bike back to the café. Although Tilly was also terribly hungry, she wasn't bonking. In the restaurant I wept uncontrollably and asked the waitress to bring me some bread. She pulled her pencil from behind her red curly hair and poised it over her order pad. "Will that be toast or plain? Wheat, rye, or sourdough?"

I just looked at her, ashen, critically hungry, collapsing before her eyes. "Right. Bread," she said, and hurried two enormous garlic loaves to the table. After a meal of seafood linguini, bread, baked potatoes, salad, fruit pie and espresso, I started to feel conscious again. Outside of childbirth and a motorcycle accident, I had never felt so physically traumatized. I later learned that had I gone for very much longer without food, the muscles of my heart would have eventually buckled and I could have died. I was not invincible. Even wolves need food. I had collapsed into my newfound joy and had become careless. That experience warned me to know my limitations.

How many times had I bonked in my other life off the bicycle? I bonked when my father disowned me. I bonked when I gave Matthew away. I bonked when Will disappeared. I bonked in college from loneliness. I bonked at CBN when God walked out on me. I bonked every time Kai bonked. How many times had I exhausted my reserves and become numb and desperate? In my real life, my heart collapsed one fiber at a time and I responded without seeing, reacted without feeling, and kept going blindly ahead. Where were my reserves then? Why couldn't I see how hungry I had become?

Here, on my bicycle, in the rain and shine, feeling the seasons change on my skin, having no expectations but only wonders about the next bend, there was no margin for self-pity, no room for mistakes. I met life on its own terms and it offered me the treasures of introspection, challenge, and self-assessment, wonder in the small things, gratefulness for the simple things. On my lovely bicycle, the more I experienced life, the closer I came in contact with my true face. By embracing my wild nature, I had overcome my stunted sensibilities. Wisdom and care would guard my fragrant new life.

At our next campsite, we followed behind sixteen other cyclists who were also riding from Victoria to Mexico, except they had four support vehicles, a mechanic, two cooks, checkpoints, dinners in restaurants, and they carried no bags on their bikes. When we pulled into camp completely self-contained, one of the other cyclists whistled and said, "Jeez, you girls look *awwwwesome*." Yeah, we were awesome. We had ventured out alone, under our own steam, and met the challenges of the road on our own terms.

Michael was right about respecting Mother Nature. We learned that lesson when the weather turned against us fifty-three miles north of the Astoria Bridge and the state line of Oregon. The first storm that day seemed light enough to venture forward because we had our super-duper-micro-filament-rain-resistant-one-hundred-and-fifty-dollar jackets. Four miles later we were soaked to the bone. Forty-mile-per-hour headwinds pelted us with driving sheets of rain that stung our bare legs and blasted our vision. Fortunately, we had two five-cent black plastic trash bags that we tugged over our technologically superior rain jackets for wind protection. Ziploc bags covered our shoes snapped tight with rubber bands. A glance at the odometer said we'd only gone eight miles, forty-five to go. There were no homes, no stores, no towns or restaurants, no barns, no tent clearings in the towering trees that marched right up the road, no shelter of any kind. Trying to pedal against the storm was futile. We were wet and dangerously cold. What were we doing out here? Had we completely lost our minds? Were we going to die out here? What the hell. Tilly stuck her thumb out.

A camper whizzed by and then slowed and stopped. By the time we got to it, a young, marine fisheries observer named Tracy was standing on the tailgate, which was invitingly open. He stood with his hands on his hips above us as we withered to a stop. "What the hell you boys doin' out here on a day like this?" he said, jumping down. He shoved our bikes into the back, making room next to his coon dog, Ruby. Safely in the shelter of the cab, we threw our helmets off and peeled off our soggy jackets. "Jesus Christ," he said, "you're girls."

"We're bikers," Tilly whimpered.

We were in such bad shape that Tracy took us home to his mother in Cannon Beach. She made clam chowder, gave us dry clothes and warm terry robes. We slept in clean, cozy beds as a second, even fiercer storm from Alaska vented itself upon the roof. The storm so intimidated us that we hid in the house with our Good Samaritans for three days before setting off on the road again. We still had a thousand miles to go.

I called Kai. He sounded so somber, so sad. Why was I so happy? I was moving. For the first time in the five years since I left CBN, I was moving in a direction I controlled. I was centered and focused and powerful. There was nothing I couldn't do, nothing that couldn't be accomplished. Possibilities were endless; there were no boundaries to my spirit, no filters or dilutions, nothing to divert me from the natural rhythms of earth and sky. I was part of the collective consciousness of storms and stones, of wasps and crows. I breathed the wind. I was of one mind, connected to all things, in a stream of simple purity. This was where God had been hiding, all around me, all the time.

As sublime as heaven, the road was also loaded with dangers and they were constant reminders not to take anything for granted. Logging trucks—from a distance they sounded like some great Tyrannosaurus rex charging behind us. The trucks snorted and growled at our heels, and hissed as they thundered past. Sometimes they moved so fast, they swept the air up with them, leaving us in the still eye of a hurricane. And then suddenly the turbulent air swooped in behind, nearly sucking us off our bikes. There was no room to wobble or act unpredictably. Those truckers assumed we would ride a straight line and by god, we did, head down, clutching those handlebars until our knuckles turned white.

I had hours each day to think about riding straight lines. There is solitude in riding a bicycle, hours of meditative pedaling when thoughts seem to murmur from a distance and then become clear. The idea formed in me that when I got home I would have to know where I was going and ride that line straight and true. To have a plan. To know my goal. A sense of destination. Anything less, and my focus would be lost, and I would surrender to the vacuumed rush of life passing me by. I was determined not to let that happen.

WE KNEW WE HAD FINALLY crossed into California even without looking at a map. There was a clear demarcation between sun and storms. North of us was wind, rain, and cold, and to the south, blue skies every day. Soon we crossed the Golden

Gate Bridge, three quarters of the way to San Diego.

Tilly called home from Monterey. She learned one of her best friends had died while scuba diving in the Sea of Cortez. Laura got pinned on the rocks during high tide and drowned. The terrible news hit Tilly hard. That same day signs along the road warned, "Dangerous hills and curves next seventy-four miles." Tilly's concentration was compromised and she wove her bike all over the road and finally wobbled right off the edge at the top of a hill.

I threw my bike down and ran to help her. Her arm was bruised and she was crying as cars and trucks shot by us like bullets. "Tilly, now is not the time to fall apart. Do it later, when we're in camp. You've got to hold it together or you'll get us both killed." I picked up her bike and shoved it towards her.

"I don't need practical safety tips right now," she cried back at me. "I need your sympathy."

"You don't get sympathy while we're both in danger on a busy road with no shoulder. We don't have that luxury. We have to get out of here," I stormed back at her.

We rode silently for the rest of the day. This time, Tilly bonked, emotionally. I felt responsible for the two of us. But why did I have to be so intense? So driven? That night at camp, we sat quietly gazing into the fire. We realized then how focus meant power and without it, we rode with danger.

Focus is power. I had gathered up some tremendous energy on the trip and I kept thinking that maybe I didn't want to go home where I was so powerless in my real life. How does a girl who's half wasp, half crow ever live timidly again?

FORTY DAYS INTO OUR TRIP and we rode into Big Sur where the edge of the continent plunged a thousand feet down to the savage beauty of smoldering surf. Red-tailed hawks and eagles soared the thermals and Stellar's jays darted through castle-sized sequoias. The highway ribboned around ocean bluffs and winds pummeled the headlands relentlessly. Switchback turns dipped and soared with no shoulder to protect us from the cars and trucks that rushed by. In this breathtaking and dangerous terrain I felt most alive. I would never be the same. And the question haunted me, how could I ever go home again?

Wolf Women Tilly and Danuta, and friend, on the California Coast, 1992

Two thousand miles on the odometer and we pulled into Santa Barbara. The pristine wilderness of this coastline gave way to fast cars, dense pockets of civilization, and an increasing sense of caution on and off the road. Glass and scraps of metal and garbage laced the shoulder of the highway through Malibu, Los Angeles, and as we neared San Diego. Single men living out of their cars filled the campsites now. We slept gripping our bike pumps for protection, just in case.

It was the forty-fourth day of travel, our last night on

the road, and our nostalgia was fierce. We sat by the cliffs in South Carlsbad State Beach watching the ocean swallow the sun and mourned our final campfire.

We remembered the day it rained so hard we couldn't light a fire. Wore trash bags on our heads. Had holes in our socks. Bargained chocolate for dry clothes. We howled like wolves remembering the bad days. There were plenty of wonderful, lazy days in the sunshine, but it was the toughest hills, the rainiest days, the harshest winds we reminisced about. As if the worst days were our best.

How could I rejoin a real life with social clamor and politics, the World Series, football, the daily news, and Kai? Would he respond to my discoveries? Would I be able to respond to him? Had he stayed sober? I hoped it wasn't just me who had changed during the past two months. The next day brought us to the Mexican border and a lot of high fives and welcome home celebrations with friends and neighbors.

And then the tough part began.

"Welcome home," Kai said, as he unloaded the packs from my bike. He opened the door, dumped the packs in the hallway, dragging his heels along the floor as if his shoes were too big. "Missed you." His red and runny eyes traveled over me seeking surrender, safety, a place to hide. He hugged me and turned absent-mindedly toward his leather chair. He snapped the TV on with the remote and pulled the footstool up on the recliner. "I'm glad you're back," he said, flipping through the channels.

I stood in the middle of our living room unsure of my direction. I had journeyed into an authentic life, hammered by exhaustion, forged by sun, beaten by wind, and humbled by birds and insects. I had been restored. But what for? To forget the stars and the savor of the night air? To languish by a man whose skin sweats the rancid odor of unprocessed alcohol? And what would I do about the feathers in my hair?

That night I pulled down the covers and climbed into bed. It had been a long time since I slept on a real mattress. As I fluffed the pillow my hand swept over something small and hard. An earring. A tiny pearl for pierced ears. Not mine.

It would take another year, but our marriage collapsed in the glint of that little pearl.

A Fool and a Drunk

THE CERTIFICATE ON THE WALL REFLECTED my distress: Joanne Riser, Substance Abuse and Family Counselor. Failing to recognize my own land mines, I now needed professional help to dig them up. Knowing that, I still resented the excavation of my emotional secrets, so carefully buried in the soil of neglect. I was lonely and angry.

"Why lonely?" Joanne asked.

"Kai took off for Sweden again."

"And why angry?" Joanne's voice was night-air calm.

Where do I begin to explain? Shit. Six months ago on my first day back from the bike trip, when I find another woman's earring in our bed? When Kai stomped off and got drunk when I asked about it? Or last week, when he borrowed money, jumped on a plane to Stockholm with a business class ticket—purchased for five thousand dollars on a day's notice—and we still can't pay the rent? He left all his cares behind for me to wrestle with and unanswered questions about another woman in our bed? You bet I was angry.

Joanne crossed her legs and folded her arms. Her pixie short hair spiked across her head like wind-blown flowers. "He's still drinking, isn't he?"

"Yeah, I guess so." I rubbed my knee.

"You guess so or you know so?"

"Know so." I slapped my thigh in frustration. "Damnit, why can't I be more direct about this?" We talked about denial and why he was in Sweden. Did I believe he was there on business? Yes I did. Denial again. No I didn't. Of course it was classic Kai. But why should I deny what I damn well knew?

I turned to Joanne feeling more confused than ever.

She puckered her lips, in a matter-of-fact sort of way. "Kai's an alcoholic. Always wants a buzz. If not from drinking or drugs, then he'll create chaos. Anything for excitement. Energy. A high. Even destructive. It's drama. As for your denial? How else could you have lived with it?"

"I don't want to live like that anymore." For the first time I locked my gaze straight at her. It felt pretty good to say that out loud. Something definite. I felt my shoulders ease down.

"Truth has that effect," Joanne said. "I have homework for you. Next week bring a list of all the things Danuta wants in her life. Not what Kai wants. What Danuta wants. Got it?" She gave me a look my mother used to give me.

A SHEEN OF SILVER GLANCED off the ocean, piercing the royal blue sky. I sauntered down the beach, in front of the Hotel del Coronado, a turn-of-the-century playground for the rich and famous. Still a seashore jewel, the hotel's stately white verandas and red rooflines echoed of romance. Wallace Simpson spent a summer at "The Del" and stole the heart of the Prince of Wales, dooming his future as King of England. Legend has it Thomas Edison lit the first electric Christmas tree lights here, and on this beach Jack Lemmon frolicked with Marilyn Monroe in the film *Some Like It Hot*. One of my favorite stories from The Del was that L. Frank Baum wrote several books in the Wizard of Oz series here.

It was four o'clock in the afternoon, when the world slowed to the speed of a siesta, when the spangled light would soon coax a sweater in the long afternoon shadows. I left toe impressions in the sand, and flecks of mica stuck to my feet like gold dust. I'd been following my yellow brick road for a long time. What did I want? Courage, passion, wisdom? Dorothy's red shoes and a sense of purpose?

I scrambled over a jetty of boulders where starfish muscled the rocks by the waterline. The air smacked of salt and fish as I stepped through a tangle of netting, broken sand dollars, and crab shells. A jellyfish glistened under some leathery braids of seaweed, its watery tentacles and cap now a thick puddle studded with sand. No brain, no spine, no will of its own, the jellyfish was tossed by a wave, marooned on the shore.

There were people like that. People who say they were pressed by powers beyond their control, pushing them forward, pulling them back, victims of life, tossed about with no say in the matter. People like my father, haunted by his war and scarred by his demons. Like Kai, trapped and struggling against his own hand. Like me, awash with regrets, no choices, no chances. Life wasted. Like me? A cold shiver rolled down my back.

When did I succumb to that philosophy? What day and hour did I surrender? A wasted life was the greatest sin. I didn't want to be a casualty of tides. I was not like my father. Not like Kai. Damn it. I didn't want to suffer by my own hand, to die of self-made wounds. I wanted control of my life. And choices. Most of all, I wanted to be whole, to feel the exhilaration I had on the bike trip. I hadn't lost those lessons and I wanted that feeling again, the experience of being alive.

IN THE MEANTIME, I NEEDED a full-time job. Writing a column for the local paper wasn't enough. Applications to local radio stations fell into black holes. I held garage sales and sold the last few treasures we had, including the dining room table and chairs. I contracted to ghostwrite a book and did some public relations work for a couple of companies, but it still wasn't enough. To make the rent, I sold my car. And to feel like I was getting somewhere, I continued to embrace my father's tapes and one in particular that spoke directly to me:

We drank a lot during the war. Everything got so monotonous. What do you do as soldiers, under the blazing desert sun from above and the glaring sand below, hot as hell, sitting in your tent? What do you do? You drink to pass the time. And you drink on the frontline to forget. Who cares if you're killed when you're drunk?

On one occasion, news came that our supplies had arrived four miles behind the lines. Supplies meant whisky, cigarettes, and gin. There was a corporal in our ranks who spent every penny he had on booze. When he heard the supplies had arrived, he was the first to jump to his feet and offer to go for them. It was dark, but he was anxious for a drink.

I volunteered to go with him.

We wound our way through the minefields on our hands and knees, touching the ground, sweeping between the mines. We crossed the field and ran the rest of the way. When we reached the supply line, there were lots of questions about the front and someone opened a bottle. We were toasting to the memory of this boy who got himself killed, and to the memory of that one who was wounded, and to the memory of those boys who were still alive, toasting glass after glass.

Eventually, we loaded up all the bottles and the cigarettes, but mostly the bottles. Tom stuffed his rucksack and our pockets full of bottles till we could hardly walk. We were both drunk, really drunk. At the minefields, we didn't bother to sweep for mines on our hands and knees, we happily sauntered right through them, to our trenches, untouched. It's true what they say, that a fool and a drunk are always lucky.

It wasn't true. Kai and I had run out of dumb luck years ago.

I had been so consumed with job-hunting, garage sales, and my father's book that I had forgotten to write down What Danuta Wants. Driving to the therapist's office in Kai's Cadillac, I suddenly remembered the list. Tilly was with me that day, sharing the car to run errands. She pulled a pen and paper out of the glove compartment and wrote while I drove and dictated a stream of consciousness of What Danuta Wants.

I veered around a too-slow car in front of me and darted into the fast lane. "I want happiness." I rolled down the window. A marine breeze blew at my hair and my catalogue of desires poured out of me. "Peace, gentleness." I cut into the middle lane, shot around a truck, and swung back into the fast lane. "Where was I?"

"'Time to write,' that's eight," Tilly said.

I rattled off more thoughts as Tilly wrote them down. I pulled off the exit, into the office parking lot, and slipped into a parking space.

"There you go," Tilly said, ticking off the last items. "A home in the country, riding your bike, which makes fourteen things Danuta wants. Better yet, what Danuta *needs*." She handed me the paper. "There's a difference, you know."

IN THE OFFICE, JOANNE ASKED me for the list.

I read it aloud, "I want happiness, passion, hope, choices, time to write my father's book, control of my own life, I want Kai to stay in Sweden, peace, to be in love, a home in the country, to ride my bike, freedom from stress, to plant a garden, to make a difference with my life."

Joanne raised a finger in the air. "Let's go back to the Kai thing for a moment."

I must have looked puzzled.

"Buried, in the middle of your list."

I scanned the list. "I want Kai to stay in Sweden." I blinked at the words. I didn't remember saying that. What would that mean for me? A different life? Having all those other things on my list? Making decisions just for me?

"Sounds pretty selfish," I said. "Kai needs me. He's sixty-six years old and sick."

"Some people don't get better," Joanne said. "You've cared for him for a decade. What's wrong with caring for yourself a little?"

Joanne's words burned in me. Self-sacrifice always came first in my marriage. Anything else sounded just plain wrong. But taking the bike trip was caring for me. Maybe giving myself love wouldn't be all that bad. A few days later I sat down and wrote a letter.

Dear Kai:

While you've been gone I've had some time to think.

I can no longer live on the edge of crisis, chronically suffering from lies, relapses, and anguishes. Living like this steals our soul and saps our strength.

You say you want the comforts of home again, but my love, you leave these comforts regularly.

I paused with my pen in the air. I called him "my love." Did I still love him or was that phrase a habit of longing? He was my husband. I still cared about him. So I must still love him. Or was I fooling myself?

I continued the letter.

You are not dealing with your disease and I can no longer be part of this ping-pong game. Therefore . . .

Therefore what? What does Danuta want? My pen drummed the desk, tap, tap, tap, thinking, thinking. Therefore there must be conditions. There have to be rules. Something tangible.

I have some conditions before you fly home this time.

1) Stay in Sweden. Get counseling there. The treatment there is free for you.

2) Get sober. Stay sober.

3) Have a plan. How can we rebuild our lives?

Do not come home unless you have accomplished these three things.

I reread the conditions. Tap, tap, tap. Counseling, sober up, a plan. How else could we live?

Without these conditions, my dearest, it kills me to say it, but our marriage will be over.

My heart leapfrogged in my chest. Marriage over. Did it really kill me to say it? Letting go—*tap, tap, tap, tap, tap, tap, tap*—counseling, sober up, a plan. A small part of me still believed Kai could pull this off. Still hoped. The larger part of me however . . . I didn't want to finish the thought. This was the last go-round of last conditions. I didn't have another in me.

Ten days later, Kai came home.

Drunk.

ROBIN

OREGON IN JUNE.

Eleven days of rain and counting. Still, a thirty-three-foot trailer in the Oregon drizzle was a refreshing change from the sun-bleached strain of my divorce, bankruptcy, and unemployment in San Diego. Mom, and my brother Rick and his wife, lived in a town called Veneta. Rick offered me his vacant trailer for the summer. My garage sale money gave me time to rest and plan for the future before heading back to San Diego.

Twenty minutes west of Eugene, Veneta was a good place to live while on the way to someplace else. A gateway town, it leads to the Willamette Valley on the east and the Oregon coast to the west. Venetians were rugged, independent, and private individuals. Some lived behind mounds of wild blackberry bushes, poison oak, and mustard-yellow scotch broom, with driveways that wound up long gravel roads. Others resided in modest wood-frame homes perched streetside, but no two houses looked the same. They didn't like their neighbors too close or their business too public. They were farmers and artists, writers and hippies. They grew apples, filberts, and rye grass. Some grew marijuana. They drove pick-ups, SUVs, and tractors.

I liked Veneta, a slow-moving place with a hundred shades of green, where deer and wild turkeys often held up traffic and homemade signs advertised chicken manure and apple cider presses, where rainbows arched the sky like Easter bonnets, promising better days ahead.

Fern Ridge Lake glistened on the town's northeastern edge, a fifteen-square-mile reservoir that held a seasonal inventory of water. In the summer it was the most used recreational body of water in the state. By October, the Army Corps of Engineers drained the reservoir down to a fraction of its maximum size. By winter, it was a landing field for Canada geese as the rains filled the reservoir back to capacity.

Like the geese, I had migrated to this place for a rest. Hope and expectation filled me with each passing rainstorm. Two years since the bike trip, but only months since the divorce, I needed sanctuary from the exhaustive process of dissolving one life and discovering what my next life would be. And it was a chance to connect with my brother, who never really recovered from the time we left him behind in Michigan.

Although he realized, years later, that the choice was his to stay with Dad at the time, he had a rough go of it. Dad often was petulant and moody; he and Rick fought. They came to a terse form of friendship at the end, but it changed Rick. Always a gentle spirit, he harbored resentments he couldn't fully express. His chest barreled with unspoken hurts, and, like my father, he often sought solace in the bottle.

Mom had moved near Rick several years earlier, and she responded well to the Pacific climate and the Douglas-firs. Whatever torments she suffered in Virginia Beach had long since given way to a renewed vigor and enthusiasm working as a county nurse and gardening. Years later, at the age of seventy-seven, she would join the Veneta Fire Department as a First Responder, rescuing hapless travelers whose cars wound up in ditches and herding lost sheep from country roads. When Mom, Rick, and I were together it was mostly congenial, but there was always an underlying wave of unarticulated emotions held back through years of practice—Mom's guilt for leaving Rick behind, Rick's bitterness over his sense of abandonment, and my remorse for thinking I was to blame. At least we were a family again and I found comfort in that bond.

During my summer in Oregon, I applied my time and energy to writing my father's story. His tapes had taken on a new dimension for me. With every tape I listened to, with every page I wrote, I rediscovered his courage and humanity and retooled my own identity. Working in my trailer surrounded by fir trees, I continued to reconstruct his life and write his book, doing what he could not—make his sufferings mean something. And I had the blind assurance that my own reconstructed life was just around the bend.

By August, what had been a comforting, healing existence in my trailer in June, now was feeling isolating and confining. The world waited. I had to get out. My summer was coming to an end and I had decided to head back to San Diego by the end of the month, maybe stay with Suzanne, my first angel, while I pulled my life together. A quick tour of Oregon, a visit to the volcanoes or the coast with an Oregonian guide would be a pleasant way to end my rest and recuperation here. But how to make friends fast in a strange new place?

A newspaper ad. Who would suspect that the Most Visible Woman in Christianity would place herself in the Men Wanted column of an Oregon newspaper? Besides, I wasn't looking for "men," I was looking for a little fun and friendship.

The trick was writing the ad. It sounded easy enough: Describe yourself in a nutshell.

Spiritual seeker, divorced, athletic. No. Who wants to meet a separated soul-searcher with strong legs?

Single, athletic adventurer. Sounded too much like gymnastic sex.

WF, likes walks on beach, sunsets, movies. Pathetic.

SDWF . . . Redundant. Single, divorced white female advertising in the personals was obvious.

Nut-shelling myself was going to be harder than I thought.

IN 1994, THE DAY THE ad was published, Robin Pfeiffer eyeballed the clock. Five a.m. and wide awake, dawn just a slash in the sky after a full night of relentless rain. He forced his eyes shut. He had retired a year before but it was hard to break a thirty year habit of pre-dawn hours, instant coffee, grading papers, and teaching Spanish to pre-adolescent kids, not to mention counseling their rousing hormones into civilized behaviors. Now, he had a vineyard to tend. More career than vocation, seventy acres was a lot of wine grapes. Digging posts, setting trellis wires, new plantings, watering, fertilizing, and pruning. Damn, he needed sleep.

He remembers hobbling out of bed, shuffling to the front door, and retrieving the newspaper, which masqueraded as a wet mackerel on the porch. He let Freddy, his kitty, scoot in from a long night of mouse hunting. Maneuvering to the couch, Robin's fifty-five-year-old eyes strained at the newsprint, so he slipped on his Dollar Store reading glasses and lodged them low on his nose, giving him a Founding Father look. He bought the 2.25 magnifications twenty at a time, at a buck apiece, since most of his glasses hid from him in various states of disrepair, with many bifocals found crunched under the wheels of his tractor. Pfeiffer Vineyards had great soil cultivated and fertilized with cheap Ben Franklins.

He scanned the front page of the newspaper: Rwanda was decimated by genocide; Northridge, California, recovering from the quake; scientists debated the environmental effects of the ozone depletion—enough to make you want to relocate to a new galaxy just photographed by the Hubble Spacecraft.

He thumbed his way to the Commentary section and the William Raspberry column, on to the Sports page, "Ducks Win Again." Regional section, "Housing Development Replaces Filbert Orchard." Then on to the Classifieds, Lost and Found, Thank You Saint Jude. He made his way to Auctions, farm equipment, and bulldozers. Eyes now burning with lack of sleep, but for some reason defiantly open, he scanned what was left, the Personal Ads. "Women Seeking Men."

WF, 45, educated, attractive, author, conversationalist, skier, long-distance cyclist, scuba diver, likes merlot, Mozart, cabins, rivers, and books, seeking WM 35 to 55 who knows how to spell. Box 9464.

Spell? He was the Scrabble champion of the family, and once head of the American Association of Teachers of Spanish and Portuguese, Oregon Chapter. Spanish teachers had to know how to spell. He could answer that ad. But he wasn't that desperate. Answering a personal ad, for God's sake. Still, just out of curiosity, he might call later and leave a message in the voice-message box. As he tells it, ten minutes went by. It was later. He pitched the cat from his lap and called Box 9464. What did he have to lose?

"My name is Robin. And anyone who can juxtapose Merlot, Mozart, and spelling all in one sentence has to be an interesting person. If you add sailing to the list, let's take my sailboat out on Fern Ridge Lake this afternoon. If you're interested, call me."

I figured if he knew how to spell he was a reader, and if he read, he was educated. If he was between 35 and 55, he would probably be at the top of his mark emotionally and professionally. We might have some good conversations. He used the word "juxtapose." He was multisyllabic. I took the chance. Besides, I was only looking for a date, for heaven's sake. What did I have to lose? I answered Robin's call.

When I met him at the boat dock, he looked like an amalgam of precious metals, his skin bronze, his hair silver, and the gold filling in his left front tooth flashed when he smiled. He held out his hand from his 22-foot Catalina, to help me aboard. I felt him study me. His direct, hazel eyes gleamed under haywire eyebrows that sparked out in all directions as if his mind were on fire. As he raised the mainsail, I noticed his strong legs and defined calves, suggesting he was a climber or bicyclist.

I hoisted the jib as Robin rattled the outboard motor to life, chugging us out of the marina and into the lake. Lapping water replaced the sound of the noisy engine when he turned the motor off, and the boat swayed as the sails caught wind.

"You said you liked wine in your ad. I brought some just in case." Robin produced two bottles of red wine without labels. "It's pinot noir. It's ours. We own a vineyard. We grow wine grapes." He pulled a card from the back pocket of his shorts. "Pfeiffer Vineyards," he said. "Seventy acres. Mostly pinot noir, but we grow a little cabernet, merlot, chardonnay, and pinot gris, too."

That would account for his strong legs. "You climb hills."

"Yep. Every day." He pulled a corkscrew from his other pocket. "Don't leave home without it." He laughed, and rocked out the cork. The happy, pluggy sound of the cork reminded me of a giggle.

He handed me a glass of wine. "Crystal? On a boat?"

"Only way to savor good wine," he said, putting the glass to his nose and sniffing.

"Okay, Mr. Vineyard Man, what is pinot noir?"

Holding the tiller with one hand he took a sip of his wine with the other and pursed his lips. The sails snapped full and we cut through the water. "Well." He considered every word. "Pinot noir is another name for Burgundy. We don't call it Burgundy because that's a region in France and this is Oregon. So it's known by its varietal name, pinot noir. Here's to you," he said, lifting his glass.

Robin, in the vineyard

"But, there's more to pinot than just its name. It's a difficult grape to grow in some respects. It's a moody wine. A cool climate grape. Pinot noir grapes need warm, sunny days to make sugar and cool nights to shut down and rest. Oregon is perfect for these vines."

"And what about the taste?" I asked, fascinated as he revealed, layer upon layer, his passion for the grapes.

He took a sip and swirled it around in his mouth, speaking softly now.

"Complex," he said. "Like plums and wet earth. On your tongue, it gives a tingle, roll it around your mouth, and there's the fruit. Swallow, and its flavor lingers against the back of your throat. In a word, elegant." He took another sip, considered it, and said, "It's like an old friend." He watched me over the rim of his glass, and then smiled, his lips glistening with a trace of wine.

I was suddenly quite breathless and felt myself blush.

"Ready to come about," Robin said.

I clutched my wine glass between my knees and released the port jib line. The boom slapped to starboard and we changed seats to the opposite side of the well. I pulled in the jib line and fastened it to the cleat in a figure eight. The boat quickened.

"You know how to sail," Robin said.

"I'm from San Diego. Used to a little sailing," I said.

It was a handsome day—the sun, soft and warm, the wind gusting at a sailor's tempo. As the boat sliced through the water, Robin's sunglasses slid to the deck floor. I picked them up and gave them to his waiting, outstretched hand. We did that exchange as though we had done it a thousand times before, as if I had handed him his pipe, or the newspaper. I shrugged it off—just my vivid imagination.

He didn't ask me any personal questions, for which I was grateful, but I wondered if he recognized me. "I told you my name was Dee on the phone but my real name is Danuta." I paused, waiting for a reaction, a sign of familiarity. Did he know? Had he seen me on television? I wasn't that person anymore and I was tired of explaining why.

"Hmm," he said. "That's a pretty name. What language does it come from?"

"Polish, my father's side." I felt relieved.

He nodded like he was having an internal conversation that pleased him. He trimmed the jib and the sail snapped to life. He filled my glass again. We talked about my father's recordings and the biography I was writing.

"What was it like to hear your father's voice after all that time?"

"Shattering. Amazing. I cried. Even Walt cried." I found myself drifting with the wind, with the sails, thinking about Walter weeping for my father. "Funny, but after all those years, he was still affected by my father's aura, but then people seemed compelled to love my dad. Once they heard his stories and saw the talent he had as a sculptor, they were hooked." A warm wave splashed over the railing.

"You must have loved your father very much."

I thought of the beatings I took from his belt when I was little, how he taught us to ski and speak Polish, his bedtime stories, his terrible moods, ducking his punches at sixteen, and the curses he threw at me.

"Yes," I said. "I loved him."

Robin turned the boat about and I hiked in the jib. Sailing back to the dock, the low sun gave the water a Midas touch. He apologized for having to dash off, saying he promised to help pour wine at the Scandinavian Festival that night for his mom's Soroptimist club.

Civic minded, I thought as he steadied my hand and helped me off the boat. I tried to avoid his eyes burning into me as he said, "I don't know about you, Danuta, but all my

antennae are out. Something's going on here. I know you. I've known you for a long, long time." And then in a lighter tone he said, "Could we meet later on this evening at the festival—under the water tower in Junction City?"

What did he mean? What antennae? I mumbled something about if I can, I will. When I got back to the trailer, I decided not to try to find Junction City. Robin told me it was only fifteen miles away but I wasn't used to dark, unlit country roads. Besides, I didn't want to give in to "antennae."

I busied myself on my father's book and worked through half the night while Robin waited till midnight, standing alone under the water tower.

Robin and Danuta on their fourth date in August, 1994. Eight days later, Robin proposed.

A Leap of Faith

ROBIN ADJUSTED THE BLANKET ON THE TOP OF the hill overlooking his vineyard. He had called me the day after I spurned our appointment by the water tower, undaunted. "The sunset's really something from here and we might see the Three Sisters." Over the eastern horizon, three snow-capped mountains looked like silver forks piercing pink and blue clouds. Below us, grape vines in straight neat rows marched up steep rolling hills. A fast-running creek below the vines fed a large sparkling pond. I told him how it reminded me of a story of the perfect spot, from a book by Carlos Castaneda.

Before I could finish he said, "It's a series of books on the teachings of Don Juan. There's a chapter where he describes finding the perfect spot, where he had to roll around and around until he found it."

I stared at him, beginning to understand what he meant about antennae. "He rolls around for hours," I said.

Robin overlapped my story, "He rolls off the porch."

"And then he's on the ground," I added.

"And when he finds his perfect spot, he knows it. And he stops moving."

We sat in silence for a long minute. "How did you know about Castaneda and the story about the perfect spot?" I could barely hear my own voice.

"I told you before, I know you."

We talked about Castaneda and what his books meant to me and how I loved the way the author saw significance in the mundane. We talked about spirituality, and I told him I liked fairy tales as a kid and how I'd done a lot of rolling around on my own porch, searching, struggling for everything.

"Struggling for what?" he asked.

"To know God, to know my father, for love, happiness, identity, the perfect chocolate bar, you know, the usual."

"I know," Robin said.

He told me how his parents bought the land back in 1947. Raised sheep for thirty years. Never ate a single one. Couldn't eat the profits. They were literally dirt poor, living in a Quonset hut up on a ridge after the old house burned down. The hut was supposed to be a brooder house for chickens but the family moved into it instead. His dad said it was temporary. Twenty-five years later, they were still living in that tin can until his parents purchased a new manufactured home for the property.

As for the sheep, coyotes and domestic dogs roaming in packs used to tear the sheep apart for fun. Some mornings, he and his Dad would have to shoot sheep that were too badly maimed to live. He couldn't take it anymore. The first thing he did when his parents turned the farm over to the kids was to get rid of the sheep.

"So you planted grapes?"

"Long story short, a Frenchman called up one day, wanted to buy the family farm. Didn't say why. Of course, it wasn't for sale, but after a little snooping around I learned he wanted it for a vineyard. What did he know that I didn't? I checked out the climate, soil, elevations, south-facing slopes, it was perfect. So we turned the pastures into a vineyard, and that hill over there?" I followed his pointed hand and scanned the tall, dense Douglas-firs cresting to the horizon. "It was bare, too. Planted a sustainable forest."

"That was a pasture? You planted all of those trees?"

"Uh-huh, 45,000 of them."

"You *made* a forest."

"Yep. And dug out that pond down there for swimming."

I focused hard on Robin for the first time, wanting to see, really see, the man who had such an explosive sense of beauty. His body told the story. A youthful face, not so much in texture, but in expression, like a school boy. A rugged tan. Laugh lines folded by perpetual optimism fanned out in white pinstripes from the corners of his eyes. The back of his neck, sun-scorched. Little dings and cuts scarred his fingers and knuckles, as if he'd been wrestling recalcitrant tractors all his life, but his fingernails were short and clean. No designer label jeans, factory distressed to look worn and faded, his jeans were worn soft from years of use. And there was something about his right arm. It seemed different from the left, injured in some way.

Just then I spied an insect near the blanket, green as the blade of grass it seemed to guard, upright on its haunches, forearms closed together. "A praying mantis." I turned on the blanket to take a closer look. "What do you suppose he's praying for?"

Robin lay on his stomach and watched the insect with me. "You said you like fairy tales."

"Yes, do you have one for me?"

"No. I have one for me," he said. "You've noticed my right arm, how it's not like the left?" I nodded. His forearm seemed welded to his elbow in a permanent right-degree angle. To shake hands he lead with his shoulder to give the stiff arm length. He transferred forks or glasses to his left hand to eat or drink.

"Years ago, I played high school football. Five-foot-nine, I was the smallest guy on the team. So I tried twice as hard. One day, I hit the ground so hard, I pulverized my wrist. It shattered. Couldn't be fixed. It fused into one solid mass of bone. Never could bend it after that. Then rheumatoid arthritis kicked in. Clear up to my shoulder." He tried flexing his wrist; it only quivered.

He continued, "When I was younger, I used to love the fairy tale about the seven swans. Do you know it?"

"Yes," I said. "Seven brothers cursed by a witch and turned into swans. Their sister had one year to knit seven sweaters out of stinging nettles to turn the swans back into her brothers."

"Yeah," Robin said. "Even as her fingers bled, she was able to knit six-and-a-half sweaters. When the swans flew down to her a year later, she threw the sweaters over them and, one by one, they turned back into men. Except for the last swan. His sweater wasn't finished."

I saw where Robin was going with this. "Yes," I said quietly. "One brother ended up with one good arm and the other arm was a . . . a . . ."

"A wing," Robin said. "That's how I think about myself, one arm like a wing." He sort of chuckled and nibbled on a blade of grass.

My heart broke. I was in love, not with a swan, but a Robin—a beautiful Robin that planted a vineyard and a forest and dug a pond and made a paradise.

"I have a story, too," I said, catching his eye. "I have two sons, one is named Paul. The other one I call Matthew." I checked for Robin's response.

"I'm listening."

When I finished the story all Robin said was, "I'd like to be there when you and Matthew discover one another. I'd like to meet both boys one day."

I hoped he would say something like that. And I stared at the praying mantis again.

PERHAPS I WASN'T LOOKING FOR love, but I hoped for it. And I certainly wasn't advertising for a marriage partner, although I believed that one day I would marry again. But Robin's marriage proposal twelve days later still shocked me. It shocked us both.

Over dinner, drinking a deep, smoky merlot, he said, "We could continue dating for the next year or so, checking each other out, lifting the veil, so to speak. But I could spend the next 100 years with you and still arrive at the same conclusion: I knew you the day I met you. You're like a bell and every side gives the same clear ring. What if we skipped those next few years and started right now, today, building our lives together? Let's not waste another minute. Grab it now."

"*It* being?" Robin didn't hear my question.

"To lose any more time by not savoring the fruit we have now would be a true, godawful sin. If we turn around years from now and say, but why didn't we act on it then, well, it would be tragic, don't you think so too?"

"Tragic, yes, I suppose."

"We don't need to take the time that younger people have. We understand ourselves. We know each other." He scratched at an imaginary spot on the table. "It would all make sense. We could move your things to my place. You'd be out of that trailer before the winter rains begin. We're burning daylight. So, what do you say?"

"Are you suggesting we live together, because I'm not really interested—"

"Oh, God. No." Robin said, bolting forward in his chair,

spilling purple blotches on the tablecloth. "No, I meant marriage, marry, I meant we get married. Didn't I say that? I'm sure I said that."

My glass hung in midair halfway to my lips as my universe shifted through candlelight to Robin's deep eyes. "You're proposing." My face felt hot.

Now on one knee, lifting his glass up to me, he said, "Danuta, marry me?"

This was love, not blind or needy or motivated by unconscious desire. This was love, a bold, willful kind of love. Our chime rang clear and true.

"Yes," I whispered.

Wedding Day

TO POLAND

FOUR SUPERB VINTAGES HAD PASSED SINCE
Robin and I claimed a life together—happily growing grapes,
harvesting the fruit of our labors, and making fine pinot noir.
I was home, content to be the wife of a grape farmer, trellised
by his strong heart, the rugged terrain of my life leveled out
into pastures of love. I had found comfort within myself,
without angst or effort, my life arranged with everything
coming in its season.

One day, on a blustery visit to the coast, Robin asked, "If
you could wave a magic wand, what things would you wish
for?" His voice soared above the sound of the surf on the
Oregon coast, a wild, furious confluence of water and land,
black rocks and white foam boiling on a pulverized sea.

"To live with you for a million years." After these four years,
I still felt like a new bride. I threw out my hand to balance
on a slippery rock.

"Diplomatic answer. And the right one, I might add."
Robin helped me hop down onto a sandy ledge beside him.
"But what would you wish for?"

"Finishing my father's book," I said as we crossed a patch
of stones.

"And?"

"Finding Matthew."

"Go on," he said, following behind me.

"More?" I jumped down from a massive rock to the beach

below and Robin held my hand as we walked up a path to the top of a cliff.

"A happy family. A home where friends can visit. To make a difference in the world. And to go to Poland one day."

"Poland?"

"Yeah. Research my book. See where my father lived. Meet the relatives, Aunt Danuta, Uncle Richard. Ski his mountains. I've been corresponding with my cousin, Cesar, for years."

The surf hissed in the background as we walked quietly back to our hotel. I explained how I had done some research, but finding records was difficult. The International Olympic Committee couldn't find Dad's records from 1936. The war seemed to have made them disappear. "Yeah, Poland one day," I sighed. "Why do you ask?"

"One day never happens unless you make it. Let's do it. Let's go to Poland."

November, 1998, and we were on our way. Seventeen hours to Warsaw—a long time to hang in the sky. Although I was not sure what I expected to find when I got there, I hoped to have some clues into the true nature of my father, who remained an enigma to me. Why did he make it so hard for us to love him? Perhaps I could find the justification for the rage and depression that tormented him and oppressed us. I wanted to ground myself in my father's life, walk his mountains and touch what he touched, to find the truth of him and to find a part of me.

As the jet engines growled against gravity and the runway fell below us, Robin's sweaty hand clutched at my fingers in an iron grip.

"It's just the taking off and landings that get to me," he said. "I'm okay in between."

"It's the landings and the take-offs I like the best. It's

thrilling to be all wrapped up in that power and speed, don't you think?" I tried to sound reassuring but it wasn't working.

"Why don't you just get a Kawasaki, then?" Robin pulled out a book and leaned back in his seat, trying to relax.

Gaining on 35,000 feet the landscape rolled out below us, a carpet of green hills and beige farmlands in patterns becoming of a Persian rug.

"You can't see that from a Kawasaki!" I said, coaxing a foam airline pillow the size of a Tic Tac against Robin's shoulder as he read a book called *Tackling Polish Verbs*. He peered at me over his Dollar Store reading glasses, like Benjamin Franklin's good-looking brother with hair.

"*Dobranoc*, that means 'good night' in Polish." He patted my hand and went back to sacking Polish verbs.

Somewhere below, Fern Ridge Reservoir, now drained for winter rains, would welcome Canada geese and ducks seeking refuge during their lofty migrations. Here above the clouds we were making our own migration to the land of my ancestors. My heart warmed with anticipation.

Robin put down his book and picked up his CDs, *Learn Polish in Six Weeks*. His love of languages followed him everywhere and during the past few months he was determined to learn Polish before we hit Warsaw.

"You know," Robin hollered above his earphones, "Polish is the fourth hardest language in the world to learn for English-speaking people. It follows Arabic, Japanese, and Korean. This language is godawful tough." Half the Polish passengers in the plane looked up.

I pulled on his earphones, "You're shouting."

He snapped the headset back in his ear. "Oh, sorry," he hollered back.

I snuggled into the pillow on Robin's shoulder. This trip was a monumental step for me and for my father. In retelling his stories and retracing his steps, perhaps I could come to terms with the man I adored and feared; perhaps I could even forgive the father who was a puzzle to me. It would be a chance at last to put my father's life into focus. I thought of my favorite picture of my father, sitting on a fence in Europe, wearing his wool Polish army uniform. Chiseled into his youthful face were the high-boned features of Slavic stock: a gritty resolve, a determined jaw, tight, straight lines that formed his lips, and startling blue eyes. He was handsome in that photo, still full of optimism and life. The image stirred a need in me to hear his voice again.

I sat up, wrestled my Walkman from my bags under my seat, plugged in a cassette, adjusted the earphones, and fell back into his life and his war.

The Germans were in full retreat. Allies were on the move. Our destination, Dachau. Moving fast. I was a fifth wheel on the tank, riding it, sometimes driving it. Six tanks entered the gates of Dachau. I started to feel bad. I'll never forget the faces of the Americans when they saw the horror. All but one smart guy, a Nazi, had stayed behind to keep the camp in order.

"What the hell is going on here?" the captain asked.

The Nazi puffed himself up and sniffed, "This is a prison for criminals, captain, that is all. Surely you have criminals in America?" The young SS man was a perfect military soldier, obeying the party line, in perfect military order. The American looked at him in disbelief, momentarily stunned by the cavalier attitude of the German and the hideous reality of the death camp.

American Red Cross workers filled the yards with equipment, food, and doctors, quickly helping the poorest in health. The camp was full of prisoners and with the gate open, many who could not walk, crawled, weeping, to get out. Stick figure women walked around in a daze, fleshless bones with deep-set eyes bulging with fear and expectation. Many unbelieving they were saved.

Some Germans fled the very day we arrived, keeping the furnaces going full blast just the day before. Still going at it! I was sorry I went back there a second time, you know. I . . .sorry . . . I was desperately running around, looking for a familiar face. None. They were gone. They were all gone.

I had escaped Dachau in the winter of 1943 and came back in April 1945, and the camp was still full of prisoners, but the mountain of bones was bigger. They couldn't dispose of all of them, even using the bones as fertilizer for farmers. The mountain of bones was much higher. And the misery was the same. Worse. I asked to leave. I left with a very heavy heart.

I got drunk. I got so drunk.

We had sailed over the Atlantic for endless hours and now we soared above the Norwegian Sea, passed over Sweden, banked to the south and across the Baltic. Most people on the plane slept, unaware of the Milky Way, a fringe of rhinestones caught in moonlight, and the lonely tremble of jet engines hailing the stars. My watch said 3 a.m. in Oregon, and I should have been sleeping too, but I was too full of desire to know what awaited ahead, too anxious to fill in the blanks of what came before.

"Five more hours to Warsaw," Robin said before nodding to sleep.

Love had been my obsession, love of God, love of my father, and the love I shared with Robin. Unlike my father's complicated love, Robin's love did not flow in a backwash of rationalizations and conditions, but outward, unchecked, to me. And my devotion to him was as free as sunshine.

My eyes traced his profile, from the base of his nose that formed a perfect right angle to his upper lip, to his laugh lines shaped like butterfly wings. A face of clear intentions, a gentle face reflecting a generous heart, full of humanity. Loving him warmed me with the sweetness of hot chocolate.

I still had time for another tape and pull out the Walkman.

After three weeks of working the gas chambers, we became gravediggers. Our new job was to take the bodies down from the scaffolds where people were hanged twenty-four hours a day and haul them to the deep wide graves and cover the bodies with lime. The graves constantly had to be enlarged and the physical demands of digging for the dead drained us of life. If a man fell, if he was weak, he was smashed over the head with the butt of a rifle, or stabbed with a bayonet. Were we digging our own graves today?

I put the recorder away. The strength of my father's life force consumed me and sometimes I struggled to breathe, devoured by his vitality until there developed a loop of curiosity—he drove me back to him in order to know myself—my life enhanced by understanding his.

I am almost there now.

Warsaw

OUR PLANE DESCENDED THROUGH SMOKY gray clouds and lumbered across a wintry landscape. A halo of ice circled Warsaw. The wheels tugged at the runway, the engines rumbled in a last bellicose roar, and passengers applauded, relieved the long flight was over and grateful to be on Polish soil.

Robin's grip on my hand tightened and tears pooled in our eyes. "I promised you Poland, Danka," he said, using the name my father called me.

After passport checks, luggage claim, and a final nod from customs, we pushed toward a set of frosted glass doors beyond which shadows moved like ghosts. Poland waited for me in those shadows.

The doors opened in a burst of light, and I crossed the threshold to my father's world. *One day, Danuta, I will tell my story and one day, you will write it.* Now, I breathe his air. *One pole was broken, I had one pole left, and I lost the gold medal by fractions of a second.* I am on fire inside. *I now pronounce you Daddy and wife.* The soft, "shush" words of the Polish language skim the air like swallows, echoes of my father's voice. *The gas chambers and furnaces were going twenty-four hours a day. You are my sunshine. You are a whore!* I wanted to cry. *No, Daddy, please!* His presence plunged into me like an ice pick into a melon.

My heart hammered. The unknown was a tiptoe away

and suddenly I didn't feel up to the task. Weakness and doubt crowded me. Oxygen came scarce. Scanning the crowd, all I saw were eyes fly-fishing in a stream of faces, casting about for a glimmer of recognition. Occasional shrieks exploded into joyful reunions.

And then, "There he is." I spied Cesar in a white wool coat, waving an enormous bouquet of salmon-colored roses above his head.

Gushing tears, we ran to each other and hugged tightly.

"It is big time of waiting, Danuta. I am happy you are here." We were all giddy and smiling big, goofy smiles at one another. Like my father and brothers, he had the build of a downhill skier, stocky and solid. His pale skin was the color of a winter sky, but his eyes were full of summer. With a short giggle and then a hum, he searched for words in English. "Danuta, Robin, please, come, parents wait."

Packing our American luggage into a Polish car made me feel self-conscious about our bags, oversized in an undersized country.

"*Dobra*," Robin said.

"You speak Polish." Cesar laughed.

"*Tak*," Robin replied, and then managed to say in Polish, "I can speak a little."

As we traveled the outskirts of Warsaw it began to snow. Slush the color of coffee grounds heaped against the street gutters. People in dark coats bundled against the white cold walked briskly along the streets, shrinking into their scarves. Unpainted concrete buildings seemed to be pasted flat against the gray sky like giant tombstones. A commuter train brushed alongside our car, the colors of its siding grimed over by an endless winter, the window-framed faces reminding me of mournful cameos in antique brooches. Cables and telephone wires spider-webbed across the road. On our left, the emerging Poland, a sparkling new shopping mall with big picture windows and a parking lot flush with cars. On our right, the traditional Poland, a shamble of tin-roofed stalls where vendors huddled behind exposed tables of shirts and sweaters. Crates of oranges and cans of soda were stacked below summer dresses fluttering on hangers in the falling snow. Old women wearing scarves and carrying shopping bags printed with garish flowers shuffled through the stalls.

Cesar was in good spirits. "So, Danuta, we have for you, every day, something to show you. We make plans to go to Krakow to see relatives. Then to house in Rajcza, where your father grows up and to see Olenka, your other aunt. Yes? This is okay?"

"Okay!" I said, eagerly anticipating every sight and sound and smell.

A part of my father was home. I carried him in me. I was his emissary, his ambassador of longing, fulfilling what he could not, completing the one mission he was never able to achieve. The time was ripe for our healing. "We're here, Daddy," I whispered.

Suddenly, Cesar hit the brakes. Our car skidded to a stop at the side of the road. "My parents," he shouts, "they have come to meet us." A car swung around in the road and parked behind us. Cesar jumped out and opened my door.

Sleet basted my back. A woman jumped out of the car behind us, carrying roses in one hand and a red umbrella in the other. My Aunt Danuta rushed toward me. Umbrella and roses embraced me and my arms wrapped around her. All she could say was, "Danusia." All I can say is "Danuta, Danuta," back to her. Her hair smells of perfume. The fur around her collar cuddles my cheek. We two Danutas sobbed, clinging to one another as though the whole world depended on the bond between our hearts. Fists of wind pummeled us for attention and one gust punched the red umbrella inside out. We screamed and laughed and grabbed at the handle. The roses went flying. Cesar made a leap and caught the bundle under his arm. Uncle Richard made a grab for the windblown umbrella. He and Robin embraced like brothers. We clung to one another unconcerned with the storm or the cars rushing by us in the road.

A generation of waiting condensed to the spot where we stood. No wonder the snow fell like confetti and the wind gusted with joy. We closed a gap between two worlds.

Robin used his first Polish guidebook word, which sounded like "pro-sha oo-shanse," and pointed to the seat in the car. She was charmed that Robin asked her to sit down in her own language.

"Oh, pro-sha oo-shanse!" Aunt Danuta cried out. "You know Polish!" And she climbed into the car and obligingly sat down as Robin grinned with delight.

Danuta and Richard lived in a four-room apartment in the heart of Warsaw, for forty-five years paying rent to the communist state, owning nothing. Their place was impressive for the things they didn't have: no knickknacks, no paintings, no porcelain saucers from the Franklin Mint. A picture of Pope John Paul hung over the door, a calendar in the hall, a clock in the living room. Everything compartmentalized. In the kitchen, a small refrigerator, the size you might find in an RV back in the States. Three aluminum pots, nicked, scorched, and pitted, sat atop the two-burner gas stove. Next to the stove, a tiny sink with three little hooks holding three dishrags. Everything seemed miniaturized, frugal, and sparse, nothing going to waste.

I looked like Aunt Danuta, the same dominant nose cradled by apple-plump cheekbones set under big blue eyes. She didn't speak English, but she didn't need to. Hands and eyes, pointing and laughing; it was all the language we needed. Aunt Danuta was the youngest of my father's five siblings. There was an aristocracy in the way she wore her silk scarf tied just so about her neck, and the deep purple earrings that matched her sweater, and in the way her chin rose when she sank into a chair. *I am from a long line of the House of Jasterowski.* We were both from the same royal line, both shared the same heritage. Uncle Richard, wizened by an endless chain of cigarettes and breathing heavily to fill frail lungs, snapped his fingers and produced a bottle of vodka and a carton of orange juice. He pointed to us, to the drink. "Aha," he said, pouring one for each of us.

"*Nazdrowia!*" and we drank it down.

"Ah." He snapped his fingers again and pointed at the glasses.

Aunt Danuta

"No, no," we protested, as he poured another round.

He bowed in his starched white shirt, vested suit, and dapper tie, and with great dignity said, "Welcome to your home in Poland," and we drank again.

Aunt Danuta opened a book filled with dozens of pictures of Rick and me when we were little. And letters. She had saved them all. A birthday card sent from me when I was seven, my name scratched in pencil between two hand-drawn lines to keep my penmanship straight. I wrote "Happy Birthday" in Polish. Aunt Danuta handled them like jewels.

There was a picture of me in England, when I was eight months old. And Rick and me in Canada. A picture of my mother in London. "We have many letters and pictures from your father in early years," Cesar said. "But then, letters stop. We hear nothing for long, long time, until letters from you. We don't know what happens in those years."

"But, I thought he wrote all the time. He missed everyone so much. That's all he talked about."

"At first, yes, there were many letters, as you can see," Cesar said. "But after you move to Michigan, less and less, until nothing."

"Why did Johann not come to see us?" Cesar translated the question for Aunt Danuta.

"I don't know. It was his dream." I didn't know what else to say.

Danuta kissed me and stroked my face. "We always remember you, while Johann and family forgets about us," she said through Cesar.

The scattered pictures disturbed me. Why did he stop writing? A long stillness enveloped us. Thankfully, Uncle Richard snapped his fingers and pointed to the table. *Kolacja,* supper, was served. Spread upon the table were four kinds of cheese, a half-dozen sausage varieties, sliced thin as paper. Tomatoes, potato salad, tomato soup, roast beef, steaming boiled potatoes and cauliflower came at me, one after another. The aromas of pickles and garlic and gravy put my stomach on notice. I could tell I was going to love the food in this country. Robin uncorked a bottle of wine we packed in our luggage. The room filled with happy voices, laughter, toasts, and satisfied sounds of food passed around a loving table.

Before the dishes were washed, I was ready for bed. As Uncle Richard quickly unfolded the little couch in the living room, I realized it was their bed. He pulled blankets and pillows from a small cupboard and wouldn't hear of us sleeping elsewhere. They would sleep in his small office on floor cushions. I was too tired to argue.

The next morning, after a breakfast of sliced sausages, tomatoes, cheese, crusty bread, and hot tea served in water glasses, we were on our way from Warsaw to Krakow with Cesar and his wife, Elizabeth.

My heart soared. Krakow, where my father studied. Perhaps we could see his classrooms, visit the fine arts department, and maybe find someone who knew him as a student. The four-hour journey went quickly as we chatted about how similar the countryside looked to Oregon, with rolling farmland, grassy meadows, pine forests, and lakes. Then we passed a sign, *Oswiecim*. I wanted to stop there, but Cesar turned his eyes from the road to me. "This is a terrible place. You do not want to go there. In the war . . ."

"Yes, but because of my father I thought it might be good for me to see a camp for myself." Cesar did not respond; instead we passed the exit sign to Auschwitz.

"Maybe, on the way back, Cesar?" I asked.

"Yes, maybe," he said, "but we have many things to show you."

I could tell we weren't going back there. I wondered if he was embarrassed by the existence of such a horrible place. If it were me, I would want to look the other way, too. Nobody wants a memorial to man's depravity in your backyard. Still, I wished we had taken the diversion.

Krakow sat on the banks of the sparkling Vistula River and even from a distance, it looked like a fairy tale city. The ancient capital of Poland was dotted with spires and castles and cathedrals.

"Here, in Krakow," Elizabeth said, "are hundreds of schools and universities. Since the fourteenth century Krakow is center of Poland for culture and science. People do not realize, Danuta, but one time, Krakow was the cultural center of all of Europe." Elizabeth swept a strand of soft brown hair from her face. She looked like an angel from one of my father's statues.

"I never expected Poland to be so medieval and graceful," I said. "I mean, people in America imagine grand opera houses in Milan and Paris, but Poland? And universities eight hundred years old?"

"This was only major city in Poland not destroyed by bombs in last war," Cesar said.

We toured the famous Wawel Castle. "One of the most beautiful buildings in all of Poland," Cesar said. I could feel the history in every stone beneath my feet. The gothic structure held the entombed bones of kings and queens and inscriptions on their crypts told of their heroic deeds in battle, legends of Polish mythology. In spite of thousands of years of invaders sweeping across Poland from every direction, the Poles never lost their identity. My father never lost his.

Cesar

Statues of saints and angels peeked at me from the buttresses flanking the domed ceilings and the high walls of the altar and I perceived a vague familiarity to those sculptures. And then I realized; the draped robes, the empathetic postures, and sorrowful faces. These statues could have been carved in our living room back in Michigan. It was easy to see that my father studied his craft in this city, his work so much like the art of Krakow. As he said in his tapes, the University of Fine Arts in Krakow was where he experienced the happiest days of his life.

We climbed a high hill overlooking the city, where the wind curled up in my face, and our coats slapped like loose sails in the wind. "Cesar, where is the University of Fine Arts from here?" I asked, searching the skyline.

"You can just see between hills." Cesar pointed and I followed the line from his fingertip to a cluster of distant rooftops. "It is not important, there are many universities in Krakow," Cesar said.

"Yes, Cesar, I know, but the University of Fine Arts is where my father went to school. I would love to see it." Cesar and Elizabeth searched each other's face, as though searching to understand me.

"But, Danuta, in Krakow, is many schools, perhaps a different one for your father." I noticed Elizabeth engaged in an animated conversation with Aunt Danuta.

"No, no, Cesar, you don't understand. The University of Fine Arts is the school I want to see, not another one."

Cesar joined the conversation with Danuta and Elizabeth. Uncle Richard said something. I felt frustrated with Cesar. Why did he keep dismissing my requests to visit places I wished to see? Why all this hubbub and need for group discussions when I asked to visit a place that was important to me and to my father?

"My English, is not so good, eh?" Cesar said, putting his arm around my shoulder. "We see your cousin Ania now. She learns English very good in school. Maybe she explain and talk with you?"

An hour later we met Basha, my Krakow cousin, and her teenage children, Ania and Peter. They lived in a fine three-story house in the suburbs. Basha, a geography teacher in her mid-forties, was a pretty woman with short auburn hair wound in tight curls. We all piled into her house, Aunt Danuta, Uncle Richard, Cesar, Elizabeth, Robin, and me, and it was abuzz with kisses and squeals of delight. Hands flew about and voices rang out in a Polish opera of greetings. They hadn't seen each other in some time and this had become a family reunion.

"I didn't know I had such a big family. I'm having trouble keeping track of the family tree," I said to young Ania, a shy seventeen-year-old.

"This is very natural, there are many of us." Ania said, running her hand through her short tousled hair. The younger generation was taught English as a mandatory second language in school. Very much like Poland itself, they had a childlike quality about them with a fresh, honest appeal. Ania was slim and her clothing simple: slacks, black shoes, T-shirt, no make-up.

Peter, twenty-one, was more somber, but only on the surface. He loved to be hugged, though he pretended he didn't. When he spoke in English, he snapped his fingers to help him search for the right word.

"Ania, would you tell Cesar that I want to go to the University of Fine Arts to see where my father studied? He said you would understand my English better."

Ania addressed Cesar in her soprano voice, adding wonderful melodic tones to her language. Cesar turned to Aunt Danuta. They spoke animatedly to one another. Uncle Richard added something. Ania went to her mother, Basha. Now two discussion groups were going on.

"Robin, why is there always a need for long debates over simple questions?"

He shrugged. "Beats me."

Finally, Ania carefully interpreted what was said.

"Um, Danuta, Cesar and the family says that your father,

Danuta and Cesar looking for answers

um, he never went to the University of Fine Arts in Krakow? There is, we think, some mistake," Ania sing-songed. "There is a different school. It is called Istebna. Near our hometown in the mountains in the south of Poland. We are going there tomorrow."

"But not in Krakow?" I tried very hard to get this right.

"No, not in Krakow. By Rajcza, near your father's home." Everyone nodded in agreement, encouraging me to digest the answer, watching for my reaction.

This was going to be tougher than I imagined, trying to get straight answers through Polish translations. I sat down in a chair and Ania sat next to me. "Look, my father clearly stated in his memoirs that he attended the University in Krakow. Do you understand me?"

"Danuta, it is no problem, tomorrow we will go Rajcza, where my grandmother, Olenka, lives, where your father grew up. Frank, who is married to Olenka, went through the war with John. We will talk about all things tomorrow with whole family."

We finished supper with four different sausages, cheese, tomatoes, bread, torts, and cakes. Like pulling a rabbit from a hat, Robin yanked another bottle of wine from his bags.

"To the family we have found," Robin rose from his chair, *"Nazdrowia."*

"Ah. *Nazdrowia!"* Charmed by Robin's Polish, we all rose for the toast with our wine uniting a new family.

Ania and Peter

DISCOVERY

Now faith is the substance of things hoped for, the evidence of things not seen.

Hebrews 11:1

THERE IS SOMETHING COMFORTING ABOUT waking up in a city that's a thousand years old. It is the kind of reassurance that comes with the routine of days, when the sun seems to rise more from habit than nature. The day is not new but a link in a chain of other days before it and the days to come.

Sunday morning in Krakow, our third day in Poland, and the household fluttered with excitement. Uncle Richard fussed with his tie; Ania searched for her shoes. Aunt Danuta shrugged into her black fur coat and Cesar arrived grinning and humming. Elizabeth's porcelain skin shined in a blue silk suit.

I was far from shining. "Where's everybody going?" I asked sleepily, poking into the kitchen, hoping to smell coffee.

"It is Sunday. We go to church," Ania said.

"Church?"

Robin appeared around the corner. "Somebody say coffee?"

I shook my head. "Church."

"Church?"

"When was the last time you went to a Catholic Church in Krakow?" I asked.

The Most Holy Heart of Jesus Chapel was on Garncarska Street, a narrow street lined with dark apartment buildings. A nearby convent owned the two-hundred-year-old church. Thick, arched columns rose into a long hall with a magnificent domed ceiling. The pews were heavy and dark. A veil of incense skimmed the cold air. Three tall white candles burned steady flames from each side of an emerald-green altar trimmed with gold. An emerald and gold backdrop rose thirty feet high. The Catholic Church was the only place where color had been allowed to reign in Poland. A statue of Christ crucified hung on the wall, his arms wide and embracing. Paintings of angels embellished the edge of the altarpiece as though they inhabited the very structure of the church.

People poured in around us, filling the pews, pressing my elbows close to my sides. Ten-year-olds prayed next to their fathers; old women in bulky coats and babushkas prayed next to sleek young women in high-heeled black boots and fashionable black overcoats. A baby cried. Children fidgeted in their seats next to their mothers. All summoned here by their faith.

A single, clear, female voice sang from the balcony, a haunting plea building to a triumphant call to heaven. A chorus joined her and we were transported upward and inward. Aunt Danuta sang beside me, Elizabeth and Ania in front of me. Cesar knelt in prayer and Peter returned from the confessional booth. The priest appeared with ten altar boys. The congregation rose. The Mass began. God was there for them.

Robin squeezed my hand and gave me a little smile.

I envied them the comfort of their faith and pressed into the scene around me, rising with the music, inhaling the perfumed air. I wanted the God on the wall, the mystery, the certainty. Where was the golden shaft of light to anoint me? Mea culpa, mea culpa, mea maxima culpa, through my fault, my most grievous fault—here is your Bride. But the sign of the cross felt awkward and I was no longer called to communion by the ringing of the bells.

When did I stop believing in this God of vestments and miters, of blessed water in little bowls, of mortal sin, the God of punishment and abandonment, the God of my father? I had no memory of my father standing in church next to me. Why did he sleep in every Sunday while insisting on our fidelity to the Church? What did my father believe in? Wood and stone. He chiseled his relationship with God in the face of Christ, etched his faith into the crown of thorns, and placed his trust in the crafted hands of the Virgin Mary. But he didn't go to church.

Like my father, I shied away from God, losing my faith to sorrow and neglect, allowing it to ebb away one small grace at a time. The lifeline to the God of my catechism frayed until the threads could no longer sustain the weight of my needs. When the power of the sacraments and the saints no longer sheltered me from the ravages of my young life, I looked elsewhere for my salvation.

Bells rang from the altar, calling us to our feet.

If God and the saints no longer heard my prayers, who would? The answer came in college with Friedrich Nietzsche. His books taught me that in order to live life to the fullest, I had to embrace all of it, the suffering as well as the joy. By avoiding any part of life, I reduced the flame in general, including happiness. I was persuaded that it was as natural to hurt as it was to be joyful. From the moment I read Nietzsche I committed to embracing my life. No longer would I run from it, hide from it, or fear it. I would live it, free to be alive with sorrow, free to accept whatever happiness I'd find.

Before long I became an ideology addict, sampling one doctrine after another; Buddhism, Transcendental Meditation, and yoga were among the items on my philosophical smorgasbord. I became a vegetarian and learned to read palms, tarot cards, and astrological charts. I threw the I Ching, and listened to the music of Tibetan bells. But the tofu salad of my spiritual meanderings never tasted quite right, always needing more salt or more ingredients. Trying to fill the void of my childhood faith, I had become born again, and again, disheartened.

The bells rang once more, beckoning the faithful to kneel in prayer. The priest raised the Blessed Sacrament and pews emptied as people lined the altar rail to receive the body and blood of Christ.

The people in that church seemed so sure, and their eyes expressed no doubt. Their faith was in their blood. They were the living, breathing Church. I used to know that feeling of spiritual comfort, unquestionable self-rightness: my salvation assured, right and wrong clear as night and day, no room for the twilight of uncertainty. I thought I knew how to push God's buttons and exact His response.

As fundamentalist Christians at CBN, we were suspect of the salvation of those who did not speak in tongues and of those who belonged to "traditional churches." Catholics were questionable, the litany of Lutherans was under scrutiny, and some Baptists were not to be trusted. Unitarians were positively heathen and the remaining jumble of the "unsaved" fell under the dark cloud of New Age Humanists. Republicans were clearly on God's side while the Democrats were dangerously close to communists and, perhaps, the Devil himself.

When my role as a televangelist came to an end, "church elders" came to counsel me. Perhaps, they counseled, I wasn't spiritual enough. Perhaps I was being punished. Perhaps, they said, I never knew God at all.

The Mass ended; the chalice was covered and the tabernacle closed. My first Mass in thirty-five years passed without a crack of lightning, or a thunderous voice from heaven. Did I hope otherwise? There was nostalgia for my spiritual home, my first church, my first God—the innocence of a simple faith. God may have waxed and waned through my life, but my father remained a certainty. He gave me this family and a proud heritage, something to believe in. While God eluded me, my father's legacy provided roots and a strong foundation.

We exited, passing through the great doorways of the church and down the worn stone steps to the street. How many shoes had trod those stones before me, each taking a bit of dust, bowing the steps like the back of a tired horse? How many souls came to this place, some with lofty expectations, others in despair, some full of faith, some lost? How many found God? How many left disappointed?

IN POLAND, *OBIAD*, SERVED AT noon, is the biggest meal of the day. After tomato soup and potato salad, pierogies and sausages, someone passed me a muddy-looking, gelatinous mold, with bits of shredded chicken suspended in it. Basha giggled. "It is special Polish dish. Called galareta," she explained through Peter. "You must squeeze lemon on it." The quivering mass of gelatin flopped onto my plate.

"You go first," I whispered to Robin, although I don't know why I thought to trust his palate—Robin ate everything. The table fell silent. Everyone watched his expression.

"Mmm," Robin said, shaking his spoon in the air. *"Dobra!"*

There were nods and oohs and aahs and chatter resumed like an assembly of happy blue jays on a picnic table.

"It's bad, isn't it?" I asked under my breath.

Robin lifted his eyebrows, delivering the message. Thinking no one was watching, I covered my portion with a ring of sausage. Out of sight, out of mind.

"Danuta," Cesar said with a twinkle in his eye, "you do not like galareta?"

Busted.

"Oh. Yes. But I'm so full!"

Cesar and Ania chortled. "It's okay," Ania said, "we don't like it either."

Everyone erupted into hearty laughter. Robin wagged his finger at Basha, and Aunt Danuta covered her cackle with her hand. Uncle Richard hooted, "Ho, ho," and Cesar picked up my little sausage with his fork and pointed to the galareta hidden underneath. We laughed so hard we cried.

"If you don't like it, why do you eat it?" I finally managed to ask.

"It is tradition," Ania sang out, and everyone laughed again.

"Speaking of tradition, I have a toast." The eyes of my beautiful new family gazed at me, eyes I recognized, eyes like mine. "Here's to us, to the long line of the House of Jasterowski."

Cesar translated. Uncle Richard and Basha tilted their heads, as though they had water in their ears. Wine glasses froze in the air, like tulips on flesh-toned stems. Another group discussion ensued as the toast stalled and the glasses slowly floated back down to the table.

"Ah, Danuta, I am sorry, but we do not understand this toast. Perhaps you explain?"

"It's to Count Jasterowski and to us, his family," I said. "You know, Count Jasterowski, who changed his name to

Rylko, from his coat of arms?"

"Changed his coat?" Cesar pinched his shirt.

"No, Cesar, not coat, shield." I laughed.

Cesar smiled blankly. "No, Danuta, I do not understand this."

"It is the history of our family. My father told me many times. We are from the House of Jasterowski, the Polish count? He fought against the Czar, escaped with his family to the Carpathian Mountains? This is where we get our name, Rylko."

More discussion at the table, some "ahs," and talk became more lively.

"Danuta, my mother says there was a Jasterowski in the Rylko family," Cesar whispered, and I strained to hear him.

"Oh, good. For a minute there, I thought somebody turned off the lights."

"Turned off lights?"

"An American expression. Means, things get dark. People don't understand."

"Ah, turned off lights, yes I see." Cesar contemplated that for a minute. "But, Danuta, Jasterowski was woman who married a Rylko many years ago, in great-grandfather's time. It is not family name."

"No, Cesar. Jasterowski was a count. Surely, you must know that."

More discussion, except now, the conversation grew intense. Uncle Richard shook his head. Aunt Danuta punctuated her words by slicing her hand in a vertical motion across the table. Cesar spoke. Basha said something to her daughter and Ania then turned to me.

"Danuta, you must understand, Rylko name is common name in south of Poland. Jasterowski was a woman who marries a Rylko. That is all."

They all shook their heads like daisies in the wind.

"Robin, what does it mean?" I turned to Robin hoping he got a different message.

"I think it means that there was no count."

"Danuta, it is some mistake. There is no count." Cesar shrugged.

"How could that be? My mother knew about him. My brothers and I knew about him. My father told us. My mother asked for a picture of the castle, my brother wants a copy of the coat of arms. Do you understand what I mean, Cesar? The whole American family knows about Count Jasterowski!"

"Danuta," Ania said, running her hand through her hair, "my mother says to ask Olenka. She knows family history. She is oldest. She can tell us more about that side of the family."

"You mean, only Olenka knows the story? "

"Yes. We will ask her all questions in Rajcza. In family home, when we go tomorrow."

Later that night, I couldn't sleep. How did the family not know about their own history?

Robin whispered from his pillow, "It's strange, first there's the University of Fine Arts that your father apparently didn't attend, and now this Jasterowski thing. He stopped contact with his family, even while he said he missed them. Something's not coming together here."

"What's wrong is the language barrier. I'm losing something in the translation, I'm sure of it," I said. I snuggled close to him. "Once we get to Rajcza, things will be clearer."

Rajcza

POLAND LIES ROUGHLY BETWEEN THE NORTH latitudes of 50 and 55 degrees. About the size of New Mexico, if superimposed on a map of America, the southernmost point would dip into North Dakota and the northern point would be halfway to Alaska—I was all too familiar with that stretch of geography. By air, Warsaw is only thirty minutes from Stockholm and boasts a climate similar to New England. Summers are hot and humid, but winters are cold, and for me, magical.

Three cars rumbled behind us, collecting relatives on our way to Rajcza, where my father grew up, the place all the Rylkos called home. It was where my aunt Olenka and her husband, Frank, still lived. Rajcza. I've heard the name a thousand times. *Rye*, like the grass, *cha*, like the dance. RYE-cha.

Traveling through the countryside, luminescent green fringed the snow drifts like the emerald curl of a Pacific wave. Trees cuffed the edges of the snowy meadows in blue shadows and leafless shrubs tangled the snow like bales of wires. The pass through the Carpathian Mountains swept low like the back of a two-hump camel, and poured us into a maze of ranges within mountains. We cut through the West Beskids, and motored across Poland's crown jewels, the raw, sharp Tatras on the country's southernmost tip. The dense, gunmetal sky grew dark and snow fell like long strands of pearls. Our undaunted convoy fearlessly climbed those passes without snow tires, chains, cellular phones, or AAA roadside assistance, as if nothing could go wrong.

An old Abba song faded in and out on the car radio and forests scrolled by my window to the rhythms of "Dancing Queen." I thought back to how Rick loved to play his drums to the oldies, how excited he was to learn of our trip.

The road narrowed and began to wind through a slender valley. A sign read "Jelona."

Jelona. Where my father's war started. The gorge where the Germans flooded into Poland. My finger stabbed the glass, pointing at everything. "And this must be where he rode his horse to find his parents the night the Germans came. And it's where the bomb killed his friend and where my father's horse died."

Robin reached back from the front seat and squeezed my hand.

Hills rose up from each side of the road and a shallow river snaked alongside. We traveled through humble villages of stone houses; signs over some doors designated shops. A woman pushed a baby carriage along the shoulderless road. A man in a brown suit pedaled an old bicycle and pulled into the ditch to make way for a horse-drawn wagon loaded with a mountain of loose hay. A little girl bundled in a thick pink coat sat precariously atop the unruly straw like a paperweight. A black Mercedes Benz trailed impatiently behind the wagon as the driver talked on a cell phone. The horse trod wearily forward, as if unimpressed by the pace of the future storming at its heels.

After another turn Cesar said, "Danuta, here is Rajcza."

I rubbed the steamy windows with my sleeve, squeaking the glass clean for a better view. Were those my father's ski slopes? Was this the railroad station that took him to war?

And where in those mountains did Count Jasterowski build his castle? Arriving at the heart of his being and into the arms of his family, I felt my father closer to me in death than in life, his very breath still part of the air. This Polish family surrounded me with a love I seldom felt from him, making up for all that he withdrew.

"There, ahead." Cesar pointed through the windshield. "That is family home."

Just how I pictured it. Grandfather's carvings spanned the roofline, a sun with rays spreading across the gables. Yellow and white slats decorated the second-story balcony. The front garden, buried in snow, hid the earth where my grandfather had tended his flowers. Along the opposite side of the street, the Sowa River flowed beneath mounds of ice, just as my father described it. Soon, I would stand before the family crest, and bring back a copy of it for my brother. I would see Count Jasterowski's castle and take a picture of it for my mother. I would fulfill every promise to them, to my father, and to myself.

This was the place that kept him alive and fired his will to live when he peeled himself off the frozen floor in the death chamber. This home gave him the courage to defy the Butcher, to escape from the hell in which so many others had perished. The flood of all his longing was in me as we pulled off the road and into the short driveway.

There was a big sign in the front of house, a huge blue and white metal structure planted firmly in the front garden. "Is advertisement for how you say, stones for graves?" Cesar climbed out of the car. "Olenka allows sign for extra money every month."

Cesar unloaded suitcases from the trunk while Ania's mother and father, Basha and Andrej, drove up. Aunt Danuta and Uncle Richard followed behind. Elizabeth, Ania, and Peter pulled up in the third car.

On the far end of the front porch I spotted another sign, *Bar Nad Sowa.*

"Is bar. Sign means, Bar Near Sowa River. Other family members make their part of house for bar. House is put in half. Half Olenka and Frank, half bar."

The bar, right, and home, left

Before I could digest that architectural description of a divided house, Olenka came down the icy steps from the porch and ran toward us, plowing through the snow in brown slippers. A fuzzy ball of white hair bobbed toward me. "Danka. Danka," she cried. A warm smile crinkled across her kind and craggy face. Uncle Frank shuffled behind Aunt Olenka, leaning heavily on a cane, singing over and over, "Ha-low. Ha-low."

I tried to embrace them both and could easily see Uncle Frank's tears magnified behind thick glasses. Robin hugged and kissed them, patting everyone on the back. Olenka said something. I nodded and cried, understanding the emotion if not the words. No one seemed to mind the freezing cold or the threatening sky. This was home and all was well.

As we entered the house through the kitchen, I thought how my father's house had been a shrine in my head, a hand-me-down memory, and a genetic keepsake from another generation. Now this house was my own memory to hold. While everyone talked at the same time, like happy starlings nesting in a familiar tree, I pulled away from the chatter and walked through the house, entranced by the moment and the history I found there. The plastered walls gleamed with bright yellow paint. Were they yellow when my father was born? Faded blue linoleum covered the uneven kitchen floor. Did the floorboards creak when he scampered in bare feet as a child? To think my grandmother cooked and cleaned for six children in this simple kitchen with a single wooden table resting against the wall. Three stools neatly tucked below the table. A gas stove, the size of a playhouse toy, steamed with pots of soup and boiling potatoes, and meat roasted in the Barbie-sized oven. A miniature refrigerator squatted along an opposing wall next to a large aluminum sink with a big mirror. By the opening to the living room, a simple wooden cabinet held a few cups and glasses, a sugar bowl and a can of tea bags, and dishes stacked on shelves below. Through a doorway from the kitchen, I could see Olenka and Frank's bedroom with a double bed in the middle of the room and a single bed in the corner.

"Danuta. A toast. To family," Cesar called out, handing me a bottle of Polish beer and drawing me into the living room, back into the ring of starlings. *"Nazdrowia!"* Smiles and nods accompanied the clink of bottles, a refreshing pause

Frank and Olenka

after such a long and cramped ride. The winter clothes and bags and twelve exuberant Poles in one room made for cozy quarters especially with all our heavy coats and jackets piled up on a small brown couch.

A door from the living room opened to a narrow space the size of a walk-in closet with a bed and small dresser tucked inside. The room looked like an afterthought.

"So, where's everyone going to sleep?" Robin asked, eyeing all the bags.

"First we eat," Ania said, unfolding a side table into a large dining room table. Olenka and I cleared out the coats from the room; Cesar shuffled the bags.

"But there are twelve of us," Robin said. "Do we have enough chairs?" Ania pulled the table alongside the brown couch. "Here are four seats," she said.

Aunt Danuta threw a white linen tablecloth over the table and Ania and Peter brought out plates. Assorted chairs appeared and, amazingly, with a little maneuvering, a table for twelve assembled in the middle of the room.

"Feel this!" In the corner of the living room, Robin

caressed a rectangular, yellow-tiled ceramic structure that nearly touched the ten-foot ceiling. "It's a radiant electric heater," he said. From this vantage point I could see the two sisters, Olenka, my country aunt and Danuta, my city aunt, hovering over the cooking stove, giggling together like schoolgirls with a secret.

"Did you notice the plumbing in the bathroom?" Robin scratched his back against the heater like a bear on a tree trunk. "It's exposed on the outside of the walls. The toilet is separate from the bath. It's enclosed on the back porch. It must have been added on after the war. You probably have to keep the toilet door closed to keep the pipes from freezing out there."

"This house was one of the prettiest houses in Rajcza in its day, my dad always used to say."

"It's a big house. Have you seen the other rooms?"

"There are no other rooms, except the kitchen, a bedroom, and one little space here, walled off from the rest of the living room. It's half the size of a walk-in closet, enough room for a single bed."

Robin glanced at the door leading to the closet-sized bedroom. "You think that's where we're sleeping?"

"Don't know, but the other half of the house is sealed off for the bar."

Cesar handed us another beer and clinked our glasses. He explained that all the Rylkos own a portion of the family house. But one cousin wanted to use part of the house for a business. So they made their half a bar, sealed off from other parts of the house.

"No person likes this in family, but we must live with it," Cesar said, sipping his beer. "In bar is room where your father is born."

"My dad was born on *that* side of the house? In the bar?"

"Well, before bar," Cesar laughed, "when was grandmother's bedroom. Upstairs is small. Stairs are outside. For storing only," Cesar said. "Olenka says the upstairs is your part of house."

"I own a part of this house?" I felt as though I had inherited the crown jewels.

Cesar translated my surprise to the others. "*Tak. Tak,*" Olenka said, her gray, fuzzy hair bouncing with every word.

"The family always hold upstairs for you," Cesar interpreted for my aunt.

"Not only am I a Polish princess, I'm a Polish homeowner." I couldn't have been more delighted.

"Why you say 'Polish princess'?" Ania asked, setting forks on the table.

"Because of Count Jasterowski, of course." I set out an armful of wine glasses next to the plates.

"A-ha," Ania said without looking up, and then, "We all would like to be princesses, yes?"

Dinner was a hearty affair. Robin pulled out a bottle of pinot noir. That's when Frank made a beeline to the kitchen and disappeared, coming back a few minutes later with a large bottle of gooseberry wine he made years ago.

"Ya, ya, it is very good," Frank said. "I make it good."

"Frank, when did you learn to speak English?"

"Chicago, America," he said. "I come to Poland when eighteen years. Never leave. Go to war. Meet Johann, marry sister, Olenka. I stay." Frank had over sixty years to forget much of his English. He poured himself another glass of pinot as Robin poured one of gooseberry.

Frank said he was in the war with my father and Uncle Stephan, but that Stephan died eight years ago. Dad used the second story of the house for his paints and papers.

During the early days of the war when the Germans came, the family hid in the forest. The Germans took the house, the pictures, dishes, beds, chairs, until there was nothing left. They took all the food, killed the chickens, and sent it all to Germany.

Aunt Danuta spoke and Olenka nodded and said something.

Cesar translated, "They say, when the Germans go, then Russians come. They take what is left—nails out of walls, stones from steps, whole roof off house, even pipes in ground for water."

"Your aunt, she says Russians crazy. They go to second floor, get drunk, and jump to ground. Crazy. They burn what they do not take, photographs, other things, in big fire. When family comes back to Rajcza from hiding, house is bare. Grandfather makes new roof."

"Where did they hide?" I asked.

"Aunt Danuta is youngest. Climbs tree and hides. Germans do not find her. Olenka, they take and send to labor camp in Germany. Parents find Danuta, go to another village, and wait until Germans leave. Then hide again from Russians."

"But, in my dad's tapes, Danuta and Olenka were both taken by the Nazis. My father and Stephan found them during the war on a labor farm in Germany. They were not in a camp." I sipped at some water, watching Olenka over the rim of the glass.

"No. Not right," Uncle Frank said. "Olenka goes to same work camp in Germany as Johann, as Stephan. Where I go. Danuta stay with parents."

"Olenka and my father were in a labor camp in Germany? Which camp?"

"Same camp with Frank and Johann's brother, Stephan."
Cesar shrugged." I do not know name."

Two hours later, when the house turned dark and quiet
and we were under covers on the pullout couch in the living
room, Robin was still counting heads and beds.
"Danka, there are twelve people, right? But there are only
four beds. And we're in one of them. Frank and Olenka are
in another. Ania is on the single in their room. Peter is in the
closet. Where are Cesar and Elizabeth sleeping? And what
about Aunt Danuta and Richard, and Basha and Andrej?"
"I hope they're not sleeping in the bar. Maybe they're sharing beds. I hope no one's sleeping on the floor. Jeez, we could
sleep on the floor and let someone take this bed."
Robin came up on one elbow, considering the idea. "Let's
find out tomorrow."
"Robin, something's bothering me. Did you hear Frank
say he went through the war with my father? I never knew
that. I thought it was only Dad and his brother, Stephan. He
never mentioned Frank."
"Maybe your father didn't think it was important to add
Frank to his story. Lucky you still have Frank to talk to. And
he can sort of speak English, in a funny Chicago-Polish way."
Robin rolled over.
"But I'm confused about the labor camp where the family
said Olenka and Dad worked. My father never mentioned
that his sisters were with him, in fact, in the tapes, he and
Stephan pretended to be Nazis, crossed all over Germany
looking for them, and found them on a German farm."
Robin turned to me. "Must have been another time, I
guess." He kissed me on the forehead, on the nose, and on
the lips. I snuggled into him, returning his light kisses.

"No you don't, I'm onto your tricks. Don't try ambiancing me. Not in your father's house." Robin rolled off to his side again. "I love you, Danka."

I punched my pillow a couple of times, fluffing it up. "What does ambiancing mean, anyway?" Robin mumbled something about fooling around. And my last thought lingered, *I was in my father's house.*

FROST HAD FORMED ON THE inside of the single windowpane overnight. Cars and trucks sputtered and backfired past the house in this unmuffled part of the world, waking me just after 7 a.m. Olenka was making tea. *"Dzien dobry,* Olenka."

"Oh, *dzien dobry,* Danuta." She smiled and clapped her hands. It was an awkward moment; neither of us spoke the other's language and there was so much to say. She pointed to her coat, put it on, and then grabbed a shopping basket.

"Can I go with you?" She nodded. "I'll get my coat. Maybe Robin too?"

Olenka nodded. Ania emerged from the bedroom. "We go shopping for breakfast? I will come, too."

Before long, we were all outside in the snowy morning. Three men scampered up a huge snow bank from the river and crossed the street. They carried sleeping bags and walked up to the porch of our house and into the door under the *Bar Nad Sowa* sign.

"The men sleep in the snow to be first in the bar in the morning," Ania said.

I checked my watch. It was only 7:30, but the bar was open.

The snow-packed sidewalk followed the river. Along the riverbanks, drooping branches of fir trees shouldered heavy mounds of snow. Water trickled under rocks, and here and there joyfully broke out of the ice to make lush, gurgling sounds. Minutes later, we passed a huge cemetery behind a wrought-iron fence. Thousands of tombstones, large and small, with the same concrete crucifix perched as sturdy as a bird on top of each stone. Dusted in snow, they created ethereal white shoulders repeated to the horizon.

Olenka lead the way through ankle-deep mounds of crusty snow. As I scanned the names on the tombstones, one jumped out at me, "Jan Rylko." I was caught off guard. My father was buried in Michigan. But before I could catch my balance, another name caught my eye, Michael Rylko. I thought of Michael living in Seattle, happily married, the father of three. Then I saw Josef Rylko, Andrej Rylko, Rylkos everywhere. I was confused.

When I asked Ania about all the names she simply shrugged and said, "Like we tell you before, there are many Rylkos in Rajcza. Maybe one-third of all people here are Rylko. Maybe distant relatives, but not close."

Ania and Olenka pointed to three gravesites marked Michael Rylko and Basha Rylko and beside them Maria Rylko. "We are related to this Michael, your grandparents and your Aunt Maria." Then Ania pointed to two unmarked graves next to them. "And this is for Olenka and Frank, when they die." Ania's matter-of-fact tone chilled me. Olenka reached into her purse and pulled out a votive candle, lit it, and placed it on her father's grave.

"Tak, tak," she said, and we slowly walked back to the sidewalk.

"It is tradition," Ania said. "We live with the dead. We do not forget them. Everyone comes to the cemetery all the time."

Robin took my hand. "That would account for the cemetery in the middle of the village," he said. "It's much the same way in Latin American countries. I noticed it when I taught in Peru. People honor their dead. In the States, we don't like to think about it, much less be reminded of our mortality every day."

"But all these Rylkos! Not my relatives." I was still trying to connect the dots between the singular family name I believed we had inherited from Count Jasterowski to this maze of unrelated people. I still clung to the hope that the count was real.

Down the road we came to a long, three-story building, the windows decorated with paper snowflakes. "This is the school where your father goes when he was a little boy," Ania translated for Olenka. "All Rylkos go to this school."

A couple of rosy-cheeked children with brightly colored Snoopy backpacks clambered up the concrete steps and pushed open the heavy wooden doors, as my father did sixty years before. His grade school, minutes from his house, seconds from the graveyard. Another block and we passed a church with a towering steeple dominating the village square where Ania said the family went to church.

"Are there other churches here, Jewish synagogues or maybe Lutheran, you know, Protestant?" Robin asked.

"Ahh, Protestant!" Ania lit up. "No. No need. We are only Catholics."

We followed Olenka into a building that looked like a stone house, except for a sign above the door, *Mieso*. A long line formed inside the meat shop. Above the counter on the wall, dozens of sausages of all sizes, shapes, and colors hung from wooden pegs, like ribbons at a county fair. No-nonsense clerks wore white coats over their clothes. No one smiled.

Suddenly a bashing sound. Whack. Whack. Whack. I darted to the front of the crowd in time to see a female clerk hacking at a huge slab of meat. She wielded the axe high and busted down on the carcass, finally getting the desired cut. She wrapped the hunk in paper, handing it to the next person in line.

In the corner of the small room, red and yellow plastic bins held plucked chickens lying in watery pink liquid. Nothing was refrigerated. Under the glass counter, a skinned baby pig with its tail intact snuggled in a nightmare scene among giant livers and kidneys and other purple things. Thank God Olenka only ordered several strings of sausages.

One more stop at a grocer's for bread, and again, no one smiled. Canned and packaged food was stacked on shelves behind the counter, reminding me of trading posts in old Westerns. The suspicious eye of the clerks made me feel vaguely uncomfortable.

"Why isn't anyone smiling, Ania?" And why was I whispering?

"Why should people smile?"

Thinking she was joking, I said, "Because it's friendly."

"That is dishonest. Phony to smile for no reason, at people you don't know," Ania huffed, sounding quite resolute in her opinion.

"After seventy years of communism, old suspicions die hard," Robin said. "Boy, that looks delicious." He ogled the cheeses behind a glass counter.

I examined small potatoes in a box on the floor, some beginning to sprout. Back home, Safeway would have thrown them out. The tomatoes were tiny and irregular, the cauliflowers the size of my hand. "We're used to big food in the States," Robin said quietly. "Maybe the soil here is over tilled, been overused for centuries."

Back in the village square an odd-looking vehicle chugged by. The rig's back tires were sized for a big tractor, but up front it looked like a truck without a roof. The grille read

*Aunt Danuta and cousin Basha looking at Michigan
newspaper accounts of John Rylko's heroic life*

"Ford" but the mismatched headlights and the varying widths
of the tires made it look like a Picasso. Four men riding the
runningboards hugged the frame as a fifth man drove.

"Can you imagine how many engines and machines had to
be cannibalized over the years to make up that one mechanical
oddball?" Robin waved at the men on the belching machine.
The driver delivered a toothless grin. The heavy sweet smell
of horses hung in the air—big horses with massive hooves.
Several piles of manure steamed alongside the road. A col-
orless old truck choked by, followed by two passenger cars.
Rush hour in Rajcza.

It should have been simple to find the answers to my
many questions: Where did Count Jasterowski live? Why
didn't Dad mention that Olenka and Frank were held at the
same labor camp with him? Why are there so many Rylkos
when our family was supposed to be invented only a few gen-
erations ago? Why didn't Cesar know about my father's time
at the University of Fine Arts? Instead of answers, however, I
seemed to be gathering more questions.

DROPPED FRUIT

THE HOUSE WENT THROUGH A METAMORPHO-
sis from the hotel it had served as the night before. Aunt
Danuta and Uncle Richard had slept on half of Olenka and
Frank's bed, the larger bed separated into two. Cousin Basha
and Andrej slept on floor cushions. But by midmorning,
the beds were realigned to their former positions, cushions
replaced, bedrolls tucked away; our bed became a couch again
and the side-stand reconverted to a dining room table. The
transformation seemed effortless, as though the house were
used to change.

Then came the implosion. It began innocently enough,
with breakfast, full of chattering, and the table bountiful
with fresh sliced tomatoes, sausage, bread, and cheese. We
lingered over *ciastka*, sweet cakes, and a third cup of tea. We
all laughed when Uncle Frank launched into a nursery rhyme,
"Little Bo Peep."

"She lost her sheep and don't know where to find dem.
Leave dem alone. Dey come home. Wagging der tail behind
dem." He sat back in his chair with a huge grin on his face. "I
remember dis as young boy in Chicago. I remember all songs
and rhymes my mudder sing to me." Frank struggled to his
tired legs and hobbled to the porch for a cigarette, murmuring
another song he learned more than seventy years ago, "Geor-
gie Porgie puddin' and pie, kissed the girls and made them cry."

That's when the past came tumbling out of a bureau

drawer. Basha and her mother, Olenka, piled photographs onto the middle of the table. Hundreds of them. Elizabeth handed me a small black-and-white photo of my mother, Rick, and me sitting on the grass. She is wearing a white dress with big polka dots. I'm about three and Rick is about a year-and-a-half. On the back my mother wrote, half in Polish, half in English: "*To moja kochana* Mama, with all my love, Patricia." Even then she tried pleasing my father by learning a little Polish and writing "my dear Mama" to a woman she had never met. There was my school picture at eight, chubby cheeked, big-eyed, bangs and freckles. If only I had known during all those times when I felt alone that there was a family loving me half a planet away!

Olenka said something. Elizabeth translated, "Johann was like legend to us, living far away in America. He makes good life with good family. But why did Johann stop sending letters and photographs?"

Olenka watched for my answer, her capable hands clutching at a dishtowel. At eighty years old, Olenka's rugged Slavic face could be featured on the cover of *National Geographic*. Every weathered line and crease told a story, but it was her eyes that held me, sparkling like blue water.

There was that question again. "I don't know why he stopped."

"Your mother, Patricia, is she well?" Elizabeth's delicate eyes gazed lovingly at my mother's picture.

"Yes. Living in Oregon, a few miles from us."

"And your brother, Richard," Cesar asked, now rummaging through the photographs, "is he well also?"

"Yes. He lives in Oregon, too. He sends his love to you all."

How could I explain to them that we are fragmented as a family? Why Rick was left behind. Why Paul was not called my son. Why Dad left us.

"Ah, that is good." Elizabeth interrupted my thoughts. "To have family close." She was a soft woman, in her early forties and childless.

Uncle Frank returned to the table still singing, "One, two, buckle my shoe, tree, four, shut da door, five six pick up sticks."

"Seven eight close the gate," Robin sang back.

"Das right," Uncle Frank coughed. "You know dees songs, too."

"Yes, it is good to be close," I continued speaking to Elizabeth. I considered telling them how my family wanted to be close, how we struggled for that kind of intimacy, but thought it best to leave it alone. Why disrupt their image of happy American relatives? Let them have their fairy tale. It was difficult enough conveying simple things through the language barrier, much less the subtleties of a troubled family. As it turned out, I didn't have to explain anything at all. My family's troubled past in America would affect us all soon enough.

"Hey, Frank," Robin said, "when was this picture taken?"

Frank leaned on his cane and raised the picture to the light. "Oh, dat picture during da war, 1943. A picnic with da family in Rajcza. Me, Stephan, Danuta, Mudder, Fadder, and Johann."

"Picnic? During the war?" Robin studied it and handed it to me, a picture straight out of *The Great Gatsby*. My father sits on a blanket with Frank and Stephan, surrounded by his family, wearing knickers and a cap.

"But in 1943 he was in—" I didn't finish my sentence before Robin said, "Here's another one." In it, my father sits on a wooden bench in front of a hayfield. He wears a wool sport coat with those matching knickers again and clean, white socks tucked into what looks like new loafers. His handsome, clean-shaven face smiles slightly. His hands are clasped in his lap as though he doesn't know what else to do with them.

"Was this the same year?"

"Same time, 1943." Frank waved off the time like a fly from his face. "On furlough from the work camp in Dollendorf. We go on vacation to Poland." Uncle Frank favored his sore hip and he sat down gingerly in his easy chair, resting his cane against the armrest.

"On furlough? From a labor camp? In the middle of the war? Frank, that's not right," I said. "Once the war began, my father never saw his mother and father again. And in 1943, Dad and Stephan were in Dachau."

Drawn by the sounds of a conversation, the rest of the family dragged chairs and stools to the table. Cesar held up his hand, pausing the discussion to interpret for the family. When he finished, the room filled with a collision of words, bouncing between gesticulating hands and arms. They looked at me with puzzled expressions, even amusement.

After a short pause Frank said, "Das wrong. Johann with me, in Dollendorf. Not Dachau."

Robin pulled up a chair. "Wait a minute, Frank," he said, waving the picture of my dapper-looking father in knickers. "You say this picture was taken in 1943? How do you know that?"

"I remember every-ting," Uncle Frank said. "I was there. Olenka know this. Johann was with me in 1943." There was another burst of discussion and nodding heads.

Elizabeth took Robin's arm. "All family know this. Frank and Olenka are with Johann in Dollendorf in 1943."

"Wait," I said. "I've got something to show you all. It will help clear this all up." I jumped up from the table and sorted through my bags in the corner. Pulling my father's cassettes and the cassette player out, I said, "I have tapes. His own words. His voice. I wanted to surprise you. Here, he says the dates. Listen." I clicked on the machine. For the first time in more than half a century, my father's voice filled his Polish home, awakening the memories embedded in the plaster, hidden in the corners.

I had escaped Dachau in the winter of 1943 and came back in April, 1945, and the camp was still full of prisoners, but the mountain of bones was bigger.

Aunt Danuta murmured, "Johann, Johann," and grabbed Olenka's hand.

Cesar asked, "Danuta, this is Johann speaking now?"

I told him Dad left us the tapes, the story of his life. That I was using them to write his book. Cesar translated. Basha walked over to Olenka and stood behind her mother. Uncle Richard stood next to Aunt Danuta, who still clutched Olenka's hand. Andrej hushed Peter and Ania and motioned for them to sit down. My family clustered together in anticipation of my father's next words. The Requiem was about to begin.

Frank pulled forward in his chair, seeking his cane, preparing for balance. Everyone fixed their gazes on the little tape player I held in my hand, as if staring at it would increase their ability to hear.

"Danuta," Cesar said, "this is a shock for everyone, to hear Johann's voice. Play again. I will interpret for family."

I rewound the tape and played it again.

I had escaped Dachau in the winter of 1943 and came

*back in April, 1945, and the camp was still full of
prisoners, but the mountain of bones was bigger.*

"Johann," Aunt Danuta said again, still startled by her
brother's voice, her hand reaching toward the tape recorder,
trying to catch him in the air. Uncle Richard frowned and
spoke. Olenka cast a worried look at Aunt Danuta and said
something to Uncle Frank. Frank's magnified eyes behind
thick lenses stared at me. "*Nie*! No! For whole war he was in
labor camp, working in woodshop. He was with me, with
Olenka and Stephan." Frank shook his head.

"Yes, but, he was taken from the labor camp, don't you
remember, Uncle Frank?"

While Cesar translated, I searched through the box of cassettes. "He says it right here, on tape seven, listen." My father's
voice soared up from the grave and across half a century.

*The Gestapo dragged us to the meister, the owner
of the shop. He was eating his breakfast when they
barged into his kitchen, shoving us into the room. 'See
who you have working here, spies!' During a week of
interrogation, we were fed only three times. We were
starving. Finally, when they finished with us, we were
handcuffed and put on a train to Dachau.*

I felt grateful to have the tapes with me, since Uncle
Frank's recollections seemed off kilter with the facts. "So,
Frank, when exactly did Dachau happen?" I asked.

Everyone waited for his answer. I didn't take my eyes off
Uncle Frank.

"Never!" Frank thumped the floor with his cane.

"I think you're wrong, Uncle Frank. They were tortured.
You knew about that, didn't you?" I found another tape and
this time, in a soft, hesitant voice, my father uttered the hor-

rifying details of his ordeal:

And the Butcher lifted up on the locked pliers and slowly peeled back the nail from my thumb. I was shocked! I couldn't believe my eyes! And I couldn't believe my pain! My mouth was wide open, like a fish, choking on the air. Breath wouldn't come. The higher he lifted my nail, the lower I sank to the floor until I finally fainted. I couldn't stand the pain.

Cesar whispered the last words of his translation. Aunt Danuta dabbed at her eyes with a tissue. Olenka patted her shoulder. Uncle Richard bent over his chair, wringing his hands, and without raising his head, said something to Frank.

"No!" Another quick thump of his cane. Frank was unmoved. Absolute.

I tried to subdue the panic stirring in me. "Maybe you don't know the whole story? After all, you weren't in Dachau. This tape tells the whole thing." I ran the tape forward and played another section.

I remembered where I was. I am still in Dachau. I am in the Nazis' hands.

Frank commented quietly, "No. Johann never in Dachau."

"Now, wait a minute, Frank, listen to the rest. I'm sure this is all new to you." The tape continued rolling.

I touched my face. It was sticky. . . blood over my face. . . sticky over my mouth. Blood was running out of my nose. Bruises all over my body.

"*Nie. Nie.*" Olenka muttered. I would learn the Polish word for "no" all too well.

"Just a second, now, wait till you hear the rest of it."

The bitter cold woke me up. As I tried to move, I realized my body was frozen to the concrete floor. Little by little, using my hands and fingers, I tried to peel my skin off the floor.

I glanced at Frank. "Not possible!" Thump. The cane came down hard.

"Of course it's possible. These are his own words, Frank. You recognize his voice, don't you? What do you mean when you say not possible?"

Frank said nothing, a pained and pensive look settled on his face. Frustrated with trying to find sections of audiotapes, I went back to my bags and hefted out the transcript. "Look, these are my father's memoirs, all four hundred pages. I've written it from the tapes. It's the book I've been working on for years." Cesar translated. Oohs and aahs of understanding rose from my relatives. I flipped through the arsenal of memories I held on my lap until I found a section on the concentration camp.

"Look, here, he says he escaped from Dachau," I read quickly, skipping through lines. "The plan . . . we would be Gestapo guards . . . take the truck . . . loaded with prisoners through the gate. I would drive . . . between the barracks, straight to the main gate—"

Frank banged his cane again. "Impossible!"

His words unnerved me. "Frank, do you say it's impossible because you don't remember?" I looked to Robin for help.

"Frank," Robin said, "do you mean John never escaped *from* Dachau?"

"Johann never *in* Dachau," Frank said.

"But he says it right here," I cried.

"*Nie. Nie*, Danusia, please, this is not true." Frank swung his head left and right.

I tucked the pages recounting the stories I knew to be true back into the manuscript. "It's okay, Uncle Frank, we'll talk about it later." I could see I was upsetting my uncle. Perhaps his age had blurred his memory over time, and so I turned to my Aunt Olenka, thinking she might have a better memory of events.

"Olenka, here's a part of the story I think you should remember."

Olenka. . . She used to wait at the station for me, as I came back from school. I fought a man who tried to rape her.

"*Nie,*" Olenka moaned.

"*Nie?*" I repeated. "Olenka, I'm sorry, it upsets you to remember?"

There was some conversation. Cesar turned to me and said, "Danusia, Olenka says there was no one who tried to rape her."

Aggravated by my inability to reach them, I tried again, "What about this, Olenka? Remember when my father pretended to be a Nazi and he and Stephan came looking for you and Aunt Danuta in Germany?"

I took the helmet off, 'It's a disguise!' My brother came from behind me, 'Olenka, we are not German nationals! They're just useful uniforms.' Her face suddenly brightened up and she ran towards us, threw her arms around us. We all cried. We found Danuta on another corner of the farm and embraced.

"*Nie,*" Frank said, thumping the cane. My stomach cramped. I looked to Olenka, who shook her head. "No one tries to rape Olenka. Danuta not in Germany. No Nazi disguises," Frank said.

The dishtowel fell from Olenka's fingers. She stared at me, with her hand on her heart, as if making sure it was still beating. Aunt Danuta's chin quivered and her lips turned watery. Ania, Peter, Elizabeth, and Cesar all spoke at the same time, each trying to decode my father's words.

I asked Robin if the translations might be the source of all this confusion.

"They seem to understand well enough," he said.

I shuffled through the manuscript looking for another story. "Frank, the Pyrenees, do you remember when they got lost crossing the mountains?"

We were weak, cold, and disoriented, stumbling and pulling each other along in the snow. There was no way back.

My eyes locked on Uncle Frank. He sat as still as a stone and said nothing. I read more.

. . . we were starving, getting colder, desperate. We learned later we had been in the mountains for twenty-one days.

Thump! Thump! Thump! The pain in my stomach became more severe. "Danusia, it never happen this way. We all the time in labor camps." Frank muttered something to Richard, who responded in a low voice.

"What about the Normandy Landing, 1944?" I said.

We were filthy and exhausted, coughing and choking from the sea water. Blood mixed with the sand. Hand grenades through the air . . . pinned down . . . had to withdraw . . . the artillery . . . German machine guns from the left bank . . . withdraw . . . circle round . . .

run for our lives.

"Impossible!"

Robin started to say something, but I didn't want to hear it. I had to find a piece of my father in these pages. Again, I read,

> *It was May, 1944 . . . the Battle of Monte Cassino, the biggest battle on the Western Front . . . the worst battle I ever saw.*

"No." Frank was unswerving.

Robin and the rest watched in horror as Frank and I went at it, volleying for the truth, my father's words contending against Frank's memory and the ongoing thud of his cane. My hands shook, the pages blurred in front of me. I read on, disregarding the ceaseless rejections, fighting to stay in denial of the inevitable:

> *. . . three years at private school . . . a scholarship to the University of Fine Arts in Krakow.*

"*Nie, nie, nie.*" Frank insisted.

> *I was taking languages, psychology, sculpturing, stone, wood, marble, painting, drawing, and draftsmanship . . . sent to Zagreb, Yugoslavia . . . scholarship . . . then Germany on scholarship to Milan for six months . . ."*

Danuta waved her hand in the air, like a wand trying to erase the words.

Cesar translated, "No. That's not right. He went to a small art school in Istebna, a small village, not far from here. War came, and no time to finish his education."

"Are you trying to tell me he never went to college? Never had a scholarship?" I felt my father slipping through my fingers, my life slipping through the cracks in his stories. Aunt

John Rylko on vacation

Danuta came over to me and tried reading over my shoulder. She stroked my hair. She couldn't read the words, but somehow it must have comforted her to try. Ania spoke to Peter, but they didn't look up at me.

"Is that what you're telling me, Aunt Danuta? He never went to the University of Fine Arts? Are you telling me he lied about that?" I realized that for the first time, I used the word "lie." I turned to look up at her pained expression. I felt sick.

"There must be some mistake. My father said he fought in North Africa, in tanks against Rommel. Is that right, Uncle Frank?"

"Yes, we in North Africa," Frank said. "Dat is correct. Johann in Egypt, 1944."

"Yes. Right. See? And he fought Rommel at Tobruk, right?" Finally! I took my first full breath in an hour.

"Johann never *fight* in Africa, only goes there after war to help with British. Clean up bases." Quicksand. My God, what was going on?

> *In Palestine, we joined up with a British commando training camp. I trained as a skydiver, learned how to use a knife, how to utilize the night, how to use my fists and my guns.*

"*Nie.* Not right." The thud of the cane wrenched at my gut. If only I could have heard a whisper of uncertainty, just a little hesitation in Uncle Frank's voice, but he left nothing to cast a shred of hope upon.

"Why not, Frank, why not right?" I slapped the table with my hand in frustration. The solid substance of the wood felt surprisingly good beneath my palm. Photographs spilled like tears onto the floor.

"He escaped from a stalag with the help of his friend, Henry, who became a doctor in Germany . . . ." I stammered out a story I remembered.

But the staccato of rejection continued. "No. No escape. No Henry." The words tore into me like shrapnel. Certainty bled out of me, and with it the life I had believed in.

"Impossible, Danusia."

The picture of my father sitting on a bench with clean white socks and knickers blazed up at me from the table. My father on a picnic in Poland, when he should have been dying in Dachau. The smiling proof on his face stared at me but I still couldn't absorb it.

Robin tried a different tack at getting to my uncle's story, "Wait, let's back up. Frank, you said you spent the whole war with Johann?"

"We meet in stalag in 1939. Then go to work camp in Dollendorf to 1944. Five years through whole war we are in camps together—always together."

"Yes, but how did you get vacations in a labor camp?"

"In da camp, we work hard. After six or nine months, Johann works for a meister in woodshop, until 1944. He must come in to camp every night."

"But it was still *forced* labor, right?" I asked, sensing a small concession from Uncle Frank.

"Yes. Forced. But we get ten marks a month for soap and bathroom things."

"You were *paid?*" Robin's voice rang with surprise.

Uncle Frank got up slowly from his chair. "Not paid for work, but money for little things. To live."

"Okay, but Frank, a furlough from a labor camp?" Robin asked.

"The meister good friend with Johann, gives us restricted papers. We leave for few weeks only."

"But," Robin asked, "once you got out of the camp and got home, back to Poland, why not just stay?" He turned to me, "It just seems incredible that they had a vacation in the middle of the goddamned war. I mean, how many other soldiers or POWs got furloughs?" Even Robin got caught up in the confusion now.

"Must go back. Olenka stays behind in camp like hostage."

"Could my father have been in Dachau after the labor camp, Frank?" I still hoped for a flicker of light, a dent in his memory, some fragment of truth in the rubble of lies.

"No. Stephan, Johann, and me, go through war together

in camp. All the time, together." Frank shuffled out to the kitchen. He put on a coat and went onto the porch for a cigarette. The rest whispered among themselves.

Elizabeth patted my arm. "I'll make some tea."

"Everything is all mixed up. I need to go over his tapes again, read the transcripts. I must have missed something." I stared at the yellow, plastered walls. The Pope above the doorway seemed to stare back at me with the same disbelieving eyes of my aunts and uncles.

"I don't think you missed a thing." Robin sounded resigned and gave a deep sigh.

Everything I had ever believed about my father, about myself, about my family, who we were, was in these tapes, this manuscript. It was all my father left us. There simply had to be an explanation.

Frank came back into the room. "Danusia," he said, "you ask. It's okay."

The sweet man patted my knee. I thought at that moment how difficult it must be for Uncle Frank, to disavow the words of his friend, his comrade in arms, his brother-in-law, to reduce my father's memories into a heap of distortion and illusion.

"I hear da words but dey are wrong. Not right. I remember."

"Frank," I said softly, "are you telling me my father spent nearly the entire war in a labor camp? Never left? Never escaped?"

"No, never escaped."

"But he was tortured, Frank, horribly tortured, and Stephan, too."

"No!" Thump. Frank was getting frustrated.

"You heard my father say it." A stab of pain twisted inside

of me. I knew Frank was telling the truth, but now I didn't want to hear it.

"Never!" Frank bit into that word like he would never let go.

"But he suffered. My mother believed it. My brothers. All our lives, we believed he was hurt in the war. He told everyone. That's why he was so angry and depressed."

Elizabeth spoke. "Danusia, Olenka and family don't understand this. Johann was angry?"

"He was hard on us. Beat us when we were little. Unfaithful to my mother." Aunt Danuta covered her mouth and began to cry again. Uncle Richard kissed her and wiped her cheek with a hanky from his pocket. I shouldn't have said that. I shouldn't have betrayed him. There was more to him than that. "He loved us. He taught us to ski. He wanted us to compete in the Olympics, like he did." I scanned their faces.

"Olympics?" Cesar asked.

I felt a chill. I wrote to Stockholm and got the reply from the International Olympic Committee, "John Rylko's name does not appear on the competitors' list." The hair rose on the back of my neck. Oh, God, not this.

"Olenka says he was good skier, but never Olympics, only local ski competitions," Cesar said, watching Olenka confirm with a nod.

"But the medals, downhill, cross country. He skied for Poland in 1936." My voice lost its strength. I remembered reading the words from the Polish Olympic Committee, the words I put out of my head, dismissed as incomplete information, excused as lost files, "The files of our Committee say nothing about Mr. Rylko's participation in the Winter Olympic Games in 1936."

"No, Danuta. Why would Johann say such things?" Now

Cesar sounded alarmed.

In one last attempt to prove the impossible, I pulled out the newspaper articles from one of my bags, and found the announcement of my father as the new ski instructor at a resort in Michigan, and the caption, *John Rylko, a medal winner in the 1936 Olympics.* I read it aloud and showed it to everyone. Cesar chewed the inside of his lip. Robin looked at me helplessly.

"No, Danuta, again, not right." Frank uttered those words in a slow, resolute voice. His lower lip curled out stubbornly. He sat erect and stoic in his chair. His cane quiet now and still.

"These newspaper reports are not true." Elizabeth had been standing in the doorway of the kitchen, holding a teapot, listening to us. She shook her head, not so much as to say no, but in a way that said, sorry, her soft eyes bathed in compassion.

The steady stream of negatives had completely undermined me. My uncles and aunts fell back in their chairs as my anguish echoed against them. How were they supposed to explain my father's absurd claims? He was the Anointed One. Fawned over by the family, doted upon as the youngest son, held up as the boy who made good, the talented sculptor who lived in America with his beautiful family. This was their beloved Johann. From their expressions, with each resounding "No" and "Never," they were hit with the same agonizing realization: their adored Johann, my father, lied about them. Lied about himself. Not once, but hundreds of times. They must have felt as devastated as I did. Could my father have imagined how much this would hurt? Did he never imagine we would discover the truth?

I must have looked terribly distressed. I felt conscious of them all looking at me. What were they feeling, pity, confusion, defeat? Only hours ago, their American relative was so happy with her new family, and now she had melted into a wordless despair. Aunt Danuta scooted her chair around to mine at the table and took my hand, patting it, stroking it, trying to make me feel better.

Elizabeth gave me a glass of tea. Aunt Danuta reached for the cream from the table and offered it to me, as if it were an apology. I gently accepted it.

"Danusia," Elizabeth said, "we can't understand what happened to Johann, but your Aunt Olenka says it is only good story, yes? Johann was like all mountain people, they tell good stories."

"Mountaineering stories?" I scoffed, and by the look on her face, even Elizabeth knew it was a meager offering. These stories were the backbone of our lives, not some mountain myth.

Was there nothing left? I turned to Cesar. "Was he engaged to Stephanie, did she die in the gas chamber?"

"No," Cesar said for Olenka. "There were many girls. No Stephanie."

I had no choice but to endure the nightmare, to seek out the bottom, to hope for an end to this litany of lies. I offered up each remaining claim like a soap bubble, to watch it burst. I knew what the answers would be before I asked the questions.

"Count Jasterowski? His coat of arms, and his castle?"

"Danusia," Elizabeth said, "Olenka says three hundred years ago there was a woman," she counted on her fingers, "six times great, yes? This great-grandmother was named Jasterowski. She married a Rylko. During revolution, they hide from the Swedes. So they come to Rajcza, live in simple house. They have nine children. Two of the brothers then marry two sisters from another family. They make two branches of Rylkos. We come from one branch. But not royalty."

The fairytale came to a close when the final bubble burst and the castle disappeared.

I thought of my father, dazzling in his white parka, white gloves, and skis, and the crowd, cheering on the White Pole. I remembered the story as I had heard it hundreds of times before:

> *I climbed with one pole. My lungs ached for air, my heart pounded in my head. I got to the top. And then downhill, through the checkpoints and over the finish line. I was completely drained. I took second. I lost by three-tenths of a second.*

But I lost a lifetime. There was no White Pole.

My aunts looked pale. No one made a sound around the table, as though we gazed at my father's grave and wondered where the body went. I tried to say something but my voice caught in my throat. I shot a glance at Robin sitting to the other side of me. He pressed his leg against mine.

In the quiet eye of the storm of memories that swirled about us, each of us seemed to evaluate the relationship we had with a man who was a brother, a friend, a father, and now, something else. Maybe we were wrong. Memories couldn't be trusted. Perhaps we made a mistake, misunderstood something, overlooked something. But we'd all have to be wrong to make my father's story right.

We had drained the day of its light. In one greedy gulp, we had swallowed the sun. The bright and shining star that had once adorned the apex of the family tree had fallen, tarnished and frail. John Rylko had been exposed, as naked as he stood shivering in the death-camp snow in front of the

Butcher. Except there was no death camp. And no Butcher.

The family talked quietly among themselves, occasionally someone threw a furtive glance at me that spoke of shame, mine or theirs, I wasn't sure. I suppose it was still too unthinkable to cast guilt on a dear departed son. Robin suggested we take a walk.

I stood on the icy banks of the Sowa River feeling bruised by the sledgehammering words, impossible, *nie*, and never. Snow fell like spilled milk. I saw no splendor in the Tatra Mountain light, and no grandeur in the landscape.

I swiped at a low-lying branch burdened with snow, and a shrapnel of white spit into the air.

"What will I tell my mother? She put up with so much shit from Dad, and for what? She wanted a picture of the castle. What will I tell Rick? He tried to emulate a war hero. He wanted to carve the coat of arms. Instead of bringing back their dreams, I'm bringing back a nightmare. I'm so damned angry, I can't think straight." I pitched a snowball into the cold river. "He used us." Another snowball plopped into the icy waters. "That bastard."

It felt good. Throwing the damn snowballs. Into the damn river. Packing the snow. Punching the air. Spewing my anger. Another snowball zinged the air, but it wasn't mine. "Yes!" Robin shouted. He understood. In spite of my miserable state of mind, I smiled.

"No damned castle!" My snowball slammed into the river.

"No damned Olympic medals!" Robin's ball smashed against a tree.

"No damned House of Jasterowski." My pitch hit a log in the stream.

"And no damned Dachau." A burst of water and ice.

"What a couple of odd, Oregon ducks we must seem."

Robin's warm breath made puffballs around his face. "Two grown-ups, Americans at that, throwing snowballs and screaming next to a river in Poland." Robin gave a high-pitched giggle that sounded like gulls on a beach. Rolling hiccups of laughter gurgled out of him. His cackling became infectious and soon I began to laugh until my stomach hurt. Then tears came, streaking icicles down my cheeks; a hot sob of an orphaned emotion gutted my giddiness. Another sob. No daring escapes, no heroics, no nothing. Betrayal buckled me to my knees. Robin sank next to me.

In the fresh fallen snow, I welcomed the cold that crept through my legs and the soft burn of my skin as it turned numb. Emptiness always feels cold; it is a dismal hollow of glacial proportions. This was where the grand journey of expectation had led, to a bleak landscape of my identity.

I felt lost, grieving not for my father's bones and sinews, nor the stillness of his vigorous heart, but for a personality I thought I knew. By coming to this house to feel closer to him, I found a vast and colder distance. An arm across my shoulder roused me. I looked at Robin. I had come halfway around the world searching for grounding and foundation. And in Robin I saw all that I had longed for: mercy and love, hope and happiness; they were all there, in him.

Robin's voice was steady. "Come on," he said, lending me a hand and hoisting me out of the snow. "Let's go warm up. I know a little bar, it's near the river. Not too far from the house."

CRUSH

THE *BAR NAD SOWA* WAS NEARLY EMPTY WHEN we arrived, with two men sitting at the far corner table. One man had slumped over the table clutching a half-empty glass of beer, the other guy was passed out in his chair. On the table, empty vodka bottles posted the rounds to oblivion and ashtrays brimmed with half-smoked cigarettes that smoldered like forgotten days. Behind the counter stretched across the end of the room, an old woman watched a black-and-white television set. She seemed to be watching the Polish version of *Jeopardy* judging from the canned sound of the audience, the ringing bell, and the fast-talking host.

In spite of the clientele, the bar was rather pleasant. White lace curtains hung over the windows and the walls sported the same cheery yellow paint as the rest of the house. Six tables covered in blue and white plastic tablecloths dotted the room. We ordered two beers and slipped into the table farthest away from the two drunks.

After a bit Robin said, "Was this a total surprise to you? I mean, didn't you have some nagging voice that told you things weren't adding up? Any irregularities in his story?" Robin quaffed his beer.

"Not once. These stories were so embedded in me that I had no reason to doubt them. Look, it's like this. Your mom is missing her right thumb, right?"

"Yeah. She fell in front of a trolley in Boston when she was a young girl. It sliced her thumb from her hand."

"Right. That's what she told you. But let's just suppose years later you meet a relative who said your mother never fell in front of a trolley, that her thumb was severed during a knife fight with her boyfriend. And she never lived in Boston; she was a prison escapee living in Detroit. You'd be stunned, and hurt, like I am now. You build a foundation on the history you're given. No dissection, no analysis, no cause for suspicion, you believe."

"But you're not a child. You're a journalist. You ask questions. You've worked on this book for years. Didn't you research these stories?"

I thought of my shelves of books and research papers on World War II. How everything fit together. "The events happened. They just didn't happen to him. My father must have heard the stories from other soldiers, and became one of the hundreds of thousands who fought in North Africa, Italy, and France, who endured the Gestapo, and concentration camps. Who was I or anyone else to doubt him? But then, the missing Olympic records—"

Just then, Cesar came through the front door. Robin motioned to the woman at the counter, pointing to our beers. "This is called Zywiec beer," Cesar said.

"Jiv-y-ets," we repeated.

"Yes, it comes from town not far from Rajcza. We call this *pee-vo*, meaning to you, beer."

A blast of cold air rushed in as Uncle Richard appeared in the doorway and asked to join us, ordered himself a *pivo*, and patted Robin on the back. We nursed our beers for a few moments, then Cesar motioned with his head, "Danuta, your father was born there, where table is. That was bedroom for grandfather and grandmother. All children born there,

Olenka, Danuta, too."

I looked toward the far end of the room where the two drunks slept and tried to imagine my grandmother lying upon her bed, laboring with child. My father taking his first breath in this room. His lungs burning with life. His existence greeted with tears. How my grandfather must have felt. What dreams they had for him, to become a priest or a doctor. This room held him. What would they say now of their baby boy who split and divided his family because we could not stand up to the false standards he imposed?

This was the room where I was born, too. My genetic links materialized in a home that was now a haven for alcoholics in a house divided in half. I studied my beer. While I had crossed a continent and an ocean seeking truth, my father had crossed an ocean and a continent to evade it.

"Cesar, Uncle Richard, did my father say anything that was true? I mean, what about the first three weeks of war. Surely, as a young soldier he fought for Poland."

"Ah, yes, Danuta, my father says that is true. When war starts, Johann was in Jelona, not far from Rajcza."

"With the artillery, riding a horse, setting up lookouts around these hills? That is true?"

"Yes." Cesar nodded emphatically.

"I never thought I'd hear that word."

"Danusia, we have at home a picture your father made of horse, with bombs, and he is falling off horse," Cesar said.

"Yeah, I know the story!" I bounced in my chair. "He was galloping down a hillside, to warn a group of soldiers at a lookout that the Germans were coming. A shell exploded under his horse. The horse died."

"Yes. Johann writes letter to family from the frontline with picture. My father says he fight Germans for three weeks."

"That's good. Good." I took a long deep breath. We all smiled, nodding at each other.

After a short silence, I asked Cesar, "What else is true in the tapes you heard?"

"Danka," Robin sipped at his *pivo*, "your father fused truth and fiction for so long, about so much; I don't think we'll ever know what really happened."

"But why be a storyteller?"

"A storyteller? Look, no one gets hurt if the deer had a bigger rack, or the fish got longer in the telling of it. Your father wasn't a storyteller. How long are you going to avoid the "L" word?"

Robin's eyes riveted me to my chair. The "L" word. I wanted it to mean "love." The love between a father and child. The word seldom used by my father. I believed he loved me. He could show tenderness. Like not shooting the deer when he took me hunting. Like the fireside stories of witches. The soups he cooked up out of thin air. He was a gentle man in my childhood.

"You mean, when am I going to call my father a liar." The word slurred out of my mouth, a moldy aftertaste of a word. As ugly a word as there ever was. Liar. "Well, imposter maybe."

Robin leaned over the table. "An imposter is someone who can't live *as* himself. A liar can't live *with* himself. Your father couldn't live with his conscience. Took it out on you guys. And to invoke images of Dachau where people truly suffered and died, just to enhance his own ego. That hurts everyone who suffered the truth." Robin took a swallow of beer as if washing his mouth of a bitter taste.

Robin was right, stealing the honor of those who earned it and pasting it onto his chest, his falsehood was authenticated by honorable people. Reinforced by others, my father's fraud was complete. But he was punished for it; surrendering to his own deceit, his soul withered in anger and depression, driving us away.

I felt worse than ever. "Look, he was a Polish immigrant in a new land. He wanted a new life. Lots of people change their names to Americanize themselves. And maybe he felt guilty for not suffering enough. He was in a work camp, not a concentration camp, so he built a huge new life out of his imagination."

Robin eyed me with skepticism.

I knew what he was thinking. My father's false identity was not simple benign imagination; driven by ego, it created a life force of its own, recreating the past, imprinting itself on a family with such ferocity it forced into question our own identities. False identity passed on to Paul, and to Matthew. Rick will have to live up to a different hero, and my mother will have to resolve the love she had for a fictitious legend. We had lost the face in the mirror.

The bar door opened and a cold draft ran up my back. Uncle Frank had hobbled up the icy steps and entered the bar. "Olenka don't like bar in house, so I don't come to bar. But for now, I come." He put his fingers up to his lips and winked. "I have a *pivo* with you."

We scooted around to make a space for him at the table.

"Not good to hear about Johann, not for me, not for you," Uncle Frank said. "But I tink he doesn't come back to Poland because he must marry a woman here," Uncle Frank said, glancing up in acknowledgment to the woman who brought his beer.

"What woman?" I perked up.

"Woman who waits for him to come back. But he marry your mamma, Patricia, instead."

Uncle Frank nodded, but I said, "To avoid an entire country and your family because of a woman?"

Uncle Frank pulled a cigarette from his shirt pocket, lit it, and exhaled a long, cloudy trail.

Cesar absentmindedly scratched at his beer glass and abruptly slammed his hand down on the table. "Now, I remember something," he said. "Many years ago, Stephan reads London newspaper with story about Johann during the war. Story Stephan doesn't like. He writes something to Johann and then all news from Johann stop. Maybe he finds Johann lying."

From behind the bar the television rang out, "Ding! Ding! Ding!"

"Here's how I see it," Robin said. "The truth was catching up to him. First, he was engaged to a woman he didn't marry. That burned a bridge right there. And then, if his brother Stephan discovered he lied about the war, that must have caused a rift."

That made sense. Knowing his lies were exposed to Stephan, he would have to sever contact with the rest of the family because he figured everyone would find out. He couldn't live with both worlds, the truth in Poland and the lies in America. And maybe that's why he didn't have any Polish friends. They'd have picked his stories apart, asked questions he couldn't answer. Other Poles would have exposed him. He'd have to avoid those who were really in the war.

Cesar and Frank surmised that Dad made friends with Germans in America because he had befriended so many Germans in the labor camp during the war. Germans had become friends, not enemies. At that point, one of the drunks in the corner vomited over himself. It was time to leave the *Bar Nad Sowa*.

I RUBBED MY SORE, RED eyes. Sleep wouldn't come. Robin lay beside me, deep in slumber, rhythmically breathing.

Dad didn't think I'd be so thorough, that I'd actually visit Poland. I could see why nobody checked his stories; how do you doubt a man who carves the face of God?

What did I know about him for sure? He wanted to be more than the man born on the other side of this wall. His life was a myth of his own making, masquerading weakness as strength, awarding fear for love, and trading idolatry for respect. But I had to remember, he was a young man, fraught with flaws and disappointments, like so many finding their way. And there was another side, the man whose hands gleamed from the humus he dug from under a log, whose silhouette wavered against the blaze in the hollow tree. To me, he was the father I married, the man who eclipsed the sun. His was the gentle hand resting on my shoulder as the deer leapt away from his halfhearted arrow. The sculptor who carved gods out of stone. He was the father who was coming at Easter. The man who asked me for forgiveness. He created a myth and I tried to live up to it—and was stronger for doing so, regardless of the truth of it.

I watched the full moon glinting through the tiny window above me, shredding the clouds of the passing storm, spilling over the covers of the bed. Soon it would climb high atop the gabled roof of this house, where it had gleamed upon my father half a century ago as surely as it shone upon me now. Romanticized by poets and exploited by pirates, the moon spoke of the hidden and the veiled, not the harsh bleach of sunlight, but the satin caress of a lunar shade. I could almost see his face—the man in the moon—a harbinger of seasons signaling from the shadows when to plant and when to harvest, guiding us by his half-light. This is how we made our way, my father and I, in the shadow of reflected light under this Carpathian moon.

MATTHEW

LATE SEPTEMBER IN OREGON. THE WINE GRAPES are sweet and harvest is due. We struck a bargain with nature: a pledge of labor for a season of fruit. The rewards of sun-scorched skin, sixteen-hour days, and the passion for growing came together in exchange for a harvest, filled with hope and expectation.

Purple clusters took on the bronzy sheen of an autumn sun. Golds and reds fired the edges of ever-shorter days. Winter grays bullied the blue from the sky along the Coast Range. Storm clouds strung across the Pacific like pearls on a necklace, each a foreshadow of rain—torrential, unrelenting rain, the kind of rain that makes your shoulders ache and hunkers your gaze to the ground. A cold, mud-making rain cementing cows in their pasture and rotting the hooves off sheep. Five months of rain forcing hibernation and the comfort of books, cast-iron stoves, and long nights of Scrabble in front of the fire.

Gray rain is vital, greening Oregon's Willamette Valley, invigorating dense Douglas-firs. But too much or too soon and disaster will strike the grapes with destructive mold and irreversible rot. The noble fruit must be picked, fast. Rain was coming. We raced the storms to gather 160 tons of grapes. Inside each grape, the seeds were brown and the sugars and acids lined up like Jupiter and Mars on the cross hairs of the winemaker's scope—sugar for alcohol, acid for flavor. Seventy acres of pinot noir and pinot gris draped the trellis wires in lush ribbons of fruit. The vineyard buzzed with pickers and tractors, forklifts and trucks.

Robin forked the half-ton bins onto the flatbed truck and trailer while I spent the morning plowing through bins of grapes, checking clusters for rot, pulling leaves, and dodging the wasps feasting on the syrupy sugars. My back ached and my arms and jeans were stiff and sticky with fruit juice. Slogging in boots heavy with mud from an early drizzle, I felt my shoulders loosen under the woolly sauna of my jacket as the midmorning sun steamed out the dampness from my clothes. The plaid jacket, bought when Pendleton still meant Oregon wool, had a rip under the arm big enough to drive a dozer through, but I considered it good ventilation, and it was warm. I had come a long way from the fashions of Tinseltown, as Robin called San Diego, to being the wife of a farmer.

God, how I loved this. The work, the grapes, the dirt. I had learned to love the dirt, clean dirt, the kind of dirt that made good wine. The kind of wine that Robin says makes you fall to your knees and weep. Most of all, I loved Robin who grew up here, rooted as firm as his vines, honest as the soil, rugged as the land, with sympathies as deep as Crater Lake.

It was nearly lunchtime and I ran to the house to make sandwiches for the crew. I had just finished and was putting away the bread when the phone rang. The voice on the other end said, "Um, hi. Is this Danuta Rylko?"

"Yes, Pfeiffer now. What is this regarding?" I hoped the caller got the message that I didn't have any time to waste.

The caller said, "Um, well, it's about the son you had in Anchorage in 1967."

I squeezed the phone closer to my ear, and sought the kitchen counter for support. "What?"

"Well, I just thought if you're *that* Danuta Rylko, then I

think it's me. I mean, I think I'm your son."

My heart jackhammered against my chest. The caller continued, hesitant, but persistent.

"So, I was wondering, maybe we could talk or something, if you have the time . . ."

I stumbled into a chair. "Matthew."

"Who's Matthew?"

"It's you. The name I gave you."

"You named me? Really? I never thought . . . you named me. Well, my name *these* days is Troy."

I wrote "Troy" on the back of an envelope I found on the table. My son, but not mine. Not a baby, but a man now.

"I've been waiting for you." I hung my head in my hand; my face felt hot.

"Really?"

It had been twenty-nine years and six months since I heard Matthew's voice, a cry really, from a distance I could not breach. Until now. "Where are you?"

"Phoenix."

"That's a long way from Alaska." I wrote "Phoenix." I didn't want to lose him again.

"And you're in Oregon. Guess we both moved on a bit. I hope it's okay, you know, me finding you."

"Oh God, yes. It's just a wonderful shock to hear you suddenly, all grown up. I figured, when you were ready—how'd you find me?"

"The Internet. Pretty easy, really. Once I got my real birth certificate and found your name on it. I got the hospital records, too. They said you cried."

"Yes."

He cleared his throat. "Wow. I'm kinda nervous. Never thought I'd make it this far. Did you ever try to find me?"

Troy and Danuta

"I wanted to, a million times. I didn't want to interrupt your life or upset your parents. It had to be your decision."

"I can understand that. I don't know what to say now."

"Say anything. Just let me hear your voice!"

"Okay, like, how'd you get to be in Alaska and end up in Oregon?"

"That covers a lot of ground, literally. I guess the story starts with my father, your grandfather. In Michigan. When Paul was born."

"I have a grandfather?"

"Had. Had a grandfather."

"Oh. So, who's Paul?"

"Paul was why we went to Alaska. God, I'm not making much sense am I?" I scratched at the black grape juices that had hardened on my jeans.

I had spent years rehearsing for this day, what I would say, how I would explain. My father's life. His effect on us. Lies and counter-lies. Secrets and discoveries. Who we thought we were and who we became. And Alaska. It's the story I'd been waiting to tell. And now the day is here, and all my words are gone.

Patricia Michelle, 2009

Epilogue

MY MOTHER'S HANDS ARE FRAIL. HER FINGERS, still baring the clean and clipped discipline of a once-competent nurse, are now incapable of slipping a photograph into the sleeve of an album. I ask her if she remembers the faces in the old photos of our lives in Michigan and Alaska. She smiles and quietly says, "Yes." She answers as if to a voice other than mine.

Neither possessed by the past nor roused by the future, my mother lives in the absence of both with no need of memories, content with the small tasks of rinsing dishes in cold water and folding laundry into little towers of towels. She leaves the photos, unrecognizable to her, stacked in a tidy pile on the table. She drifts out to the patio to listen to birds, to wave at airplanes thousands of feet above, and to repeatedly call the dog "a good boy."

My mother, the lover of bridges, is fading away, a translucent link to my past. I search her eyes, looking for the woman she once was—and sometimes, when her wretched arthritic bones make her gasp in pain, I catch a glance of that stubborn grit, that chin tilted up like a soldier, not giving in to any of it, fighting for her dignity, fighting for every inch of herself, fighting to merely exist. And then comes anger, wrung from the frustration of a collapsing mind. It is hard to see her this way, shrinking from life.

I could not bring myself to tell her that Rick had died—as much from his tortured soul as his troubled heart. He was only fifty-eight. Actually, we lost him the day we left him behind in Michigan. Though it was his decision, he never

Michael

forgave us. I could not tell my mother that in his final hours, he did not ask for us, nor wanted any gathering in his name, as if he wanted to erase any memory of his ever having lived. If I had told her, she would mourn him, forget, and once reminded, mourn again. I could not do that to her. Besides, she is in an age of forgetfulness and the torch of memory had long ago been passed to me. So, I mourn him for both of us. And I will remember him for all of us.

It is Michael, my younger brother, who comes fetching wistfulness and flowers to rekindle the edges of Mom's amnesia. He talks of his three beautiful and bold daughters, her grandchildren, their soccer games and grades, his work at the EPA protecting rivers and waterways. She gleams at him with affection like a brightly polished kettle, but says nothing, and then gazes at the sky and the streaking white contrails of her jet planes. Michael soon melts into silence and they sit quietly sipping tea.

And Paul—the child born in fear, the son we both raised, the man with two mothers—he visits with breathless enthusiasm. Recently, he's been bringing his caged bird to entertain

Mom, a bird he adopted after a friend left town. The cockatiel is lame, but out of its cage, it learned to fly. Kindred spirits, that bird and Paul, each ensnared by circumstance, but each determined to soar.

Paul

Life is full of hard lessons written in books as heavy as stones: how to deal with betrayal, live with acceptance, eventually, how to forgive. My mother mastered those books years ago and tucked them away on a shelf she no longer reaches. But I do. I remember everything: My father's chiseled chin, his blue eyes that lied without blinking. His glorious statues, his life, a movie of his own making. A man of flaws. Had his life not been cut short, he might have come clean, explained himself, and made amends. At least, that's the ending I choose.

For all the things I needed from my father, he gave me this: the power of the story, the purpose of the myth, lessons I carry, more ballast than burden. I embody the attributes my father could only imagine; I had only to believe in them. Now, I know, my mother was the hero in our family, and I am the hero of my own story.

As for God, we have come to a divine understanding, He and I. I will not deify the unknown simply because it is unreachable. I choose not to vanquish reason for faith, nor surrender knowing for belief. Yet, with an open heart, I allow for mystery to ever inspire me. In this vineyard cathedral, I honor the Infinite, pulsing in the beat of birds and crickets, stones and stars.

As for love, here it breathes with Robin, my shepherd, and my grower of grapes.

Mateo and Jasmine, my grandchildren, stand before me poring over the photos where my mother had stood moments before. They are just embarking on their journeys. "Little Matthew," the blond, blue-eyed boy of seven, says, "You wanna go looking for tadpoles, Grandma Dee?"

For someone who was unable to raise her children as her own, Troy's children provide an unexpected joy. Hand in hand, we walk to the pond. Peering into the water, our reflections gaze back at us with a look of surprise, then suddenly disappear, dappled by the leap of a frog.

ACKNOWLEDGEMENTS

THIS BOOK HAS TAKEN MANY turns, and has had as many endings as there are to an on-going life. A loving friendship and eternal thanks to The Writers of the Round Table—especially, Kathleen Cremonesi and Jacquie Manning, who endured this book for sixteen years and provided encouragement, dedication and skill through its ever-changing edits and revisions until its minutiae had been all but memorized. My sincere thanks to the late Cary English for making me dig deeper.

Many thanks to my editor, Ross West, who picked editorial ticks out of a grassy field of commas, hyperbole, transitions and exclamation points! Thanks go to a superb proof reader, Jackie Melvin who knows, among other things, how to spell Ziploc. Thank you to my publisher, Patricia Marshall of Luminare Press, who brought this project to a beautiful, solid form with enthusiasm and grace. You made it so much fun for me. Many thanks to Conrad Pfeiffer, a research librarian who dug up data no one else could find. And thanks to Claire Flint for designing a cover that pulsed with the image of my father with his work.

A profound blessing goes to my mother for her tenacious support, uncompromising courage and the graphic memories she shared with me until there were no memories left. May you rest well beneath the trees. To my Dad, who was, after all, just a man, whose torments I tried to understand and whose flaws I have forgiven as I hope to be forgiven of mine. My heartfelt gratitude goes to my dearest Robin, a human being who loves beyond words.

A deep appreciation goes to the late Joseph Campbell,

whose wisdom taught me that to experience wonder is far more satisfying than merely having faith that wonder exists.

And finally, my gratitude to all those included in this book; I have tried above all to be fair. I thank you for sculpting me into the person I have become.

Made in the
USA
Monee, IL